Developing Proofreading and Editing Skills

fourth edition

SUE C. CAMP

Glencoe McGraw-Hill

New York, New York   Columbus, Ohio   Woodland Hills, California   Peoria, Illinois

Credits

Page 51, top: By permission. From *Merriam-Webster's Collegiate®
Dictionary, Tenth Edition* © 1999 by Merriam-Webster, Incorporated.
Page 51, bottom: By permission. From *20,000+ Words, Tenth Edition.*
(Glencoe/McGraw-Hill, Westerville, Ohio, 1996, p. 233).

Glencoe/McGraw-Hill
A Division of The McGraw·Hill Companies

Send all inquiries to:
Glencoe/McGraw-Hill
21600 Oxnard Street, Suite 500
Woodland Hills, CA 91367

ISBN 0-02-805002-9

Printed in the United States of America.

1 2 3 4 5 6 7 8 9 0   024   05 04 03 02 01 00

CONTENTS

"You never get a second chance to make a first impression." This saying emphasizes the importance of getting a message right the first time. You must ensure that your written communications are correct—both to avoid costly and embarrassing errors and to project a positive image of you and your organization.

A business letter, for example, may be the first contact your company has with a potential customer. Through that letter, your company has the opportunity to create a favorable first impression and thereby encourage the potential customer to become a new customer and, subsequently, a satisfied customer.

Developing Proofreading and Editing Skills, Fourth Edition provides instruction and exercises designed to sharpen your proofreading and editing skills. You will learn how to detect and correct errors in typing, spelling, capitalization, plurals, possessives, punctuation, numbers, grammar, sentence structure, and formatting. In addition, you will learn how to edit documents so that they are clear, concise, and complete.

NEW TO THE FOURTH EDITION

In response to feedback from users of previous editions, several changes and new additions have been made in *Developing Proofreading and Editing Skills,* Fourth Edition:

- Keyboarding errors are covered in one chapter instead of two.
- Spelling is discussed in a separate chapter that also covers word usage.
- Each chapter contains two additional end-of-chapter Application exercises.
- Four new chapters cover important topics: *Chapter 8* discusses **sentence structure** and ways to correct run-on sentences, fragments, and dangling and misplaced modifiers. *Chapter 11* reviews how to proofread **multiple-page documents** such as reports, manuscripts, and minutes of a meeting. *Chapter 15* polishes your **language use** by describing how to maintain a consistent

point of view as well as eliminate biased language and clichés. *Chapter 16* gives an overview of the importance of proofreading and editing when using **voice-recognition technology** to prepare documents.

- A CD-ROM packaged with this book contains two Application exercises from each chapter. The CD-ROM also contains Review Modules that provide proofreading and editing practice from a variety of occupational areas. The Review Modules are challenging, real-world documents that were modified to include errors that frequently occur in business writing. Each document on the CD-ROM appears in two versions: a Microsoft® Word version and a Corel® WordPerfect version.

SPECIAL FEATURES

Developing Proofreading and Editing Skills has a variety of special features designed to help you develop your proofreading and editing skills.

- **Pretest** and **Posttest** exercises offer assessment at the beginning and the end of the course.
- **TIPS** (<u>T</u>echniques <u>In</u> <u>P</u>roofreading <u>S</u>kill) features in each chapter offer helpful shortcuts and pointers to use in fine-tuning your proofreading and editing skills.
- **Software TIPS** features offer advice on using software tools such as spell and grammar checkers for on-screen proofreading and editing.
- **Whoops!** margin features highlight errors that have appeared in print, often with embarrassing consequences.
- **Net Link** margin features point you to Web sites and other Internet sources for additional coverage of topics or for additional practice.
- **Checkup exercises** in each chapter are designed to provide immediate reinforcement of chapter concepts. Answers to the Checkups appear in the back of this book so you can check your work.
- **Application exercises** at the end of each chapter contain a variety of documents to proofread and edit, such as letters, memos, e-mail messages, spreadsheets, faxes, and databases.

USING THIS BOOK TO DEVELOP YOUR SKILLS

Exercises in *Developing Proofreading and Editing Skills* are designed to help you recognize errors and use appropriate revision symbols to correct errors. The exercises gradually increase in difficulty, allowing you to build confidence and skill in proofreading and editing.

As you work through a chapter, complete each Checkup exercise as you come to it. After completing the Checkup, turn to the back of the book and compare your answers with the answer key. If you answered correctly, continue working through the chapter. If you answered incorrectly, review the chapter until you understand why you made the error or errors.

Each chapter ends with Applications numbered A, B, C, D, E, and F. Complete the Applications as your instructor directs. Applications A and B cover concepts in the current chapter while Applications C and D sample concepts in the current chapter plus previous chapters. Application E covers material in the current chapter while Application F is cumulative. Applications E and F appear both in the book and on the CD-ROM. Answers to Applications A and B are in the back of the student edition; answers to Applications C, D, E, and F are in the *Instructor's Manual and Key.*

Being able to proofread and edit your work will move your performance to new levels. Study the exercises diligently; avoid peeking at the correct answers until you have given each exercise your best effort. Please accept my best wishes as you begin studying this text.

I would like to dedicate this book to my two grandsons: Charles Ben Camp, III and John Mattison Camp, II.

Sue C. Camp

ACKNOWLEDGMENTS

The following educators provided helpful comments and suggestions regarding development of the fourth edition of *Developing Proofreading and Editing Skills:*

Vicky Charlston
Portland Community College
Portland, OR

Patricia R. King
Blackhawk Technical College
Janesville, WI

Joyce B. Lyons
Wytheville Community College
Wytheville, VA

Dona Orr
Boise State University
Boise, ID

Kathi Refosco
The Training Place
Western Maryland Consortium
Oakland, MD

Brenda Thomas
MTI College of Business and Technology
Sacramento, CA

Elva Wigle
Northern Virginia Community College
Annondale, VA

Pretest

Part 1. Is the copy in the first column identical to the copy in the second column? If it is, write *Yes* in the space provided. If it is not identical, write *No*. Circle the errors in the second column.

1.	Ms. Judi Norton 1654 Meadowacre Drive Cincinnati, OH 45021	Ms. Judi Norton 1654 Meadowacre Drive Cincinati, OH 45021	1. _____
2.	Flight 1564 Orlando, FL 10/23/03	Flight 1564 Orlando, FL 10/32/03	2. _____
3.	Dr. A. J. Marinelli drajmarinel@bnet.net	Dr. A. J. Marinelli drajmarinel@bnet.net	3. _____

Part 2. Proofread each of the following sentences for errors in keyboarding, spelling, word use, capitalization, word division, punctuation, grammar, sentence structure, number style, and consistency. Use revision symbols from the inside front cover to mark corrections.

4. We lived in Richmond Virginia before moving to Seattle.

5. Both of the career counselors has experience in human resources.

6. This proposal should be be sent to all managers.

7. You may call our toll-free number 24 hours a day for customer assistence.

8. My computer passwords is easy to remember.

9. The family room measures eighteen by twenty-four feet.

10. Helen's and Jason's business is doing better than they expected.

11. November 5 2003, is the date we will move to our new headquarters.

12. Most of teh time the customer is right.

13. Please call I if you have any questions about the investment plan.

14. Alana is the project manager;Jean is the editor.

15. Of the 12 high school students, two were selected as interns.

16. Call me about the contract first thing in morning.

17. Melanie, Ethan and Charles are in charge of handling new accounts.

18. The computer comes with a 17 inch monitor.

19. These are our goals for next year to increase sales, streamline operations, and offer stock options to all employees.

20. Whom is the manager in charge of the project?

21. Please complete both sides of the from.

22. Monica asked for someone to head the fund drive she also asked for volunteers.

23. Charles Schultz our new manager is known for developing innovative products.

24. The program is explained in detail in the appendix see page 120.

25. After reviewing the complaint the mediator suggested a compromise.

26. Brendan's apartment in Chicago is near lake Michigan.

27. Invoices 1357, 1360, and 1359 have not been paid.

28. We need to update our policys on computer use.

29. Some one in accounting should audit all records each month.

30. Our programs for computer sales need to offer customers affordable, convenient, and reliable service.

31. Neither of the partners are going to the conference.

32. We need to wiegh all options before deciding what action to take.

33. Most of our departments were effected by the merger.

34. Each programmer is responsible for completing their portion of the program.

35. Let's see if Lukes suggestion will help us improve our service.

36. Over thirty percent of our employees are under the age of 40.

37. The accident occured just after midnight.

38. Victor made more sales than any other associate but he was not promoted.

39. Pat will you write the advertising copy?

40. The art museum is in a building that is ninety five years old.

41. Her latest book is titled Smart Investing In Stocks.

42. Are you sure your scheduled to attend the conference?

43. If you decide to take the earlier flight. Call me before you leave.

44. Alonzo's new music store is open until 11:00 p.m. each day.

45. We advice our clients to review their investments once a year.

46. The meeting was held to elect new officers, for making plans, and to get acquainted.

47. Three attornies from our office are representing the plaintiffs in the case.

48. When will the final report be ready for mailing.

49. The product launch is scheduled to take place at 2 pm this Friday.

50. This Summer, I will make my third sales trip to Singapore.

Keyboarding Errors

OBJECTIVES

After completing this chapter, you should be able to:

1. Define *proofreading* and *editing*.

2. Describe four approaches to proofreading documents.

3. Identify misstrokes, repetitions, omissions, transpositions, and spacing errors in written documents.

4. Proofread names, addresses, telephone numbers, and other numbers.

5. Use appropriate revision symbols to correct misstrokes, repetitions, omissions, transpositions, and spacing errors.

Written communications serve a vital role in every organization. Managers and employees use memos, letters, e-mail messages, reports, spreadsheets, and other documents to convey essential information to people inside or outside their organizations. Applying proofreading and editing techniques can help writers convey this essential information correctly and effectively. Assuring that information is conveyed correctly requires skill in proofreading; assuring that information is conveyed effectively involves skill in editing.

Keep in mind the difference between preparing a document for a class and preparing a document in the workplace. In the classroom, one error in a document prepared for a grade may be acceptable. However, most business executives would consider a letter with even one misspelled word as unacceptable.

PROOFREADING

Proofreading is the examination of a document to find errors that should be corrected. Proofreading tasks range from simple to complex—from checking to see that nothing was omitted to checking for consistency in format.

There are four approaches to proofreading written communications: verification proofreading, partnership proofreading, proofreading on the computer screen, and proofreading without referring to an original document.

- **Verification proofreading** involves comparing the final copy with a previous draft to make sure that the material has been keyboarded correctly. This is the easiest form of proofreading.

- **Partnership proofreading** involves two people—the document preparer reads aloud from the draft as a second person verifies the final copy. Although time-consuming, the partnership approach is often the best method for proofreading statistical and technical documents.

- **Proofreading on the computer screen** is similar to proofreading printed copy, but you must adjust to viewing material on the computer screen. Also, you must be adept at using various software tools that can assist you in detecting errors in written copy.

- **Proofreading without an original document** is the most challenging form of proofreading. Because you do not have a comparison document to use for verification, you must check the content word for word. For example, if you composed a letter on the computer, you would not be verifying written copy; instead, you would be checking for errors in content, format, grammar, capitalization, word usage, number usage, punctuation, spelling, and keyboarding.

You must be familiar with all types of potential errors. *Developing Proofreading and Editing Skills* shows you how to identify errors, demonstrates how these errors frequently occur in business writing, and provides practice in detecting and marking these errors with revision symbols (also called proofreaders' marks). Revision symbols are used to indicate corrections and changes to be made in a uniform, easy-to-follow way. Each revision symbol will be introduced in this book as you need it; however, you may want to take a quick look at the complete list of revision symbols on the inside front cover.

EDITING

Editing involves revising a document to make it more effective. Think of the editing process as polishing a communication. For example, compare the following sentences:

> Enclosed herewith please find a copy for you of the pamphlet on the health concern of increasing the number of childhood immunizations.

> Your copy of the pamphlet on increasing childhood immunizations is enclosed.

The first sentence has 22 words and the second sentence has only 11 words. Both are grammatically correct, but the second sentence is easier to read and understand and is more concise. Editing improves a document by increasing its effectiveness.

Proofreading and editing have been somewhat simplified because most word processing programs have features that will find misspelled words or indicate that the sentences in a document are either too long or too short. You should be familiar with all of the tools that are available with your software. However, you must not rely completely on these tools to catch all errors. You should be able to identify errors without assistance. Often, the software will highlight a possible error and you must determine if there is an error and, if so, how to correct it.

PROOFREADING BUSINESS DOCUMENTS

Proofreading business documents such as letters, memos, spreadsheets, and reports is a vital part of communicating effectively. Everyone who writes and prepares correspondence and other documents must develop skill in detecting all types of errors. One way to sharpen your proofreading skill is to learn to detect keyboarding errors. The most frequent keyboarding errors include the following:

1. Misstrokes (striking the wrong key, letter, number, or symbol)

   Please complete the application from. (*should be* form)

   July 5 is Independence Day. (*should be* July 4)

2. Omissions (accidentally omitting keystrokes or words)

   The purpose was to unit the two political factions. (*should be* unite)

   Notify her as soon possible. (*should be* as soon as possible)

3. Repetitions (adding unneeded keystrokes or words)

   Harrison meet me at the airport yesterday. (*should be* met)

   Look on the the Web site. (*should be* on the Web site)

Do you think that a spell checker would detect the misstrokes, omissions, and repetitions in the preceding examples? Most spell checkers would have missed all but the last error, the repetition of the word *the*. A spell checker usually will not detect errors in misused but correctly spelled words such as typing *from* for *form* because both of these words are in the software dictionary. However, some spell checkers will highlight certain words that may be confused, such as *right* and *write*.

Keyboarding errors can be detected using verification proof-reading. Verification involves comparing an original or other source document (such as a handwritten draft) with the typed information on the computer screen or with a final printout. This chapter will give you practice in using verification.

PROOFREADING NAMES, ADDRESSES, AND TELEPHONE NUMBERS

Names, addresses, and telephone numbers appear frequently in written documents. Customers, patients, and business contacts expect to have their names spelled correctly. Business professionals rely on accurate addresses and telephone numbers to assure correct delivery of messages. Incorrect information is useless.

Many companies are conducting business abroad. Thus, you must be alert to checking names and addresses for individuals from other countries. Much care should be given when proofreading names and addresses used in the international business arena.

Names

Always verify the spelling of a person's name. Misspelling a person's name can be embarrassing for you and offensive to the person.

The following tips will help you to proofread names.

TIPS

PROOFREADING NAMES

- Check the spelling of each part of a person's name (first, middle, and last), and check any initials.

- Carefully check the spelling of unusual or unfamiliar names.

- Verify possible alternate spellings of names (for example, *Stephen* or *Steven*? *Katherine* or *Catherine*?)

- When using courtesy titles, make sure the appropriate one is used: *Mr., Ms., Miss, Mrs.,* or *Dr.*

Completing the following Checkup will help you to be alert to potential errors in names.

Are the names in Columns A and B identical? If they are, write *Yes* in the space provided. If they are not, write *No* in the space provided. Circle the errors in Column B.

A	B	Yes/No
1 Mr. Larry W. Berstorff	Mr. Larry M. Berstorf	1. _____
2. Ms. Alicia Ann Efird	Mrs. Alicia Ann Efird	2. _____
3. Dr. H. Baxter Smith, Sr.	Mr. H. Baxter Smith, Sr.	3. _____
4. Guillermo Navarez	Guillermo Navarez	4. _____
5. Jessica Allen Van Buren	Jessica Allen Van Buren	5. _____
6. William Wray Bergman	William Ray Bergman	6. _____
7. Ky Chin Nguyen	Ky Chin Nquyen	7. _____
8. Ms. Katherine R. Roessner	Ms. Catherine R. Roessner	8. _____
9. Manuel J. Rojas	Manuel J. Rojas	9. _____
10. J. William Scharnitzke	J. William Scharnitzke	10. _____
11. Melinda Fritz Schaffer	Melinda Fritz Schaeffer	11. _____
12. Hengky S. Jjakra	Hengky S. Jjakra	12. _____
13. J. Franklin Widenhouse	J. Franklin Widanhouse	13. _____
14. Josephine H. Hilderbran	Josephine H. Hilderbran	14. _____
15. Dr. Michelle Mendehall	Dr. Michelle Mendehall	15. _____
16. Teresa Rudisill McDowell	Teresa Rudisil McDowell	16. _____
17. Mrs. Elizabeth Berry Thomas	Mrs. Elizabeth Berry Thomas	17. _____
18. Gretchen Joy Nicholls	Gretchen Joy Nichols	18. _____
19. Wyatt J. Roggenkamp, III	Wyatt J. Roggenkemp, III	19. _____
20. Leslie Sherrill Mitchell	Leslie Sherrill Mitchell	20. _____

SOFTWARE TIPS

Spell checkers will detect unfamiliar proper nouns, such as the names of individuals, indicating that they may possibly be misspelled. If you use certain names frequently, you should add them to your software dictionary. Once the names are entered correctly in the software dictionary, the spell checker will recognize them and not highlight them as potential misspellings.

Addresses

Proofreading addresses involves checking people's names as well as street addresses, post office box numbers, city names, state abbreviations, and ZIP Codes. International addresses often include postal codes instead of ZIP Codes and also include a country name.

Street Names and Numbers and Post Office Boxes

Verify street names and numbers and post office box numbers. Striking the incorrect key can misdirect your mail and cause a delay in delivery. Study the following tips to help you learn to proofread addresses.

TIPS

PROOFREADING ADDRESSES

- Check each keystroke when verifying addresses.

- Check for errors at the end of words and within numbers. Errors frequently occur in these places.

- Check each part of an address to make sure every detail is correct.

- Make sure the last line of an address includes only the city, state, and ZIP Code. For international addresses, make sure the country name appears by itself on the last line of the address.

CHECKUP 1-2

Are the addresses in Columns A and B identical? If they are, write *Yes* in the space provided. If they are not, write *No* in the space provided. Circle the errors in Column B.

A	B	Yes/No
1. 1342 Heather Way	1344 Heather Way	1. _____
2. 6728 Third Avenue North	6728 Third Avenue South	2. _____
3. Post Office Box 86856	Post Office Box 86856	3. _____
4. 1432 Heritage Lane	1432 Heritage Lane	4. _____
5. 1534 Cypress Boulevard	1534 Cypress Boulavard	5. _____
6. 6005 Rue Saint-Laurent	6005 Rue Saint-Laurent	6. _____
7. 3265 43rd Avenue, NE	3265 43rd Avenue, SE	7. _____

A	B	Yes/No
8. Piazza Emilia, 8	Pizza Emilia, 8	8. _____
9. 1545 Hawthorn Circle	1545 Hawthorn Circle	9. _____
10. 3627 Ashbourne Drive	3627 Ashbourne Drive	10. _____
11. 6034 Tittabawassee Road	6084 Tittabawassee Road	11. _____
12. 1331 Sierra Vista Court	1331 Sierra Vista Court	12. _____
13. 4564 Westchester Street	4564 Westchester Street	13. _____
14. 7261 Nottingham Drive	7261 Knottingham Drive	14. _____
15. Post Office Box 72638	Post Office Box 72638	15. _____
16. 325 Playa Del Rey	325 Playa Del Reyes	16. _____
17. 3263 64th Avenue, SW	3263 64th Avenue, SW	17. _____
18. 728 Gehring Road	728 Gehgring Road	18. _____
19. 1231 Altamonte Springs Road	1231 Altamonte Spring Road	19. _____
20. Post Office Box 24487	Post Office Box 24587	20. _____

City Names and Country Names

City names pose a challenge when proofreading because they are not always spelled as they sound. In addition, some city names are pronounced the same but have different spellings.

Juneau, Alaska	Phoenix, Arizona
Englewood, New Jersey	Inglewood, California
Pittsburg, Kansas	Pittsburgh, Pennsylvania

Country names also can be challenging to proofread due to their spelling and pronunciation. Check a dictionary or an atlas to verify the spelling of a country name.

Ethiopia	New Zealand	Philippines	Ukraine

State Abbreviations

The U.S. Postal Service recommends using two-letter abbreviations for states and territories of the United States when addressing envelopes. Most business writers also use these abbreviations for the inside addresses of letters. However, the name of a state appearing within the text of a document is usually not abbreviated. A list of these abbreviations is provided in the Appendix of this book.

When using the two-letter state abbreviations, type them in all-capital letters and use no periods after or space between the letters. Leave one space between the state abbreviation and the ZIP Code, as in the following example.

Net Link

The World Wide Web offers a variety of sources of geographic information. One good source for verifying the names of countries is the World Factbook that appears in the publication section of the U.S. Central Intelligence Agency Web site. The World Factbook includes an alphabetical list of countries around the world and describes each country's geography, population, government, and economy.

Mrs. Julia S. Harris
16497 Dillinger Court
Baltimore, MD 21237

Addresses on envelopes may be typed in one of the following ways. Both styles can be read by U.S. Postal Service optical character reader (OCR) scanners that are used to sort mail electronically.

Inside Address Style

This traditional style uses capital and lowercase letters plus any needed punctuation. With the traditional address style you can use the same block of information for both the inside address of the letter and the envelope or mailing label, which saves typing the information twice.

Ms. Sally Anderson
921 Eveningstar Drive
Westerville, OH 43901-2396

All-Capitals Style

The U.S. Postal Service particularly encourages businesses that send high volumes of mail to use the all-capitals style for addressing envelopes. When typing addresses using this style, limit the line length to 28 keystrokes.

MR JEFFREY R GOLDBERG
BRITTON FURNITURE INC
3572 GILLIGAN ST
EUGENE OR 97401-1024

Unlike the inside address style, the all-capitals style is inappropriate for the inside address of letters.

CHECKUP 1-3 Are the abbreviations in Column B the correct two-letter abbreviations for the states or territories listed in Column A? If they are, write *Yes* in the space provided. If they are not, write *No* in the space provided, and write the correct abbreviation in the last column.

	A	B		Yes/No?	Correct Abbreviation
0.	California	CL	0.	No	CA
1.	Illinois	IN	1.	_____	_____
2.	Oregon	OR	2.	_____	_____
3.	Texas	TS	3.	_____	_____
4.	Pennsylvania	PN	4.	_____	_____
5.	Ohio	OI	5.	_____	_____
6.	Utah	UH	6.	_____	_____

A	B	Yes/No?	Correct Abbreviation
7. Vermont	VE	7. _____	_____
8. Arizona	AZ	8. _____	_____
9. Wyoming	WG	9. _____	_____
10. Connecticut	CO	10. _____	_____
11. Oklahoma	OK	11. _____	_____
12. New Jersey	NJ	12. _____	_____
13. New Hampshire	NH	13. _____	_____
14. Colorado	CL	14. _____	_____
15. Indiana	IN	15. _____	_____
16. Maine	MA	16. _____	_____
17. Maryland	MD	17. _____	_____
18. Idaho	IO	18. _____	_____
19. Montana	MA	19. _____	_____
20. South Carolina	SC	20. _____	_____

ZIP Codes

ZIP Codes are used to help deliver mail more quickly. A ZIP Code represents a geographic area, such as part of a city. The U.S. Postal Service uses ZIP+4 Codes (nine-digit ZIP Codes) to designate specific addresses within a delivery area, such as an office building or a city block. On U.S. mail, the ZIP Code appears on the last line of the address.

Cactus Air Express
835 Huntsville Drive
Suite 15
San Antonio, TX 78230-2395

The U.S. Postal Service particularly encourages businesses to use the ZIP+4 Code due to the high volume of mail businesses receive and suggests that letterhead stationery include the ZIP+4 Code. Proofreading ZIP Codes and ZIP+4 Codes is important because the post office uses optical character readers to scan these numbers, which permits automatic sorting of mail.

Instead of ZIP Codes, international addresses often have postal codes. The postal code appears on the same line as the name of the city or town. The country name is typed in all-capital letters on a separate line, as in the following example.

International Marketing Limited
Suite 440 Anaya Place
8895 Anaya Avenue, Makati City 1273
PHILIPPINES

Because the ZIP Code and international postal codes are necessary parts of an address, be alert to incorrect ZIP Codes and postal codes in the exercises in the rest of this book.

Net Link

For information on addressing mail for both U.S. and international destinations, access the U.S. Postal Service Web site at **http://www.usps.com.** Included on this site are instructions for addressing mail, a ZIP Code lookup, and a list of commonly used abbreviations for addresses.

Are the ZIP Codes and ZIP+4 Codes in Columns A and B identical? If they are, write *Yes* in the space provided. If they are not, write *No* in the space provided. Assume that the number in Column A is correct and write the correct number in the last column. Be sure to proofread the numbers you write in the Correct Number column.

	A	B		Yes/No?	Correct Number
0.	37916	37918	0.	No	37916
1.	36619	36619	1.	_____	_____
2.	93542-2251	93542-2215	2.	_____	_____
3.	85037	85087	3.	_____	_____
4.	91731-3317	91731-3317	4.	_____	_____
5.	71119	71119	5.	_____	_____
6.	02186	02185	6.	_____	_____
7.	31419-5634	31419-5664	7.	_____	_____
8.	64153	64153	8.	_____	_____
9.	62204-4531	62204-4531	9.	_____	_____
10.	53224-3697	53224-3687	10.	_____	_____
11.	32714-2782	32714-2782	11.	_____	_____
12.	23321	23321	12.	_____	_____
13.	63147	68147	13.	_____	_____
14.	43567	43567	14.	_____	_____
15.	06851-7834	06851-8834	15.	_____	_____

Are the addresses in Columns A and B identical? If they are, write *Yes* in the space provided. If they are not, write *No* in the space provided. Circle the errors you find in Column B. Assume that the addresses in Column A are correct.

A	B	Yes/No?
1. Mr. David Alexander Reilly and Associates Suite 102 15 Oak Drive West Creek, NJ 08095	Mr. David Alexander Reilly and Associates Suite 102 15 Oak Drive West Creek, NJ 08095	1. _____
2. Ms. Sydney Taylor Exports Unlimited No. 6 West Patel New Delhi 108 110 INDIA	Ms. Sydney Taylor Exports Unlimited No. 6 West Patel New Dehli 108 110 INDIA	2. _____
3. Dr. Harold Vasquez 285 East Wind Drive Columbus, OH 44340	Dr. Harold Vasquez 285 East Wind Drive Columbus, OH 44430	3. _____

A	B	Yes/No?

4. *Mrs. Leanne Waling*
   320 Water Street
   Whitby, ON KIN 4B6
   CANADA

   Mrs. Leanne Waling
320 Water Street
Whitby, ON KIN 4B6
CANADA

4. _____

5. *Mr. Robert Tyrrell*
   DesignMaster Inc.
   733 S. Topaz Avenue
   Yuma, AZ 85362

   Mr. Robert Tyrrell
DesignMaster Inc.
733 S. Topaz Avenue
Yuma, AZ 85362

5. _____

Telephone Numbers

An error in recording or transcribing a telephone number can be costly. A search for the correct number can be time-consuming and fruitless.

There are five acceptable formats for telephone numbers, as shown in the following examples.

704-555-3219
(704) 555-3219   (One space follows the parenthesis.)
704/555-3219
704.555.3219   (Using periods follows the style used for Internet addresses.)
1-704-555-3219   (Hyphens separate all elements when an access code precedes the telephone number.)

International telephone numbers may have a sequence of three or four numbers: an international access code, a country code, a city code, and the local number. Not all international telephone numbers contain a city code.

011-254-2-555-747   011-510-705-4972
(with city code)   (without city code)

The following tips will help you to proofread telephone numbers.

TIPS

PROOFREADING TELEPHONE NUMBERS

- Read each telephone number in parts. For example, read the number 919-555-8321 in three parts: "nine-one-nine, five-five-five, eight-three-two-one."

- When proofreading columns of telephone numbers, check that all parts, such as hyphens and parentheses, are aligned.

- Check that each number has the appropriate number of digits.

Keeping in mind the importance of accurately recording, reporting, and proofreading telephone numbers, complete the following Checkup.

CHECKUP 1-6 Are the telephone numbers in Columns A and B identical? If they are, write *Yes* in the space provided. If they are not, write *No* in the space provided. Circle each error in Column B.

	A	B	Yes/No?
1.	317-384-2385	317-384-2835	1. _____
2.	402-549-6517	402-549-6517	2. _____
3.	516/432/7828	516/432/7828	3. _____
4.	(206) 532-4841	(260) 532-4841	4. _____
5.	1-800-303-3827	1-900-303-3827	5. _____
6.	405.534.8824	405.533.8824	6. _____
7.	(801) 529-4821	(801) 529-4821	7. _____
8.	322/672-7783	322/672-7783	8. _____
9.	011-52-16-541-2386	011-52-16-541-3286	9. _____
10.	1-888-860-5492	1-888-860-5492	10. _____
11.	(505) 389-6687	(505) 889-6687	11. _____
12.	913-351-4957	913-351-4857	12. _____
13.	011.27.782.4893	011.27.782.4893	13. _____
14.	(616) 782-5938	(616) 782-5938	14. _____
15.	1-800-562-3381	1-800-562-33881	15. _____

PROOFREADING OTHER TYPES OF NUMBERS

Reading, reporting, and typing numbers accurately is essential in business communications. Numbers are used frequently in writing ages, dates, decimal fractions, dollar amounts, times of day, and weights and measures.

Spell checkers will not find typographical errors in numbers. Thus, you should train your eyes and mind to be alert to numbers. Why are numbers important? Consider the consequences of these two number errors:

1. On Mrs. Madison's employment records, her salary was listed at $32,000 per year instead of $42,000 per year.

2. A business manager has reservations for the busy July 4th weekend at a resort and convention center for a convention July 3–8. However, the dates for his stay were mistakenly entered in the computer for July 4–9. Perhaps the unlucky traveler will have time to "cool off" around the pool while spending the first night of the business trip without a room.

Use the following tips to help you proofread numbers correctly.

TIPS

PROOFREADING NUMBERS

- Check all numbers as a separate proofreading step.

- Make sure that numbers make sense. For example, a newspaper advertisement mentioning an antique desk made in 1991 would have to be incorrect.

- When proofreading columns of typed numbers, check to see that all parts of the numbers are aligned (hyphens under hyphens, decimals under decimals, and so on).

- When proofreading several columns of numbers, read down each column, not across from left to right. For example, proofread columns of telephone numbers by reading the area codes down each column, then the next three numbers (called the exchange), and then the last four numbers.

- Make sure that numbers have the appropriate number of digits. Social Security numbers have nine digits separated by hyphens in this pattern: 000-00-0000. North American phone numbers have ten digits in this pattern: 000-000-0000.

- To double-check typed columns of numbers, quickly add the numbers in the first draft. Then add the numbers in the final copy. The totals should be the same. This method works well when proofreading final copy that was typed from handwritten originals.

To increase your accuracy in proofreading numbers, complete the following Checkups.

CHECKUP 1-7 In each line, two of the three items are the same, and one is different. Identify the different item by writing the corresponding column heading, A, B, or C, in the space provided.

	A	B	C	
0.	Invoice #623101-5	Invoice #632101-5	Invoice #623101-5	0. ___B___
1.	$31,396.62	$31,395.62	$31,395.62	1. _____
2.	41.487 percent	41.487 percent	41.488 percent	2. _____
3.	Pages 391–397	Pages 391–391	Pages 391–397	3. _____
4.	17 7/16	11 7/16	17 7/16	4. _____
5.	March 24, 1999	March 24, 1999	March 14, 1999	5. _____

	A	B	C		
6.	Flight BA 1073A	Flight BA 1073A	Flight BA 1072A	6.	_____
7.	0.07 grams	0.007 grams	0.07 grams	7.	_____
8.	1994-1999	1999-1999	1994–1999	8.	_____
9.	April 8, 2001	April 18, 2001	April 18, 2001	9.	_____
10.	94.4232.63431	94.4132.63431	94.4132.63431	10.	_____
11.	$5,867.34	$5,367.34	$5,867.34	11.	_____
12.	32 by 28 feet	32 by 23 feet	32 by 23 feet	12.	_____
13.	11-27-43	11-27-43	11-27-23	13.	_____
14.	Age 42	Age 42	Age 44	14.	_____
15.	2 years 1 month 16 days old	2 years 1 month 26 days old	2 years 1 month 16 days old	15.	_____
16.	Account 0298533175	Account 0289533175	Account 0289533175	16.	_____
17.	11/21/99	11/21/99	11/27/99	17.	_____
18.	$324,268.78	$824,268.78	$824,268.78	18.	_____
19.	11:59 a.m.	11:59 a.m.	11:49 a.m.	19.	_____
20.	Pages 589–597	Pages 589–598	Pages 589–598	20.	_____

CHECKUP 1-8

Are the Social Security numbers in Columns A and B identical? If they are, write *Yes* in the space provided. If they are not, write *No* in the space provided.

	A		B		Yes/No?
1.	815-56-1323	1.	815-56-1323	1.	_____
2.	024-38-5286	2.	044-38-5286	2.	_____
3.	083-50-3231	3.	083-50-3231	3.	_____
4.	941-36-7836	4.	941-86-7836	4.	_____
5.	423-48-4348	5.	423-48-4843	5.	_____
6.	695-83-4163	6.	695-83-4163	6.	_____
7.	728-53-2831	7.	778-53-2831	7.	_____
8.	051-57-5314	8.	051-57-5314	8.	_____
9.	040-78-3237	9.	040-48-3237	9.	_____
10.	845-51-4231	10.	845-51-4231	10.	_____

CHECKUP 1-9

Is the handwritten copy in Column A identical to the printed copy in Column B? If it is, write *Yes* in the space provided. If it is not, write *No* in the space provided. Circle each error in Column B.

	A	B		Yes/No?
1.	002-865-8290	002-865-8299	1.	_____
2.	Dr. Leon Leonardi	Mr. Leon Leonardi	2.	_____
3.	Rockford, IL 61109	Rockford, ILL 61109	3.	_____
4.	12-25-99	12-25-99	4.	_____
5.	Nicole Negbenebor	Nicole Negbenebor	5.	_____

A	B	Yes/No?
6. *October 28, 2001*	October 18, 2001	6. _____
7. *218/492-8820*	218/492-8820	7. _____
8. *602 Baxter Road*	602 Baxter Road	8. _____
9. *042-78-2935*	042-78-2935	9. _____
10. *089-56-1973*	089-55-1973	10. _____
11. *Avenida Varca, 8*	Avenida Varca, 8	11. _____
15402 Madrid	15402 Madrid	
12. *011-61-14-347-1793*	011-61-14-34-1793	12. _____
13. *Lincoln, NE*	Lincoln, Ne	13. _____
08512-2348	68512-2348	
14. *1-800-492-5782*	1-800-492-4782	14. _____
15. *020-45-2915*	020-45-2915	15. _____
16. *Flight LH 1829*	Flight LH 1829	16. _____
17. *Frances G. Smythe*	Francis G. Smythe	17. _____
18. *Billings, MT 59106*	Billing, MT 59106	18. _____
19. *916-924-5563*	916-924-5563	19. _____
20. *Ann J. Montero*	Ann J. Montero	20. _____

OMISSIONS AND REPETITIONS

As written communications are typed, revised, or transcribed, letters, words, or entire lines may be omitted or repeated. Such errors are common, even when using the cut-and-paste or the copy feature of word processing software. Moreover, omissions and repetitions may go unnoticed: for example, a sentence can make sense even when a word is missing. As a result, it's important that you carefully proofread for copy that may be omitted or repeated.

Proofreading for Omissions

When you are proofreading you must read for more than sense; you must read for accuracy. The following sentences make sense, but one of each pair has an error. The spell checker or grammar checker in word processing software would not catch either of the two omission errors illustrated here.

I do not want to attend the conference in Puerto Rico.
I do want to attend the conference in Puerto Rico.

Enclosed is my check for $95 for one year's subscription.
Enclosed is my check for $995 for one year's subscription.

Quite a difference! Be careful to look for omitted and repeated letters, numbers, words, and lines.

Revision Symbol for Inserting Omitted Copy

The revision symbol used to insert omitted copy is the caret (∧), as shown in the following examples.

Revision	Edited Draft	Final Copy
Insert a letter	desk is n$\overset{a}{e}$t	desk is neat
Insert a word	in $\overset{the}{\wedge}$ morning	in the morning

Here are more examples of how the caret is used:

Send the report to Ms. Eas$\overset{t}{}$man.

You should $\overset{not}{\wedge}$ work late every night.

Mail $\overset{two}{\wedge}$ copies of the contract to each author.

Let's test your ability to find omissions. The paragraph on the left is correct. Proofread the paragraph on the right and correct any errors. Use the caret (∧) to insert any missing letters, numbers, or words.

Please ship me 200 more copies of *Thinking Outside the Box* by John Miller. We are using this excellent book in our management training programs.	Please ship me 20 copies of *Thinking Outside the Box* John Miller. We are using this book in our management training program.

Did you notice these omissions in the paragraph on the right?

Line 1—A zero is omitted.
Line 1—The word *more* is omitted.
Line 2—The word *by* is omitted.
Line 3—The word *excellent* is omitted.
Line 5—The *s* in *programs* is omitted.

Proofreading for Repetitions

Repetition errors result when letters, symbols, numbers, words, or other text are mistakenly repeated. Time pressure can cause a person to misread an original document or to strike a key an extra time accidentally while typing.

The spell-checker feature of most word processing software highlights repetitions of letters that result in misspelled words. Spell checkers also highlight repetitions of single words or of numbers but usually will not highlight repeated segments of words or numbers. Note the following example:

> Of the 10 sets, 5 5 were sent as samples.
>
> Of the 10 sets, 5 were sent 5 were sent as samples.

Found in the course description for a college:
"Study Skills 200—Academiic and Personal Enhancement."

In the first sentence, the second *5* was highlighted as a repetition. In the second sentence, the repetition of *5 were sent* was not highlighted. Because spell checkers do not catch all repetitions, you need to be alert to repetitions as you proofread. Spell checkers are discussed more thoroughly in Chapter 2.

Revision Symbol for Marking Deletions

Study the following examples to learn how to mark text that should be deleted. These examples show the proper use of the delete symbol.

Revision	Edited Draft	Final Copy
Delete a letter	thought	though
	agreed	agree
Delete a letter and close up	read *or* read	red
	whomever	whoever
Delete a word	wrote two ~~two~~ checks	wrote two checks
	Near to the door	Near the door

Let's test your ability to find repetitions. The first paragraph in the following example is correct. Compare the second paragraph to the first one and correct any errors. Use the appropriate revision symbol to indicate any repeated letters, numbers, or words.

Please consider me a candidate for the computer specialist position with your company. With my background in computer systems and over five years' of related work experience, I believe that I could be an asset to your firm.

Please consider me a candidate for the computer specialist position with your company. With my background in computer systems and over five years' of related work experience, I believe that I could be an asset I could be an asset too your firm.

Did you notice these repetitions in the second paragraph?

Line 4—Five words are repeated.
Line 4—The letter *o* is repeated in the word *to* after *asset*.

The following tips will help you to find omissions and repetitions when you proofread.

TIPS

PROOFREADING FOR OMISSIONS AND REPETITIONS

- Look for omission and repetition errors especially at the beginning and end of words and sentences.

- Look for omission and repetition errors with vowels such as *a*, *e*, *i*, and *o*.

- Read for accuracy and for meaning.

Omissions and repetitions frequently occur when moving text (words, sentences, and even paragraphs) within a document. Omissions typically occur when text is cut or deleted from one location and not reinserted elsewhere. Consider the following example:

> Most of our employees prefer four days instead of five days per week to work.

Suppose you wanted to move *to work* so that it appears between *prefer* and *four*. If the words *to work* were cut from their first location and not inserted in the correct location, the sentence might read as follows:

> Most of our employees prefer four days instead of five days per week.

Repetitions typically occur when text is copied and then pasted into a new location but not deleted from its original location, as shown in the following example.

> Most of our employees prefer to work four days instead of five days per week to work.

Now that you are familiar with some of the ways that omissions and repetitions occur in day-to-day business communications, be alert to them as you complete exercises throughout the rest of this book.

Let's see if you can find the omissions and repetitions in the following example. The first paragraph is correct. Proofread the second paragraph and correct any errors. Use the appropriate revision symbols to mark the errors you find.

> Your Invoice 4314, dated May 30, 2001, was received in our Chicago office on June 4. Please note that the amount we owe your company, $31.12, was incorrectly entered as $311.20. Our check for $31.12 is enclosed to cover our account in full.

> Your Invoice 414, date May 30, 2001, was received in our Chicago office on June 4. Please note that the amount we owe our company, $31.12, was incorrectly entered as $311.20. Our check for $31.12 is enclosed cover our our account in full.

Seen in an e-mail message:
"The contcat person is Dee McFarland."

Did you notice these errors?

> Line 1—The *3* in the invoice number is omitted.
> Line 1—The second *d* in *dated* is omitted.
> Line 3—The word *our* before *company* should be *your*. The *y* is omitted.
> Line 4—The word *to* before *cover* is omitted.
> Line 4—The word *our* is repeated.

Your spell checker probably would not have caught any of the five errors in the preceding example. You are learning that you cannot rely too heavily on the spell checker in your software to detect errors. You still must read and proofread your documents.

To improve your skill at detecting omissions and repetitions, complete the following Checkup. Note that you will be comparing handwritten copy with printed copy.

CHECKUP 1-10 Assume that the first sentence in each pair is correct. Use revision symbols to indicate any changes in the second sentence. If the second sentence is correct, write *C* for *Correct* beside the item number.

1. *Zach Gilbreath's order has been scheduled for shipment next week.*

   Zach Gilbreath's order has been schedule for shipment next week.

2. *The patient's date of birth is November 13, 1977, and his Social Security number is 342-16-3922.*

   The patient's date of birth is November 13, 1977, and his Social Security number is 342-16-3922.

3. *Employees of Brenhouser Manufacturing Company gave over 99 pints of blood during the blood drive.*

   Employees of Brenhouser Manufacturing Company gave over 999 pints of blood during the blood drive.

4. *My suggestion was chosen as the best from over 2000 suggestions submitted from throughout the company's 27 locations.*

   My suggestion was chosen as the best as the best from over 2000 suggestions submitted from throughout the company's 27 locations.

5. *Our meeting will be Friday, May 19, at 2:30 p.m., in Conference Room 22.*

   Our meeting will be Friday, May 19, at 2:30 p.m., in Conference Room 222.

6. *Many people will change jobs four or five times during their careers.*

   Many people will change jobs for or five times during their careers.

7. *We attended a time management seminar.*

   We attended a time managment seminar.

8. *Follow the instructions for creating your own Web page.*

   Follow the instructions for for creating your own Web page.

9. *Several of the meeting participants were salespeople.*

   Several of the meeting participants were salespeople.

10. *Of all the candidates, only two have held office before.*

    Of all the candidates, two have held office before.

TRANSPOSITIONS AND SPACING ERRORS

Two common errors that you need to watch for in written communications are transpositions and spacing errors.

Proofreading for Transpositions

Transpositions—erroneous rearrangements of keystrokes or words—occur frequently in business writing. Note the following examples:

> Load the software on the <u>comptuer</u>. (*should be* <u>computer</u>)

> Dr. Wynn is the newest member of <u>teh</u> faculty. (*should be* <u>the</u>)

When you proofread a hard copy of a document, you can spot transpositions by reading word for word and letter for letter. If you proofread on the computer, the spell checker usually will detect transpositions that result in misspelled words. However, a spell checker will not detect transpositions that spell actual words, such as those in the following examples:

> We ordered the software for a 30-day free <u>trail</u>. (*should be* <u>trial</u>)

> Salespeople should have <u>lost</u> of enthusiasm. (*should be* <u>lots</u>)

The words *trail* and *lost* in the preceding examples are correctly spelled but incorrectly used—they would not be detected by a spell checker. You must be alert to these and other transpositions that spell actual words but are the wrong words for the context. Some other examples:

quiet *instead of* quite	won *instead of* own
there *instead of* three	form *instead of* from

Although spell checkers will detect most transpositions in words, they will not detect transpositions in numbers. Therefore, you should proofread numbers carefully.

Revision Symbol for Marking Transpositions

The revision symbol for transposing copy (∪∩) indicates that items should change places. Study the following examples to learn how to mark a transposition for correction.

Revision	Edited Draft	Final Copy
Transpose letters	teh next meeting	the next meeting
Transpose words	most the of staff	most of the staff
Transpose numbers	Invoice 4657	Invoice 4567

Study the following proofreading tips. Then complete Checkup 1-11, which will give you practice in finding transpositions.

Is the copy in Column A identical to the copy in Column B? Assume that the copy in Column A is correct and that there are some transpositions in Column B. Use the correct revision symbol to mark each error. Mark *C* for *Correct* beside the item number if there are no errors.

A	**B**
1. jmfreight@harrisville.net	jmfrieght@harrisville.net
2. October 31, 1999	October 13, 1999
3. Athens, Greece	Athens, Greeec
4. 008-56-2193	008-56-1293
5. He makes service calls every day.	He makes service calls evrey day.
6. Natalie Brooks-Peeler 420-04-2198	Natalie Brooks-Peeler 420-04-2189
7. Dayton, OH 45459-3473	Dayton, OH 45459-4373
8. Most of us received the news by e-mail.	Most of us recieved the news by e-mail.
9. Frieda bought a new car.	Frieda bought a new car.
10. The plane should be at the gate by 6:30 p.m.	The plane should at be the gate by 6:30 p.m.

The following exercise will give you additional practice in finding and marking transposition errors. It also gives you practice in finding transpositions without an original document for comparison. Be sure to read for content as well as for spelling.

CHECKUP 1-12 In each of the following sentences, use the appropriate revision symbol to mark transposition errors.

1. Age determines many our of activities throughout our lives.

   For example, children begin school at about age 5 or 6.

2. The minimum age for a driver's license in many states is 61.

   In some states a learner's permit can be obtained as early as

   age 51.

3. In many states, children need their parents to sign for a

   checking account until they turn 81.

4. Citizens must be 81 years old to vote. The voting age used to be 12.

5. Workers usually retire between the ages of 62 and 07.

Proofreading for Correct Spacing

Spacing errors frequently occur between words and numbers or with punctuation marks. Note the following examples:

Wait <u>bythe</u> water fountain. (*should be* by the water fountain)

She will leave <u>onthe</u> following day. (*should be* on the following day)

Our newest office will be in <u>Salem,North</u> Carolina. (*should be* Salem, North Carolina)

The use of standard spacing is important in making sure that written communications are correct. This section reviews basic guidelines for standard spacing, particularly the spacing used with punctuation.

Be aware that some word processing programs automatically adjust the spacing between words and after punctuation. This happens most frequently when you are using full justification. Full justification ends all lines evenly at the left and right margins. Newspaper columns are an example of this format.

Review the following summary of spacing used with punctuation marks.

1. There is no space before:
    a. A period, question mark, or exclamation point.

       Tomas painted the table.   Was the meeting canceled?

    b. A comma.

       The exhibit opens on Monday, September 5.

    c. A semicolon.

       Gary designed the Web site; Denise wrote the program.

    d. A colon.

       We offer these benefits: medical coverage, flexible schedules, and stock options.

    e. A closing quotation mark.

       Read the article "E-Commerce" in the newsletter.

    f. A closing bracket or parenthesis.

       Call your friends overseas on the weekend (when rates are lower).

    g. A hyphen.

       He is a high-ranking government official.

2. There is no space after:
  a. A period, question mark, or exclamation point when followed by another punctuation mark.

    The contract should read "on or before April 1."

  b. An opening bracket or parenthesis.

    All employees (except first-year employees) receive two weeks' paid vacation.

  c. An opening quotation mark.

    Carol asked, "Who is chairing the conference?"

  d. A closing bracket or parenthesis when followed by another punctuation mark.

    Mark Sessions gave the talk (don't you know him?).

  e. An asterisk in a footnote.

    *Based on current census information.

From a medical transcription tape: "The patient experienced pain with breeding."
Source: Medical Consultants Network, Inc.

3. There is no space before or after:
  a. An apostrophe within a word.

    It's our responsibility to provide quality patient care.

  b. A decimal point within a number.

    Grant Memorial handles 67.5 percent of all trauma cases.

  c. A dash (or two hyphens representing a dash) within a sentence.

    Contact Andy Chou—he's our attorney—and get his opinion.

  d. A colon expressing time or ratio.

    His flight will arrive at 12:45 p.m.   Our product was favored by 3:1.

  e. A diagonal.

    Margo is the owner/manager of a consulting firm.

  f. A comma within a number.

    We received 1,105 responses to our survey.

4. There is no space between:
  a. A punctuation mark and closing quotation marks, except for a closing single quotation mark.

    "I propose we expand our product line," Randy said.

  b. Two hyphens used as a dash.

    Most baseball players--including rookies--are well paid.

5. There is one space between:
   a. Single and double quotation marks.

   Lyle said, "What we need is someone who can attract important clients—a 'rainmaker.' "

6. There is one space before:
   a. An opening bracket or parenthesis within a sentence.

   Lowell Dykes (he's our product manager) made the decision.

   b. An opening quotation mark within a sentence.

   She asked, "Who will conduct the research?"

7. There are one or two spaces before:
   a. An opening bracket or parenthesis that follows a sentence and begins a new sentence.

   All board members attended the meeting. (Last year the president was ill.)

   b. An opening quotation mark that begins a new sentence or follows a colon.

   The due date for the project has been changed. "We need to recruit more programmers," was Ben's reaction.

8. There is one space after:
   a. An abbreviation ending in a period within a sentence (unless followed by another punctuation mark).

   All orders are shipped c.o.d. unless otherwise noted.

   b. A comma unless followed by a closing quotation mark.

   Benjamin Roystan, Esq., handles our legal inquiries.

   c. A semicolon.

   Tim completed his degree in August; Jan will complete hers in May.

   d. A colon within a sentence.

   I have a sentimental reason for visiting Syracuse: it is my birthplace.

   e. A closing bracket or parenthesis used within a sentence.

   Our next training seminar (scheduled for March 15) will cover customer service and e-commerce.

   f. An apostrophe that ends a word within a sentence.

   She took a two-months' leave of absence for medical reasons.

9. There are one or two spaces after:

   a. A period, question mark, or exclamation point that ends a sentence. (All of the following examples show one space.)

      We won the contract! Now the challenge begins.

   b. A period used for enumeration.

      Before buying a house:

      1. Examine your finances.

      2. Request a copy of your credit report.

      3. Discuss your housing needs with a realtor.

   c. A closing quotation mark that ends a sentence.

      Jeff said, "I want to make a change." This remark puzzled Doug.

   d. An asterisk at the end of a sentence.

      See page 305 for a detailed explanation.* Note the percentage.

   e. A colon within a sentence.

      We are proud of our record: three years without an accident on the job.

   f. A closing bracket or parenthesis that encloses a complete sentence and is followed by another sentence.

      (Refer to page 15 of the policy for details.) There are some exceptions.

   g. A dash that ends a statement that ends abruptly.

      If only we had— But why didn't you tell us?

Flexibility in applying spacing standards is acceptable in some situations. For example, most word processing programs have a default setting of one space after punctuation at the end of a sentence. As a result, it is correct to use either one or two spaces after a period or other punctuation that ends a sentence, with one space being preferred. If you are in doubt as to what spacing to use, consult a reference manual such as *The Gregg Reference Manual*.

Throughout this book, the exercises use one space after end punctuation, unless otherwise noted.

CHECKUP 1-13   Circle the appropriate number of spaces in the column at the right that correctly completes each sentence. For some sentences you may need to circle more than one number.

Number of Spaces

1. There should be _____ space(s) before a comma.   0   1   2

2. Leave _____ space(s) after a period
    that ends a sentence.   0   1   2

3. There should be _____ space(s) between
    single and double quotation marks.   0   1   2

4. Leave _____ space(s) after an apostrophe
    if it is at the end of a word.   0   1   2

5. There should be _____ space(s) after
    a decimal point within a number.   0   1   2

6. Leave _____ space(s) before an
    apostrophe within a word.   0   1   2

7. There should be _____ space(s) after
    a period following a number or letter
    used for enumeration.   0   1   2

8. Leave _____ space(s) before a colon.   0   1   2

9. There should be _____ space(s)
    after an abbreviation that ends in a period
    within a sentence.   0   1   2

10. Leave _____ space(s) after a period that
    is followed by another punctuation mark. 0   1   2

11. There is no space before a semicolon, but
    there should be _____ space(s) after
    a semicolon.   0   1   2

12. There should be _____ space(s) before an
    opening parenthesis or bracket that encloses
    material that is a complete sentence and is
    preceded by another sentence.   0   1   2

13. After a comma, there should be _____
    space(s) unless there is a closing quotation
    mark immediately following the comma.   0   1   2

14. There is no space before a diagonal, and there
    should be _____ space(s) after a diagonal. 0   1   2

15. There should be _____ space(s) following
    a quotation mark that ends a sentence.   0   1   2

	Number of Spaces

16. Leave _____ space(s) after commas within a number.   0 1 2

17. There should be _____ space(s) before an opening parenthesis or bracket that encloses parenthetic material within a sentence.   0 1 2

18. Leave _____ space(s) after an asterisk within a sentence.   0 1 2

19. When using opening quotation marks, there is no space after, but there should be _____ space(s) before when the quotation begins a sentence or follows a colon.   0 1 2

20. When using closing quotation marks, there is no space before the mark, but there should be _____ space(s) after when the quotation ends a sentence.   0 1 2

Revision Symbols for Adding and Deleting Space

The following examples show the revision symbols for adding and deleting space. Study them carefully before proceeding with the next exercise.

Revision	Edited Draft	Final Copy
Add one space	in the#book	in the book
Add two spaces	at the end.##Next	at the end. Next
Delete space	at the ba⌢nk	at the bank
Leave one space	for⌣ two days	for two days

CHECKUP 1-14   Proofread the following paragraph and use the appropriate revision symbols to mark any spacing errors.

Customer service is important in a variety of work settings— from hospitals to offices to retail stores. There are several things you can do to develop a winning customer service attitude. First, always be optimistic when you are handling a customer 's request or complaint. No matter what the situation,be positive. Show genuine interest in the customer. You can accomplish this by (1) asking the customer to explain what is wanted, (2) listening carefully, and (3) approaching the situation with a "can do" attitude. To better assist customers, familiarize yourself with the products and services your organization provides. That way you will be better equipped to handle any customer inquires. Whenever you communicate with customers, remember : put the customer first.

The following tips provide detailed suggestions for proofreading documents on the computer screen. Refer to these tips as you complete the CD-ROM applications in each chapter of *Developing Proofreading and Editing Skills*.

TIPS

PROOFREADING ON THE COMPUTER SCREEN

- Proofread the document on the screen before printing it.

- Use the proofreading method or combination of methods that works best for you.

- Scroll through the document, and proofread line by line as each line appears at the bottom of the screen.

- Move the cursor through the document, and check each word and number as you come to it.

- Run the spell checker.

- Make corrections or changes and save the corrected document.

- Print the document and proofread it.

- If additional errors are found, make the corrections and save the corrected document.

- Print the corrected document and proofread it.

As you have learned in this chapter, some keyboarding errors are obvious; others escape detection frequently. You should consider it your responsibility to find and correct errors in all written communications you proofread—no matter who prepares the document.

Application I-A

At a recent meeting staff members wrote their names and home e-mail addresses on a list to be compiled for department use. Compare the typed list on the next page with the handwritten list below. Use revision symbols to correct any errors in the typed list.

Nancy Hilderbran	nancy@lakeview.net
Harry Nelson	harryn@blueridgemtn.net
Zach W. Taylor	zachwt@hiddenvalley.net
Evelyn R. Owenby	erowenby@blueridgemtn.net
H. Gordon Wexler	wexler@lakeview.net
Catherine Mobley	catherine@hiddenvalley.net
Michael S. Miller	mike@skytel.net
J. W. Harrison	jwh@battleground.net
Patricia Abbott	patabb@battleground.net
J. B. Roland	jbroland@hiddenvalley.net
Barbara Goldberg	bgoldberg@citytower.net
Darlene S. Wray	dswray@citytower.net
Betty H. Searcey	bettys@skytel.net
Lynn S. Norman	lnorman@hiddenvalley.net
Amber B. Camp	abc@blueridgemtn.net
Sarah Ann Booth	sbooth@citytower.net
William Starnes	bill@skytel.net
Brandon Koch	koch@piedmont.net
Brady S. Bellemy	bbellemy@piedmont.net
Mary Elizabeth Wirt	mewirt@piedmont.net

Application I-A (continued)

Note that the names in this typed version of the list have been placed in alphabetical order.

Patricia Abbott   patab@battleground.net

Brady S. Bellemy   bbellemy@piedmont.net

Sarah Ann Booth   sboooth@citytower.net

Amber B. Camp   abc@blueridgmtn.net

Barbara Goldberg   bgoldberg@citytower.net

J. W. Harrison   jwh@battleground.net

Nancy Hilderbran   nancy@lakeview.net

Branden Koch   koch@piedmont.net

Michael S. Miller   mike@skytel.net

Catherine Mobley   katherine@hiddenvalley.net

Larry Nelson   harryn@blueridgemtn.net

Lynn S. Norman   lnorman@hiddenvalley.net

Evelyn R. Owensby   erowensby@blueridgemtn.net

J. B. Roland   jbroland@hiddenvalley.net

Betty H. Searcey   bettys@skytel.net

William Starnes   bill@skytel.net

Zach W. Taylor   zachwt@hiddenvallley.net

H. Gordon Wexler   wexler@lakeview.net

Mary Elizabeth Wirt   mewirt @ piedmont.net

Darlene S. Wray   dsray@citytower.net

NAME _____ DATE _____

Application 1-B

While staffing your company's booth at a conference, you asked visitors to register for a door prize in order to collect address information from them. Compare the typed list on the next page with the registration form below. Use appropriate revision symbols to mark any corrections to the typed list. Place a check mark beside each entry on the typed list that is correct.

Register to Win a Door Prize!

Name	Mr. David Stoesifer	Name	Mr. J. Michael McCabe
Company	Dexter Data Consultants	Company	City Office Services
Address	2286 Marguerite Avenue	Address	19264 Ginocchio Court
	Syracuse, NY 13207		Bakersville, CA 93363
Telephone	315-864-2613	Telephone	805-249-6734
E-mail	dstoesifer@syra.net	E-mail	mccabe@bakers.net
Name	Ms. Jacqueline McCrorie	Name	Mrs. Anita Sanchez
Company	Triangle Technology Group	Company	Rosenzwieg Center, Inc.
Address	P.O. Box 17892	Address	1386 Edgemoor Avenue
	Paducah, KY 42002		Boston, MA 02181
Telephone	502-287-6153	Telephone	617-389-4428
E-mail	jacmccrorie@stables.com	E-mail	asanchez@mass.com
Name	Mr. J. C. Delachevrotiere	Name	Ms. Benita Branson
Company	Imperial Graphics and Communications	Company	Branson Ultrasonics Corp.
Address	9218 West Florissant Avenue	Address	19236 Muirfield Court
	St. Louis, MO 63115-9218		Grand Rapids, MI 49506
Telephone	314-527-9984	Telephone	616-897-2182
E-mail	jcd@graphics.net	E-mail	bransonb@rapids.net
Name	Dr. Linda S. Spradley	Name	Dr. Donald J. Tyndall
Company	Spradley Communications	Company	Datatronics, Inc.
Address	1831 Wimbledon Court	Address	P.O. Box 2189
	South Bend, IN 46613		Broken Arrow, OK 74011-2189
Telephone	219-492-8876	Telephone	405-568-2247
E-mail	spradley@indiana.net	E-mail	djtyndall@okla.net
Name	Ms. Amanda S. Browillette	Name	Mr. Malcolm Brantley Wilkinson
Company	Professional Management Systems	Company	Multigraphics, Inc.
Address	1449 Eucalyptus Drive	Address	12423 Nuecestown Road
	Orlando, FL 32181		Corpus Christi, TX 78410
Telephone	407-397-4487	Telephone	512-675-3489
E-mail	asbrowillette@sunshine.net	E-mail	brantley@cctx.net

Application I-B (continued)

Ms. Benita Branson
Branson Ultrasonics Corp.
19236 Muirfield Court
Grand Rapids, MH 49506
616-897-2182
bransonb@rapids.net

Ms. Amanda S. Browillette
Professional Management
Systems
1449 Eucalyptus Drive
Orlando, FL 32181
407-397-4487
asbrowillette@sunshine.net

Ms. J. C. Delachevrotiere
Imperial Graphics and
Communications
9218 West Florissant Avenue
St. Louis, MO 63115-9218
341-527-9984
jcd@graphics.net

Mr. J. Michael McCabe
City Office Services
19264 Ginochio Court
Bakersville, CA 93363
805-249-6734
mccabe@bakers.net

Ms. Jacqueline McCrorie
Triangle Technology Group
Post Office 17892
Paducah, KY 42002
502-287-6153
jacmcrorie@stables.com

Mrs. Anita Sanchez
Rosenzweig Center, Inc.
1386 Edgemoor Avenue
Boston, MA 02181
617-389-4428
asanchez@mass.com

Dr. Linda S. Spradley
Spradley Communications
1831 Wimbleton Court
South Bend, IN 46613
219-492-8876
spradley@indiana.net

Mr. David Stoesifer
Dexter Data Consultants
2286 Marguerite Avenue
Syracuse, NY 13207
315-864-2613
dstoesifer@syra.net

Dr. Donald J. Tyndall
Datatronics, Inc.
P.O. Box 2198
Broken Arrow, OK 74011-2198
405-568-2247
djtyndall@okla.net

Mr. Malcolm Brantley Wilkinson
Multigraphics, Inc.
12423 Nuecetown Road
Corpus Cristi, TX 78410
512-675-3489
brantley@cctx.net

Application 1-C

Proofread the following memo. Use appropriate revision symbols to correct any misstrokes, repetitions, omissions, transpositions, and spacing errors.

MEMO TO: Esteban Lopez

FORM: Aniela Orlano

DATE: October 30,2001

SUBJECT: Menu for Board Meeting

Below is the proposed menu for the November board meeting. Please let me know by November 2 if any changes are desired.

MENU

Tomato Juice
Shrimp Cocktail
Fresh Garden Salad wit Poppy Seem Dressing
Baked Beast off Chicken
Green Deans
Buttered Yeast Diner Rolls
Cherry Cheesecaked
Iced Tea or Coffee

Application 1-D

Proofread the following flyer that is to be posted throughout the Central College campus. Use appropriate revision symbols to correct errors.

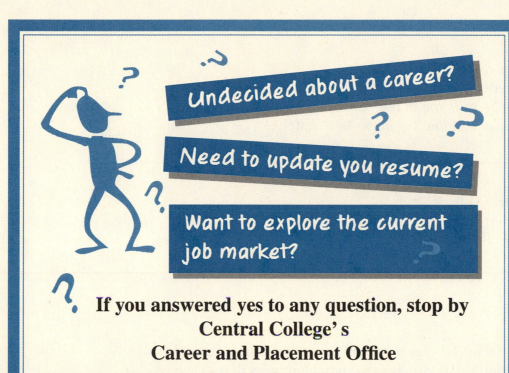

Undecided about a career?

Need to update you resume?

Want to explore the current job market?

If you answered yes to any question, stop by Central College's Career and Placement Office

We provide career planning and job placement services for both students an alumni. Stop by our office from 9 a.m. to 8 p. m. Monday through Friday in Foster Hall, Room 16, for a career assessment.

Our six full- time placement specialists will assist you with:
• Career exploration
• Job searches
• Resume writng
• Mock interviews
• Interveiws with prospective employers

Call our career hotline today!
212-555-2273

CD-ROM Application 1-E

Using your word processor (Microsoft® Word or Corel® WordPerfect), open the file DPES01E from the *Developing Proofreading and Editing Skills* CD-ROM. A copy of the memo is shown here. Make the changes listed below, then run the spell checker. Save the revised memo using your initials in place of the DPES. Proofread the memo on the screen and make any additional corrections. Save and print the corrected memo.

1. Change the date to *August 31*.
2. Change Frederick Conner's extension number to *4283*.
3. Change *the to* to *to the* in the second sentence.
4. Delete the second *that the* in the last sentence.

MEMO TO: Patrick Tracy

FROM: Candice O' Leary

DATE: August 13, <small><YEAR></small>

SUBJECT: New Telephone Extensions

Below is a list of changes in telephone extension numbers. These are in addition the to numbers for new employees that I gave you last week.

Harriet Allen	4206
Frederick Conner	4238
Phillip Littlejohn	4289
Glenda Milsap	4278
Benita Alveraz	4265

Please make these changes and bee sure that the that the entries appear in the online directory.

CD-ROM Application I-F

Using your word processor, open the file DPES01F from the CD-ROM. Proofread the letter to Mrs. Pruitt on the screen and correct any misstrokes, omissions, repetitions, transpositions, and spacing errors. Run the spell checker, then save the letter using your initials in place of the DPES. Proofread the letter on the screen, make any additional corrections, then save and print the letter.

April 17, <YEAR>

Mrs. Kelley Pruitt
Nations Hardware Store
3481 South Tryon Street
Charlotte,NC 22811

Dear Ms. Pruitt:

Thank you for using our travel services on our recent trip to Kansas City. I hope that attending the annual Kansas City Hardware Exposition was beneficial to you.

In reviewing your travel arrangements for next month, we noticed that you have scheduled a family trip (for people) to Orlando, Florida, and a business trip (on person) to Atlanta, Georgia. We took advantage of the recent reduction in airfares and saved you $50 per person on the flight to Orlando and $25 on your trip to Atlanta. (You may have red about the lowered rates in the in the newspaper.) Your net savings of $225 has been credited to your personal account ($200) and your corporate account ($25).

I own four tickets to Walt Disney World a at recent travel convention. These tickets are enclosed for you and your family.

Sincerely,

Andrea Marvin
Travel Consultant

kd
Enclosures

Spelling and Word Usage

OBJECTIVES

After completing this chapter, you should be able to:

1. Apply basic spelling rules to spell words correctly.

2. Identify and correct errors in using homonyms, false homonyms, and words that may be written as one word or two words.

3. Use a dictionary, wordbook, reference manual, spell checker, and grammar checker to verify spelling and to select the appropriate word.

4. Consult a thesaurus to find synonyms and antonyms for vague or overused words.

5. Use appropriate revision symbols to indicate corrections in misspelled or misused words.

In some cases, spelling errors may be amusing to readers but they are embarrassing to the person who made the error. Consider the following error that appeared on diplomas given to one graduating class of the U.S. Naval Academy:

The Seal of the Navel Academy is hereunto affixed.

Confusing the spelling of two similar words such as *naval* and *navel* is a common error in business writing. A good proofreader would have detected such an error.

This chapter will give you practice in correcting misspellings that break spelling rules as well as mix-ups in using sound-alike words and words spelled as one or two words. You will also become familiar with using print and electronic resources to verify spelling and to select synonyms and antonyms.

SPELLING RULES

There are many variations in spelling patterns in the English language—so many, in fact, that there are few spelling rules that do not have exceptions. The following basic rules, however, will help you to avoid many of the most common spelling errors. Pay careful attention to these rules.

1. **Ei and ie.** Usually, *ie* is used when the sound is *e*, and *ei* is used when the sound is *a* or appears after the letter *c*.

ie: piece	believe	field	relief
ei: weigh	neighbor	eight	vein
receive	receipt	ceiling	perceive

2. **Final silent e.** A final silent *e* is usually dropped when a suffix beginning with a vowel is added to the word (a *suffix* is a word ending).

   use + able = usable   response + ible = responsible

   disclose + ure = disclosure   expense + ive = expensive

   believe + ing = believing   size + able = sizable

   Words ending in *ee* (*agree, see*) do not drop an *e* when a suffix beginning with a vowel is added (*agreeable, seeing*).

   A silent *e* is usually retained when a suffix beginning with a consonant (any letter other than *a, e, i, o, u,* and *y*) is added to the word.

   achieve + ment = achievement

   hope + ful = hopeful

   late + ness = lateness

   immediate + ly = immediately

   Exceptions

   acknowledge + ment = acknowledgment

   judge + ment = judgment

   nine + th = ninth

   Note: Both *acknowledgment* and *judgment* have two different spellings. The preferred spellings are shown here.

3. **Words ending in ie or y.** For words ending in *ie*, change the *ie* to *y* before adding *ing*.

   lie + ing = lying

   tie + ing = tying

   For words ending in a consonant plus *y*, change the *y* to *i* before adding a suffix.

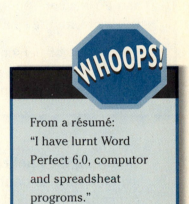

WHOOPS!

From a résumé:
"I have lurnt Word Perfect 6.0, computor and spreadsheat progroms."
Source: Accountemps

temporary + ly = temporarily   rely + able = reliable

heavy + er = heavier   easy + est = easiest

If the suffix itself begins with an *i*, do not double the *i*.

library + ian = librarian   apply + ing = applying

For words ending in a vowel plus *y*, keep the *y* when adding the suffix.

play + er = player   say + ing = saying

employ + ed = employed

TIPS

IMPROVE YOUR SPELLING

- Identify word endings or combinations of letters (such as *ie* and *ei*) that present you with spelling problems. Familiarize yourself with the spelling rules for these situations.

- Keep a list of personal spelling demons—words that are a challenge for you to spell correctly. Memorize these words and watch for them in the documents that you proofread.

4. **Doubling the final consonant.** A final consonant for a one-syllable word is doubled when the word ends in a single consonant preceded by a single vowel and a vowel begins the suffix.

plan + ing = planning   slim + est = slimmest

cup + ed = cupped   fat + y = fatty

A final consonant for a one-syllable word is not doubled when the suffix also begins with a consonant.

cup + ful = cupful   seam + less = seamless

For words of more than one syllable that end in a single consonant preceded by a single vowel, double the final consonant before a suffix beginning with a vowel *if the last syllable of the root word is accented*.

refer + ed = referred   (accent on *fer*)

begin + ing = beginning   (accent on *gin*)

occur + ed = occurred   (accent on *cur*)

forget + ing = forgetting   (accent on *get*)

Exceptions

Two words familiar to computer users do not fit these rules:

format + ing = formatting   program + ed = programmed

5. **Special problems.** Beware of words ending in *ant, ent, ance, ence, able, ible, ise,* and *ize.* These words are very troublesome because they do not follow any set rules. When you are not absolutely sure of the spelling of a word with one of these endings, look it up.

ant	defendant, resistant
ent	dependent, persistent
able	dependable, reasonable
ible	feasible, flexible
ance	assistance, importance
ence	intelligence, occurrence
ise	enterprise, advertise
ize	summarize, recognize

Note: A few commonly used words end in *yze: analyze, paralyze.*

Even in today's high-tech world, informal communications may still be handwritten for convenience. Checkup 2-1 will give you experience in detecting misspelled words in handwritten documents.

CHECKUP 2-1 Circle the misspelled words in the following sentences, and write the correct spellings in the space provided. A sentence may have more than one misspelled word.

1. *Rain suits should be waterproof, not merely water resistent.*

   _____

2. *The prefered method of payment for the carpetting is by credit card.*

   _____

3. *Exerciseing three times a week will help keep your weight at a managable level.*

   _____

4. *Cathy, the sales manager, said that appearances can be deceiveing.*

   _____

5. *Both attornies summarised their arguements before the jury.*

   _____

6. *After reviewing her acheivements, the committee awarded Irene the full scholarship.*

   _____

7. *Meera refered to the patient's chart to see if there was any gain in wieght.*

   _____

8. *Fax machines should be available on each floor of the building. The equipment should be dependible and inexpensave to operate.*

   _____

9. *Brent's hobby of tying flys for trout fishing has turned into a very lucrative business.*

   _____

10. *Shelly asked for my assistence in planing the training seminar.*

   _____

REVISION SYMBOLS FOR MARKING SPELLING AND WORD USAGE ERRORS

The following revision symbols are used to mark errors in spelling and word usage. Some of these symbols were first introduced in Chapter 1.

Revision	Edited Draft	Final Copy
Change a letter	dependant	dependent
Change a word	sight	cite
Delete a letter and close up	useable	usable
Insert a letter	leisurly	leisurely
Transpose letters	reciept	receipt
Insert a space	We maybe traveling.	We may be traveling.
Delete a space	Every one will attend.	Everyone will attend.

Use appropriate revision symbols to correct the spelling errors in the following sentences.

1. Sam recognised the missing child from the poster in the post office lobby.

2. After hiking for 12 miles, Alice eagerly cuped her hands to catch drinking water from the cool mountain stream.

3. Al's computer was programed correctly for document formating.

4. Karel was flying to Maryland this weekend for a conference and was temporaryly delayed because of bad weather.

5. We are hopful that his latest acheivements will influence the contest judges.

6. During the remodeling process, the cielings in all eight rooms will be lowered and painted white.

7. Even though the perishible items were ruined, all of the canned food items are useable.

8. Edward's positive attitude was detected immediatly.

9. After only six months on the job, Abigail was promoted to assistent manager.

10. As a student, I must find a job that allows flexability in arrangeing my work hours around my class schedule.

SPELLING CHALLENGES

As you proofread, you must be prepared to deal with the challenges of words that sound alike but are spelled differently, words that sound somewhat alike and are often confused, and words that may be spelled as either one or two words.

Homonyms

Homonyms—words that sound the same and are spelled similarly but have different meanings—frequently cause problems. Use a wordbook, a dictionary, or a reference manual to check the spelling of these similar words. Some of the most commonly confused homonyms appear in the following table.

ad (advertisement) **add** (to join or combine)	**overdo** (do too much) **overdue** (past due)
allowed (permitted) **aloud** (spoken)	**pain** (hurt) **pane** (glass panel)
assistance (aid) **assistants** (helpers)	**pair** (one and one) **pare** (to cut) **pear** (fruit)
bare (empty; uncovered) **bear** (to carry)	**passed** (gone by) **past** (beyond)
beat (to hit) **beet** (vegetable)	**patience** (tolerance) **patients** (ill persons)
board (wood) **bored** (weary)	**peace** (serenity) **piece** (portion of)
brake (stop) **break** (cut)	**plain** (simple) **plane** (aircraft)
buy (to purchase) **by** (near)	**principal** (main) **principle** (a rule)
capital (seat of government) **capitol** (building)	**raise** (to lift) **raze** (to destroy)
cereal (grain) **serial** (in a series)	**right** (correct) **write** (to compose)
cite (to refer to) **sight** (a view) **site** (a place)	**some** (a few) **sum** (total)
coarse (rough) **course** (path)	**stationary** (still) **stationery** (paper)
council (a meeting) **counsel** (to advise)	**their** (possessive) **there** (a place) **they're** (they are)
discreet (secretive) **discrete** (separate)	**threw** (tossed) **through** (during; ended)
dew (moisture) **do** (to accomplish) **due** (payable)	**to** (toward) **too** (also) **two** (one and one)
fair (equitable; just) **fare** (a charge)	**undo** (unmake) **undue** (not called for)
hear (to listen) **here** (at present)	**waist** (body part) **waste** (to destroy)
hole (opening) **whole** (all)	**wait** (pause) **weight** (heaviness)
its (possessive of *it*) **it's** (it is)	**waive** (to let go) **wave** (gesture)

(continued)

EASILY CONFUSED WORDS
HOMONYMS

knew (aware of)	**ware** (goods)
new (original)	**wear** (to have on)
	where (in a place)
leased (rented)	**weak** (feeble)
least (slightest)	**week** (seven days)
loan (lend)	**weather** (atmospheric conditions)
lone (alone)	**whether** (if)
mail (postal items)	**who's** (who is)
male (masculine)	**whose** (belonging to someone)
meat (food)	**you're** (you are)
meet (to convene)	**your** (belonging to you)

Checkup 2-3 will give you practice in finding errors in correctly spelled but incorrectly used words. Some of the incorrectly used words appear in the preceding table; others do not.

CHECKUP 2-3   Use appropriate revision symbols to mark the incorrectly used words in the following sentences. Some sentences may be correct. Write a *C* for *Correct* beside the item number if the sentence contains no errors. You may need to use a dictionary or a wordbook to complete this exercise.

1. Do you know weather Carol will coordinate the relief effort for flood victims?

2. Once you are threw with your orientation, you will be given a project to manage.

3. The new headquarters will be built on a sight near the interstate highway.

4. Most of us were two absorbed in our work to pay attention to the public address announcement.

5. The hospital took a pole of employees to get their reactions to the upcoming merger.

6. What is the basis for the reporter's story?

7. The Red Cross requests donations from individuals to help pay for disaster aide.

8. Each intern will be pared with an employee who will serve as a mentor.

9. Do you know if you're schedule includes a sales trip to Dallas?

10. Given the circumstances of the case, the attorney thought the verdict was fare.

Pseudohomonyms

Pseudohomonyms or "false" homonyms are words that sound somewhat alike but, when pronounced correctly, they do not sound exactly alike and they also have different meanings. The following table lists some of the most often confused pseudohomonyms.

EASILY CONFUSED WORDS	
PSEUDOHOMONYMS	
accept (take or receive) **except** (exclude)	**ensure** (to make certain) **insure** (to guard against)
access (admittance) **excess** (too much)	**expand** (to stretch) **expend** (to use)
adapt (to adjust) **adept** (skilled) **adopt** (to select)	**farther** (distant) **further** (go beyond)
advice (recommendation) **advise** (to inform)	**fiscal** (financial) **physical** (bodily)
affect (to change) **effect** (a result)	**intense** (focused) **intents** (goals)
alternate (a substitute) **alternative** (a choice)	**later** (in the future) **latter** (recent)
appraise (to assess) **apprise** (to inform)	**liable** (responsible) **libel** (slanderous comment)
beside (next to) **besides** (in addition to)	**loose** (free) **lose** (to fail) **loss** (something lost)
choose (to select) **chose** (had selected)	**moral** (ethical) **morale** (feeling)
complement (a complete set) **compliment** (praise)	**persecute** (to harrasss) **prosecute** (to sue)
conscience (moral sense) **conscious** (aware)	**personal** (private) **personnel** (workforce)
detract (take away from) **distract** (to divert attention)	**precede** (go ahead of) **proceed** (move forward)
device (instrument) **devise** (to plan)	**propose** (to suggest) **purpose** (aim)
disapprove (to reject) **disprove** (to prove false)	**quiet** (silent) **quit** (to give up) **quite** (rather)
disburse (to distribute) **disperse** (to scatter)	**respectfully** (courteously) **respectively** (separately)
elicit (to draw out) **illicit** (unlawful)	**suit** (a legal action; clothes) **suite** (group of items) **sweet** (sugary)

(continued)

EASILY CONFUSED WORDS
PSEUDOHOMONYMS

eligible (qualified)	**than** (otherwise)
illegible (unreadable)	**then** (additionally; formerly)
eminent (prominent)	**thorough** (complete)
imminent (upcoming)	**through** (during; ended)

When you encounter pseudohomonyms in material you are proofreading, be sure to question the usage of each word. Use a dictionary or a reference manual to verify your word choice.

CHECKUP 2-4 Use appropriate revision symbols to mark incorrectly used words in the following paragraphs.

Many companies have adapted a casual dress policy for their employees. Employees may have the option of wearing casual dress one day each week or every day of the week. A casual dress policy has a good affect on employee moral. Dressing casually has aloud employees to be more relaxed and comfortable while performing their jobs. This relaxed atmosphere leads to greater productivity.

In many workplace settings, casual dress consists of coordinated outfits that are less formal then business suites. Depending on the company, casual dress may consist of khaki slacks and a sweater or jeans and a sweatshirt. Companies make it convenient for employees by recommending a variety of casual dress choices to chose from.

Sent as part of an e-mail message: "Please provide an account number too charge the costs against."

One Word or Two?

There are many commonly used words that may be written as either one or two words. Which form is used depends on the intended meaning. For example:

Wrong: Sally soon mastered the <u>every day</u> routine of the office.

Right: Sally soon mastered the <u>everyday</u> routine of the office.

Wrong: Sally attended <u>everyday</u> of the conference.

Right: Sally attended <u>every day</u> of the conference.

Spell checkers are of little use in detecting errors in words that can correctly be written as either one word or two words. If the grammar checker highlights a word or words as a potential error, the user still has to decide which form is correct: one word or two words. Refer to the following table for some commonly confused words.

EASILY CONFUSED WORDS
ONE WORD OR TWO WORDS

almost (nearly) **all most** (all very pleased)	**everyone** (everybody) **every one** (each person)
already (previously) **all ready** (prepared)	**indirect** (not direct) **in direct** (in contrast to)
altogether (completely) **all together** (in a group)	**into** (within) **in to** (to go in)
always (at all times) **all ways** (by every means)	**maybe** (perhaps) **may be** (might be)
anymore (any longer) **any more** (additional)	**nobody** (no person) **no body** (no group)
anyone (anybody) **any one** (any one person)	**onto** (moving forward) **on to** (proceed to)
anything (any thing at all) **any thing** (only one thing)	**someday** (in the future) **some day** (any day)
anyway (in any case) **any way** (by any means)	**someone** (some person) **some one** (any one person)
awhile (for a short time) **a while** (a short period of time)	**something** (any one thing) **some thing** (a particular thing)
cannot (unable to do) **can not** (cannot help but)	**sometime** (at no specific time) **some time** (a period of time)
everyday (ordinary) **every day** (each day)	**upon** (on) **up on** (on top of)

The next Checkup gives you practice in deciding whether to use one word or two. Some of the words appear in the preceding table; others do not.

CHECKUP 2-5   Use a dictionary to help you determine which of the two words in parentheses is correct. Circle the correct word.

1. Cathy said that she (maybe, may be) transferred to Arizona.

2. (Everybody, Every body) was on time for the meeting.

3. You should try to (instill, in still) the value of hard work in your children.

4. Max suggested that we do (something, some thing) to recognize exemplary employees.

5. Mrs. Trexler decided that she will apply for the job (anyway, any way).

6. The manager said that he would be out of the office for (awhile, a while) this afternoon.

7. The speaker said, "Let's go (onto, on to) the next agenda item."

8. Kevin is (indirectly, in directly) responsible for the rate increase.

9. Do you have (anymore, any more) stationery?

10. A sales representative will call you (sometime, some time) soon.

Compound Nouns

Compound nouns—nouns formed from joining two or more words—are often misspelled. Many compound nouns are spelled as one solid word while others are spelled as two separate words.

The following compound nouns are always spelled as one solid word; they are sometimes mistakenly spelled as two separate words.

airfare	salesperson
checklist	setup
database	software
eyewitness	spreadsheet
feedback	timetable
goodwill	upgrade
paperwork	workplace
passport	workstation

The following compound nouns are always spelled as two separate words.

cash flow	real estate
check mark	time frame
half hour	word processing

CHECKUP 2-6 Use appropriate revision symbols to mark any incorrectly spelled compound nouns in the following sentences. Write a *C* for *Correct* beside the item number if the sentence contains no errors.

1. All of our associates handle both commercial and residential realestate.

2. You may pick up a pass port application at any post office.

3. Anthony Reeves was named the outstanding sales person for the year.

4. Computer Works offers software upgrades at low prices.

5. Most of the feed back from customers has been helpful.

6. Who designed the check list for preparing contracts?

7. Fidelity Investing updates its online stock report every halfhour.

8. Spread sheets may be used to calculate budget costs.

9. We have a six-month timeframe for completing the project.

10. Excellent customer service generates good will for an organization.

HELPFUL TOOLS

There are a variety of tools for verifying the spelling of words. You can use a dictionary, a wordbook, or a reference manual to verify spelling or word usage and use a thesaurus to find synonyms or antonyms for words. Automated resources for checking spelling include a spell checker, a grammar checker, and a thesaurus.

TIPS

When you are proofreading someone else's writing, don't rely on that person to have spelled all words correctly. Even people with the best education misspell words.

Dictionary

Millions of dictionaries are sold each year, because everybody needs one. If you consider yourself a poor speller, don't worry. You can greatly improve your spelling skills by paying special attention to a few general rules and by getting into the habit of using a dictionary. Whenever you're not sure of the correct spelling of a word, look it up in a dictionary or a wordbook.

Your dictionary is a valuable tool. As you can see by the entries for *counsel* in Figure 2-1 on page 51, the dictionary tells you more than just how to spell the word. It shows you how to divide the word at the end of a line (*coun-sel*). It tells you *counsel* is both a noun (n) and a verb (vb), and it lists the principal parts of that verb (*counseled* as in "I have counseled" and *counseling* as in "I am counseling") with the preferred spelling listed first. The dictionary also gives the different meanings of *counsel* as well as examples of how the word is commonly used in phrases and sentences. As a further help, synonyms for *counsel* are shown in all-capital letters (*deliberation, consultation, purpose, consultant, advise,* and *consult*).

Net Link

For a challenge and some fun while improving your spelling and word use skills, go to the Merriam-Webster® Web site at **http://www.m-w.com.** Besides allowing you to look up words in the Merriam-Webster® dictionary or the thesaurus, the site offers an assortment of word games to test your spelling and vocabulary skill.

¹**coun·sel** \ ¹kaun(t)-səl\ *n* [ME *conseil,* fr. OF, fr. L *consilium,* fr. *consulere* to consult] (13c) **1 a :** advice given esp. as a result of consultation **b :** a policy or plan of action or behavior **2 :** DELIBERATION, CONSULTATION **3 a** *archaic* : PURPOSE **b :** guarded thoughts or intentions **4 a** *pl* **counsel** (1) : a lawyer engaged in the trial or management of a case in court (2) : a lawyer appointed to advise and represent in legal matters an individual client or a corporate and esp. a public body **b :** CONSULTANT 2

²**counsel** *vb* **–seled** *or* **selled**; **-sel•ing** *or* **-sel•ling** \-s(ə-)lin\ *vt* (14c) : ADVISE <~*ed* them to avoid rash actions –George Orwell> ~ *vi* : CONSULT <~*ed* with her husband>

Figure 2-1. Dictionary entries for *counsel.* Note the use of *counsel* as a noun and as a verb.

Source: By permission. From *Merriam-Webster's Collegiate® Dictionary, Tenth Edition* ©1999 by Merriam-Webster, Incorporated.

Wordbook

Wordbooks are helpful spelling references. Although they do not list all the information given in a dictionary, wordbooks do provide the essential word information most business writers need, and they provide this information in a handy format. For example, Figure 2-2 shows a page from the wordbook *20,000+ Words* by Mary Margaret Hosler.

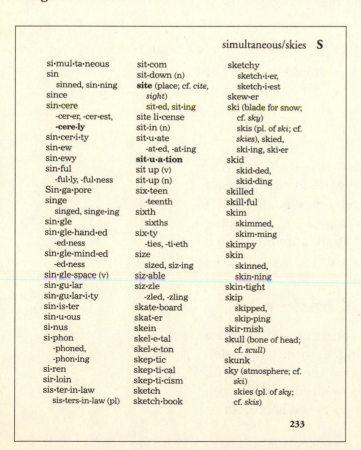

simultaneous/skies **S**

si·mul·ta·neous	sit·com	sketchy
sin	sit-down (n)	sketch·i·er,
sinned, sin·ning	**site** (place; cf. *cite,*	sketch·i·est
since	*sight*)	skew·er
sin·cere	sit·ed, sit·ing	ski (blade for snow;
-cer·er, -cer·est,	site li·cense	cf. *sky*)
-cere·ly	sit-in (n)	skis (pl. of *ski;* cf.
sin·cer·i·ty	sit·u·ate	*skies*), skied,
sin·ew	-at·ed, -at·ing	ski·ing, ski·er
sin·ewy	**sit·u·a·tion**	skid
sin·ful	sit up (v)	skid·ded,
-ful·ly, -ful·ness	sit-up (n)	skid·ding
Sin·ga·pore	six·teen	skilled
singe	-teenth	skill·ful
singed, singe·ing	sixth	skim
sin·gle	sixths	skimmed,
sin·gle-hand·ed	six·ty	skim·ming
-ed·ness	-ties, -ti·eth	skimpy
sin·gle-mind·ed	size	skin
-ed·ness	sized, siz·ing	skinned,
sin·gle-space (v)	siz·able	skin·ning
sin·gu·lar	siz·zle	skin·tight
sin·gu·lar·i·ty	-zled, -zling	skip
sin·is·ter	skate·board	skipped,
sin·u·ous	skat·er	skip·ping
si·nus	skein	skir·mish
si·phon	skel·e·tal	skull (bone of head;
-phoned,	skel·e·ton	cf. *scull*)
-phon·ing	skep·tic	skunk
si·ren	skep·ti·cal	sky (atmosphere; cf.
sir·loin	skep·ti·cism	*ski*)
sis·ter-in-law	sketch	skies (pl. of *sky;*
sis·ters-in-law (pl)	sketch·book	cf. *skis*)

233

Figure 2-2. Sample page from a wordbook.

Source: 20,000+ Words, Tenth Edition (Glencoe/McGraw-Hill, Westerville, Ohio, 1996, p. 233).

This wordbook gives you the spelling and word division for each entry and, where appropriate, lets you know whether a term or expression is written as one word, as two words, or as a hyphenated word. For example, *skateboard* is written as one word. *Sit up* is written as two words when used as a verb, but *sit-up* is written as a hyphenated word when used as a noun.

Verb   *Sit up* straight when the photographer takes your picture.

Noun   Sarah includes 50 *sit-ups* in her daily exercise routine.

This wordbook also notes frequently misspelled plurals such as *skies*, and it distinguishes among other words that might be confusing. Refer to the wordbook page shown in Figure 2-2 to determine which spelling is correct in the following sentence:

We selected a (cite, sight, site) for our new building.

Site is defined as a place; thus, *site* is the correct spelling in the example above. Notice that both *cite* and *sight* are listed as words that may be confused with *site*. (*cf.* is an abbreviation for *confer*, which means "compare").

The wordbook also lists the forms of words that often cause spelling problems. Note, for example, that the *y* in *sixty* is changed to *i* to spell *sixties* and *sixtieth*. Check the wordbook page shown in Figure 2-2 to verify the correct spelling of the underlined words in the following sentence:

The skiers skied down the slope as though they were skiing on air.

A wordbook can be a valuable reference and should be a part of every business professional's library.

Reference Manual

For detailed information on spelling rules and sound-alike words, consult a reference manual such as *The Gregg Reference Manual* (Glencoe/McGraw-Hill, Columbus, Ohio). A reference manual such as this one will provide spelling rules and examples and also definitions for help in selecting between words that are commonly confused or that may be spelled as one or two words.

Spell Checker and Grammar Checker

Most word processing programs have a spell checker that checks a document for errors—particularly spelling errors. The spell checker highlights, or in some other way makes the user aware of, words that are either misspelled or not recognized by the spell checker. The user must then decide whether the word is correct or incorrect.

The spell checker or "spelling verification" has a dictionary of words that it recognizes. Users can add words that are particular to their discipline or occupation, such as law or medicine. For example, proper names and technical terms can be added to the dictionary so that the spell checker will recognize these words and not highlight them as potential errors.

Keep in mind that using a spell checker to verify spelling can lead you to develop a false sense of security in terms of finding and correcting errors. Look at this example:

It has been too months sense hour last meetnig.

The only error the spell checker would find would be the misspelled word *meetnig*. Did you find three more errors? The sentence should read as follows:

It has been two months since our last meeting.

A spell checker generally does not identify words that are correctly spelled but incorrectly used. Therefore, it would not identify the misused words *too*, *sense*, and *hour* in the previous example. Other commonly confused words such as *council-counsel*, *overdo-overdue*, and *weather-whether* will not be highlighted by the spell checker when they are used incorrectly.

A grammar checker, if available with your software, may point out the possibility of an error in some words that are frequently misused. In Figure 2.3 below, read the sentence and the message that is displayed when using the grammar checker in Corel® WordPerfect. The word *effect* is highlighted, and the message displayed on the screen indicates that the word *effect* may be confused with the word *affect*. The grammar checker gives a brief definition of *affect* and *effect*. It's up to the user to decide which word should be used. You must be familiar with the meaning and use of such confusing words in order to choose the correct word. The grammar checker cannot make the correct choice for you.

Figure 2-3. Grammar checker in Corel® WordPerfect.

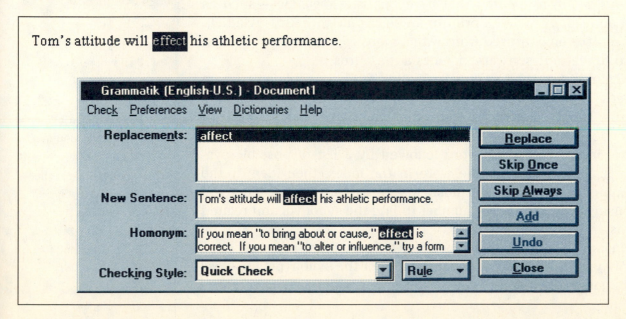

Although the spell checker and grammar checker in software programs catch most spelling and word usage errors, as a professional, you should be able to detect such errors on your own without assistance.

Thesaurus

A thesaurus contains a list of words and their meanings. You can use a thesaurus to help you find *synonyms*—words with similar meanings—such as *begin* and *activate*. You can also use a thesaurus to find *antonyms*—words that have opposite meanings—such as *neat* and *sloppy*. Using a print or an electronic thesaurus will help you replace an overused word with a more appropriate word. Most word processing software includes a thesaurus.

Figure 2-4 at the top of page 55 illustrates a sample entry from *Roget's International Thesaurus*, *Fifth Edition*, a well-known thesaurus. This version of a thesaurus is organized by categories, with *effect* being one word in a category. Words are listed alphabetically in the index, with each word followed by a list of possible synonyms. Simply look up the word in the index, then identify the meaning from the list that most closely matches the meaning you are using. Go to the entry number to find the synonym and related terms.

In Figure 2-4 the words in boldface type are the words most commonly used to express the idea. Note that the synonyms for *effect* are organized by parts of speech, beginning with nouns and verbs.

Net Link

Roget's Thesaurus, a well-known reference source, can be accessed on the Internet. Using a search engine, conduct a search for *Roget's Thesaurus*. Once at the thesaurus site you can look up a word by using the alphabetical index or searching for a word by category.

886 EFFECT

NOUNS **1 effect, result,** resultant, **consequence,** consequent, sequent, sequence, sequel, sequela, sequelae; event, eventuality, eventuation, **upshot, outcome,** logical outcome, possible outcome, scenario; **outgrowth,** spin-off, offshoot, offspring, issue, aftermath, legacy; **product** 892, precipitate, distillate, **fruit,** first fruits, crop, harvest; development, corollary; derivative, derivation, by-product

2 impact, force, **repercussion,** reaction; backwash, backlash, reflex, recoil, response; mark, print, imprint, impress, impression

3 aftereffect, aftermath, aftergrowth, aftercrop, **afterclap,** aftershock, afterimage, afterglow, aftertaste; wake, trail, track; domino effect

VERBS **4 result, ensue, issue, follow,** attend, accompany; **turn out, come out,** fall out redound, **work out,** pan out <nonformal>, fare; have a happy result, turn out well, come up roses <nonformal>; turn out to be, prove, prove to be; **become of,** come of, come about; **develop,** unfold; **eventuate,** terminate, end; **end up,** land up <Brit>, come out, wind up

Figure 2-4. A sample thesaurus entry for *effect*.

Source: From "886 Effect" from ROGET'S INTERNATIONAL THESAURUS, 5th EDITION by PETER MARK ROGET. Copyright © 1992 by HarperCollins Publishers, Inc. Reprinted by permission of HarperCollins Publishers, Inc.

Whether in print or electronic form, using a thesaurus can help you improve your writing. Suppose you are typing a document and want to replace the word *just* in the following sentence because it does not convey your intended meaning of being unbiased.

> Both attorneys want a legal settlement that will be just for everyone.

Using the electronic thesaurus, you would first select the word *just* and then access the thesaurus. The thesaurus would list several synonyms for *just*, similar to those shown in Figure 2-5. Of the synonyms listed, the two most appropriate choices would be *fair* and *equitable*.

Figure 2-5. Grammar checker in Microsoft® Word.

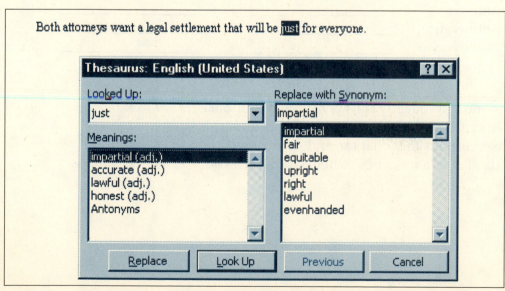

The following Checkups will give you practice in using a thesaurus to find synonyms and antonyms.

CHECKUP 2-7 For each of the following sentences, use a thesaurus to look up each italicized word and replace it with an appropriate synonym. If you have access to word processing software, type each italicized word and look it up in the electronic thesaurus. *Note*: There may be more than one appropriate synonym for each word.

1. Every year, our university plans an educational *trip* for students.

2. The results of the employee survey are *important* and indicate that a policy change is needed.

3. An accountant must make sure that all of the financial reports are *correct*.

4. The antique desk that was bought for this office is both functional and *beautiful*.

5. Aline Bonfim is a *superior* employee and has won the Employee of the Year Award.

CHECKUP 2-8 For each of the following words, write two antonyms in the spaces provided. Use a thesaurus to verify your choices. If you have access to word processing software, type each of the words and use the electronic thesaurus to select appropriate antonyms.

1. old   Antonyms: _____ _____
2. vague   Antonyms: _____ _____
3. late   Antonyms: _____ _____
4. important   Antonyms: _____ _____
5. beneficial   Antonyms: _____ _____

A list of 500 of the most frequently misspelled words in business writing appears in the Appendix of this book. Words from this list are used in the exercises in this chapter and throughout the rest of this book. Use this list as a reference to help strengthen your spelling skills.

Application 2-A

Proofread the following memo. Use revision symbols to indicate misspelled and misused words as well as errors in words that should be written as one word or as two words. Use a thesaurus to select an appropriate synonym for *noncompulsory* in the third paragraph and for *brochures* in the fourth paragraph.

MEMO TO: Steve Berkowitz, Sales Coordinator

FROM: Alice Daves, Human Resource Coordinator

DATE: April 8, <YEAR>

SUBJECT: Fringe Benefits

As a new associate, you are now illegible for most of the fringe benefits offerred by our company. You will be pleased to know that you will not have a brake in your health plan coverage during your employment transition.

Your life assurance plan is now in affect, and your retirement plan will begin after you have been employed for won year. To take advantage of our retirement plan, you must make a contribution of up to five percent of your salary. Your contributions will be matched by the company. Most associates take advantage of the five percent maximum.

You maybe interested in enrolling in noncompulsory coverage at your own expense. We have arranged for dental and vision insurance premiums too be deducted from your check.

Within the next two weeks, you will be recieving brochures that explain each of these benefits in detail. After you have had an opportunity to read the information provided, please let me know if I can help you with your fringe benefit selection in anyway.

1. Synonym for *noncompulsory*:   _____

2. Synonym for *brochures*:   _____

Application 2-B

E-mail messages, though often quite informal, should be correct. Proofread the following two e-mail messages. Use appropriate revision symbols to mark misspelled and misused words as well as errors in words that should be written as one word or as two words.

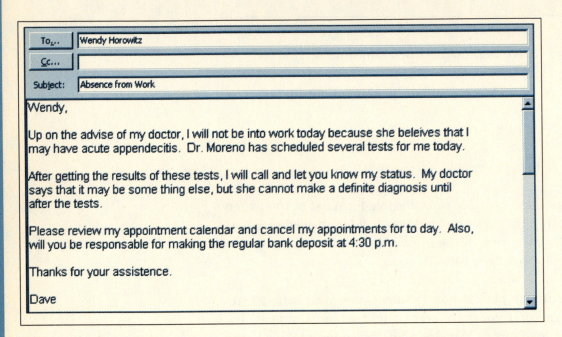

To...   Wendy Horowitz
Cc...
Subject: Absence from Work

Wendy,

Up on the advise of my doctor, I will not be into work today because she beleives that I may have acute appendecitis. Dr. Moreno has scheduled several tests for me today.

After getting the results of these tests, I will call and let you know my status. My doctor says that it may be some thing else, but she cannot make a definite diagnosis until after the tests.

Please review my appointment calendar and cancel my appointments for to day. Also, will you be responsable for making the regular bank deposit at 4:30 p.m.

Thanks for your assistence.

Dave

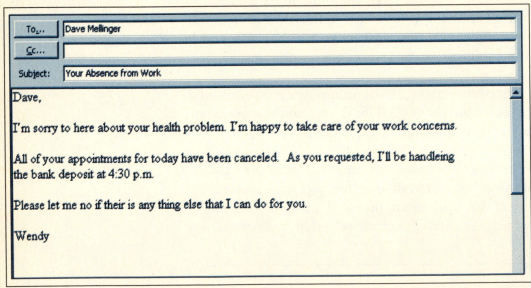

To...   Dave Mellinger
Cc...
Subject: Your Absence from Work

Dave,

I'm sorry to here about your health problem. I'm happy to take care of your work concerns.

All of your appointments for today have been canceled. As you requested, I'll be handleing the bank deposit at 4:30 p.m.

Please let me no if their is any thing else that I can do for you.

Wendy

Application 2-C

Proofread the following letter written to a client of Aetna Realty Services. Use revision symbols to correct any spelling or word usage errors as well as other types of errors.

Aetna Realty Services
2058 W. Cambridge Drive, Eugene, OR 97403-2058
Phone: 541-555-7325 / FAX: 541-555-7337

September 3, <YEAR>

Mr. Dennis Trenjan
Facilities Manager
Aurora Energy Services
906 Treemont Drive, Suite 15
Eugene, OR 97404

Dear Mr. Trenjan:

Aetna Realty Services in is the process of having sum repairs done to the entrance and loading dock of your building. Please be adviced that during the next few weaks we will have contractors working in these areas during regular business hours. The work to be done will include repairing cement and installing an awning. We will also have suit numbers painted on the loading dock doors.

We expect that these upgrades will cause minimal disruptions to your business. Thank you in advance for your pateince and cooperation. Please contact me should you have any questions or concerns.

Sincerely,

Patrice V. Curtis

Patrice V. Curtis
Managment Services Coordiator

Application 2-D

Proofread the following draft of a letter to be sent to a prospective guest of Cowboy Dave's Dude Ranch. Use revision symbols to indicate any spelling or word usage errors as well as other types of errors.

Cowboy Dave's Dude Ranch

2315 Ranchero Road, Cheyenne, Wyoming 82009-1523
1-800-555-3892
cowboydave@ranch.net

March 28, <YEAR>

Mr. Steve Brower
3636 Summer Hill Drive
LosAngeles, CL 90043

Dear Mr. Brower:

Thank you so much for your interest in visiting Cowboy Dave's Dude Ranch. We have a board spectrum of activities that your family will enjoy.

Guests may choose from three levels of horseback riding trials: beginning, intermediate, and advanced. Each of these trails is supervised, and instruction is provided as needed. As a special threat for children, we offer pony rides and a visit to our diary farm where they can milk the cows. At night, you may want to sit a round the campfire and sing traditional ballads and folk songs as will as listen to host stories about haunted caves. You may also choose to relax in your log cabin.

A brochure listing all of our activities is enclosed. Our van can meet your plane and bring you directly to our ranch. Please make your reservations early because we are feeling up fast for the summer months. Please call us at 1-800-555-3892 to make your reservations.

Sincerely,

David Dillon
Owner/Operator

dnp
Enclosure

CD-ROM Application 2-E

Using your word processor (Microsoft® Word or Corel® WordPerfect), open the file DPES02E from the CD-ROM. A copy of the memo is shown here. Make any needed corrections in spelling and word usage, then run the spell checker/grammar checker. Use the thesaurus feature to find a synonym for *proportion* in the second paragraph. Save the revised memo using your initials in place of the DPES. Proofread the memo on the screen and make any additional corrections. Save and print the corrected memo.

MEMO TO: Stephanie Marcos—Sales Manager

FROM: Abigail Miller—Manager

DATE: August 25, <YEAR>

SUBJECT: Increase in Sales Commission

Beginning September 1, we will have a knew sells commission rate of 10 per cent on all cruises. As you know, we have been offering 8 percent. This new rate has been made possible bye continually improving our productivity and reducing our administrative costs.

This increased productivity and the cost reductions are indirect proportion to the amount saved by our implementing soft ware that automatically searches for the lowest available fairs.

Thank you for recommending the new software. We would not have up graded the software with out your recommendation.

CD-ROM Application 2-F

The following copy is a draft of a company's smoking policy. Using your word processor, open the file DPES02F from the CD-ROM. Proofread the policy on the screen and correct any errors. Run the spell checker/grammar checker, then save the revised policy using your initials in place of the DPES. Proofread the corrected policy on the screen, make any additional corrections, then save and print the corrected policy.

Smoking Policy

Beginning October 30, smoking will be prohibited in our office complex accept inn designated areas. The designated areas include the patio at the east wing entrance and the and the first floor lounge besides the mail room.

Reimbursement of up to $300 per employee is offered for any one who documents medical expenditures related to braking the smoking habit. This offer is extended for medical expenses incurred though end of the calendar year.

Violaters of the policy will receive a written reprimand in their personal folders.

Policy #823

October 1, <YEAR>

Capitalization

OBJECTIVES

After completing this chapter, you should be able to:

1. Apply basic capitalization rules as you proofread.

2. Detect and correct capitalization errors that frequently occur in business writing.

3. Detect and correct capitalization errors in memo and letter formats.

4. Use appropriate revision symbols to indicate capitalization errors.

Capitalization is used to give importance and emphasis to words. Notice how the capitalized words in the following example stand out from the rest of the sentence.

Jon works as a computer analyst for America Online.

In order to capitalize words correctly, you must be familiar with capitalization rules. This chapter presents basic capitalization rules that are most often applied in business writing.

APPLYING THE RULES

Capital letters play a very special role in business writing. For example, capital letters are used to indicate the names of particular people, places, and things. Capital letters also have particular uses in letter and memo formats, which will be discussed in Chapter 10.

Study the following capitalization rules carefully. Knowing the rules presented in this chapter will help you to detect and correct capitalization errors as you proofread.

Basic Capitalization Rules

Besides the rules for capitalizing the first word of a sentence and capitalizing proper nouns, there are other capitalization rules that are equally important to know.

1. Capitalize the first word in each sentence. Also capitalize the first word of an item in a list or an outline.

   Please reply by e-mail today.

   Use the software to:
   - Create forms.
   - Design newsletters.
   - Develop brochures.

2. Capitalize proper nouns—the names of particular people, places, and things.

Mrs. Jeanne Spragins	Tao Song Hue
the Serengeti Plain	Lake Michigan
Pyrex plates	the Internet
Brennen Corporation	Hewlett-Packard
Dallas, Texas	Frankfurt, Germany

   Youth Assistance Program of Cleveland County

3. Do *not* capitalize common nouns—nouns that refer in general to people, places, or things.

street	hotel
building	company
employee	woman
city	committees
state	river

SOFTWARE TIPS

Most word processing software has an automatic correction feature that can decrease the frequency of capitalization errors. When activated, the automatic correction feature will either highlight a potential capitalization error or will automatically capitalize text according to the style set up in the software. For example, most programs will capitalize a word in the following situations:

- The letter *I* when used alone.
- The days of the week.
- The first word in a sentence.

Most programs will allow you to "turn off" this feature and let you make your own capitalization decisions.

4. Capitalize titles when they appear before a person's name. Do *not* capitalize titles when they follow or further explain a person's name, except in an inside address or the writer's identification of a letter.

Dr. Alexander Strokanov, visiting professor from Russia, telephoned Barry Hambright.

Dr. Alexander Strokanov, Visiting Professor   Sincerely,
Department of Social Sciences
Springs University
Altamonte Springs, FL 32714

                                                        Nancy Piper
                                                        Sales Manager

5. Capitalize the days of the week, months of the year, holidays, and religious observances. Seasons of the year are *not* capitalized.

Monday, Tuesday	May, June, July	Labor Day
Fourth of July	Martin Luther King Day	Thanksgiving
Kwanzaa	Yom Kippur	Easter
spring	fall	

6. Do *not* capitalize *a.m.* or *p.m.*

11 a.m.   5 p.m.

7. Use all-capital letters for certain abbreviations (shortened forms of words or phrases) and coined acronyms (abbreviations that are pronounced as words). Some abbreviations mix capital and lowercase letters. Check a dictionary or a reference manual to verify the capitalization of abbreviations and acronyms.

Abbreviations:

Mr.	Ms.	Ph.D.	Dr.
Sr.	Inc.	CPA	CEO
HTML	ATM	NCAA	IRS

Acronyms:

SADD (Students Against Drunk Drivers)

PIN (Personal Identification Number)

FAQ (Frequently Asked Questions)

HUD (Housing and Urban Development)

WATS (Wide-Area Telecommunications System)

Cathy studied BASIC and COBOL when she was in college.

Erin Crowe is a CPA.

Patrick Brown, Ph.D., has a counseling practice in Huntersville.

8. All-capital letters may be used for titles of literary works such as books and pamphlets; however, initial capital letters in italics or with an underscore are more commonly used. To be consistent, use the same style within a communication. When using initial capital letters, capitalize the first and all other words that are not articles (*a, an, the*), short prepositions (*of, at, for*), or short conjunctions (*and, or*).

Paula recommended the book SOFTWARE FOR CHILDREN.

Or

Paula recommended the book *Software for Children*.

9. In titles of articles, use initial capital letters for the first word and all other words that are not articles, short prepositions, or short conjunctions. (Article titles are enclosed in quotation marks.)

The title of Sam's article is "Surfing the Internet."

Net Link

For more information on acronyms, connect to the Internet and search for the WorldWideWeb Acronym and Abbreviation Server, or type the URL **http://www.ucc.ie/info /net/acronyms** to go directly to the Web site. This Web site lets you search for an acronym and review its definition plus any related terms.

TIPS

CAPITALIZING IN TITLES

Be familiar with the following words that generally are not capitalized when they appear in titles of books or articles.

Articles—*a, an, the*

Prepositions—*in, at, for, by, on, of, to, up*

Conjunctions—*and, or, but, nor, as*

Note: These words should be capitalized when they appear as the first or last word in the title of a book or article.

CHECKUP 3-1   In each of the following sentences, which of the two terms in parentheses shows the correct capitalization? Circle the correct term.

1. Leif Anderson wrote the book entitled (SUCCESSFUL EXPORTING, Successful exporting).

2. We bought 10 sets of Corning (Dishes, dishes) at a yard sale on Friday.

3. Tanya's article, "Speaking (For, for) Success," will be published in our July edition.

4. You should mail the package by 8:30 (A.M., a.m.)

5. Dr. Anthony Negbenebor, a (Professor, professor) at Grimsley University, is an expert in international exporting.

6. Most banks and federal offices will be closed on Labor (Day, day).

7. Please see that each information packet contains the following:
   - (Employee, employee) handbook
   - (Health, health) plan enrollment forms
   - (Guide, guide) to the company Intranet

8. Most of our customers use (Credit Cards, credit cards).

9. Your attorney, (Ms., ms.) Susan Washburn, has approved the new contract.

10. James D'Antonio is the (OSHA, Osha) inspector for our area.

Here are some additional capitalization rules that are important to know.

10. Capitalize points of the compass (or their derivatives) when they are used to specify a definite region. Do *not* capitalize them when they are used only as a direction or general location.

    The best market for that product is on the East Coast. (Definite region)

    Moss Lake is west of the interstate highway. (Direction)

    The movie plot begins in the Deep South. (Derivative used as definite region)

    Speedy Flight Delivery Service plans to build a small airport on the east side of town. (General location)

    Capitalize points of the compass that appear in mailing addresses.

    1500 East Main Street   12 Southwest Boulevard

11. Capitalize nouns that are followed by numbers or letters that show a sequence, such as account numbers, flight numbers, invoice numbers, and so on.

Account 30426	Room 212
Flight 138A	Item C
Invoice 8163	Policy 22490
Exhibit 12	Building 4C

    Note: Do not capitalize the words *page, line,* and *paragraph* when they are followed by a number.

12. Capitalize the names of people, races, and languages.

Hispanics	African Americans
Indonesian	Portuguese

13. Capitalize the names of specific courses. However, do *not* capitalize the names of academic subjects or areas of study unless they contain a proper noun.

Economics 102	Computer Science 230
allied health	French literature

14. Capitalize the names of trademarked items—items that are licensed to a particular company. Also capitalize the names of computer companies and products as they are shown on the company literature. Some of these names use a style that has an initial capital letter plus a capital letter within a word.

Trademarks:

Kleenex	Band-Aid
Scotch tape	Yellow Pages

Computer Names:

PowerPoint	JavaScript
AltaVista	WordPerfect

TIPS

CAPITALIZATION REFERENCE

Consult a comprehensive reference manual, such as *The Gregg Reference Manual*, for detailed information on capitalization rules. Besides presenting basic capitalization rules, this reference manual also covers special capitalization situations and gives examples of exceptions to rules.

CHECKUP 3-2 In each of the following sentences, which of the two terms in parentheses shows the correct capitalization? Circle the correct term.

1. Tanesha is majoring in (Computer Science, computer science).

2. Did you reserve a seat on (Flight 1628, flight 1628) to New York?

3. The rehabilitation center will be built (South, south) of the expressway.

4. Our school system has seen an increase in the number of (Hispanic, hispanic) students.

5. Have you taken (Medical Office Procedures, medical office procedures) 201?

6. My homeowner's insurance, (Policy 301429, policy 301429), was issued two years ago.

7. My knowledge of the (Japanese, japanese) language is limited.

8. We use (JavaScript, Javascript) to program our Web site.

9. The new site for our research facility is on the (West Coast, west coast).

10. Doug will create the (PowerPoint, powerpoint) slides for our presentation.

Capitalization Rules for Letters and Memos

The following rules deal with capitalization in letter and memorandum formats. After studying these rules, you may want to refer to the illustrations of letter and memo formats shown in Chapter 10.

15. Use capitals appropriately in memorandum guide words when typing a memo on plain paper. Use either all capitals or initial capitals only.

Date:	**MEMO TO:**
To:	**FROM:**
From:	**DATE:**
Subject:	**SUBJECT:**

Capitalize the words following the guide words—except for prepositions. Note the following example.

MEMO TO: John Smythe, Assistant Manager

FROM: Sally Lamb, Sales Director

DATE: March 5, <YEAR>

SUBJECT: Updated Health Benefits

16. Use all capitals for two-letter abbreviations for states and territories used in mailing addresses. For international addresses, use all capitals for the name of the country that appears on the last line of the mailing address.

Dr. Karel Rybnicek
St. Anne's Medical Center
8246 Washington Avenue
Covington, KY 41017

Mr. Philip Rowe
4 Bay Tree Avenue
Canberra, NSW 3441
AUSTRALIA

Refer to the Appendix for a complete list of two-letter abbreviations for the United States.

17. When using the simplified letter style, type the subject line and the writer's identification in all-capital letters. (See Chapter 10, Figure 10-7, for an example of the simplified letter style.)

ALVAREZ LICENSING AGREEMENT

JEFFREY W. PATTERSON, PRESIDENT

18. Capitalize the first word in the salutation of a letter. Within the salutation, also capitalize all nouns and titles.

Dear Mr. Allen:

Ladies and Gentlemen:

Dear Ms. Ziegler and Professor Marcos:

19. Capitalize only the first word in the complimentary closing of a letter.

Sincerely,

Sincerely yours,

Very truly yours,

Cordially yours,

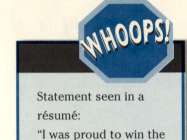

Statement seen in a résumé:
"I was proud to win the Gregg Typting Award."
Source: Accountemps

SOFTWARE TIPS

Word processing programs such as Microsoft® Word and Corel® WordPerfect include memo templates—memos with the guide words and formatting already set up. These templates vary in the use of capitalization for guide words. For example, memo templates may use all capitals, initial capitals, or all lowercase letters depending on the style of the template.

Complete Checkups 3-3 and 3-4 to test your knowledge of capitalization rules.

CHECKUP 3-3

The capitalization is correct in the following letter. To make sure you know why each underlined letter or item is correctly capitalized or not capitalized, write the number (1 to 19) of the rule that applies.

Rule Number

<u>J</u>uly 3, <YEAR>   1. _____

Lena Alexander, <u>Ph.D.</u>   2. _____
1432 <u>E</u>ast Lexington Boulevard   3. _____
Boston, <u>MA</u> 02160   4. _____

Dear Dr. <u>A</u>lexander: 5. _____

Thank you for your fax order for disposable contact lenses. As you
requested, the order is being shipped by <u>UPS</u> with delivery guaranteed   6. _____
by 10 <u>a.m.</u>, Thursday, July 5. Your order will be delayed one day due   7. _____
to the <u>F</u>ourth of July holiday.   8. _____

Enclosed with your lenses is a complimentary copy of a short
pamphlet, <u>*Is Laser Surgery for You?*</u>, which may be of interest to you.   9. _____

Please call one of our eye care professionals if you have any questions.

<u>S</u>incerely yours,   10. _____

In each numbered line of the following letter, which of the two choices in parentheses shows the correct capitalization? Circle the correct choice.

1.   (September, september) 15, <YEAR>

      Mrs. Regan Kennedy
      3218 Prescott Road
2.   Akron, (OH, Oh) 44313

      Dear Mrs. Kennedy:

3.   Congratulations! Your (Credit Application, credit application) has been approved.

4.   Your (References, references), Mrs. Kennedy, have a high opinion of you and your ability to meet your financial obligations. All of the responses to our inquiries were positive.

5.   You may use your Mason's (Charge Account, charge account) begin-
6.   ning today. You will receive a 10 (Percent, percent) discount on any
7.   purchases you make during (October, october). This discount is in
8.   addition to the already low prices during our (Fall, fall) sale.

9.   Sincerely (Yours, yours),

      Gretchen Mason
10.   Credit (Manager, manager)

      djf

REVISION SYMBOLS FOR CAPITALIZATION

The following revision symbols are used to indicate changes in capitalization. Review the symbols to see how to change capital letters to lowercase letters and lowercase letters to capital letters.

Revision	Edited Draft	Final Copy
Capitalize a letter	europe	Europe
Lowercase a letter	State Legislature	state legislature
All capitals	html	HTML
Lowercase a word	15 PERCENT	15 percent
Initial capital only	AGENDA	Agenda

Another revision symbol often used with capitalization is the symbol used to indicate *stet* or *do not change*. This revision symbol consists of dots under the indicated change and directs the typist to ignore the change that was marked and to use the original text as printed. Look at the way the stet mark is used in the following examples.

Revision	Edited Draft	Final Copy
Stet (do not change)	price is only $19.95	price is only $19.95
	Bart works at Netcom.	Bart works at Netcom.

Completing the following Checkups will give you practice in using revision symbols to mark corrections in capitalization.

CHECKUP 3-5

Each group of words has been marked with revision symbols. In the space provided, write how the final copy should appear.

0. My cousin moved to maine.
0. <u>My cousin moved to Maine.</u>

1. Carlos Tolemea is a cpa.
1. _____

2. MAYOR Godfrey was reelected.
2. _____

3. We bought a book by professor Nelson.
3. _____

4. The article profiles a College Professor at work.
4. _____

5. We have Flight Reservations for today.
5. _____

6. She arrived at 8:30 A.M.
6. _____

7. dear Mr. and Mrs. Harris:
7. _____

8. Read the book entitled <u>Health for College Students</u>. 8. _____

9. The library is closed on labor day. 9. _____

10. Wholesale Prices are increasing. 10. _____

TIPS

MARKING CORRECTIONS

Use a pen with brightly colored ink, such as red, for marking corrections while proofreading. Using a bright color makes it easier to spot corrections that need to be made.

CHECKUP 3-6

The copy in the first column represents a draft. The copy in the second column represents the desired final copy. In the draft column, use appropriate revision symbols to indicate the changes that must be made to yield the final copy.

Draft	Desired Final Copy
1. Call on sunday morning	Call on Sunday morning.
2. We close at 8:45 P.M.	We close at 8:45 p.m.
3. Bev learned Fortran in college.	Bev learned FORTRAN in college.
4. Ask jill Kline to attend.	Ask Jill Kline to attend.
5. The building site is South of town.	The building site is south of town.
6. Gary interviewed at ibm.	Gary interviewed at IBM.
7. I bought maxwell house coffee.	I bought Maxwell House coffee.
8. Our BOARD meeting is Friday.	Our board meeting is Friday.
9. Which States are on the border?	Which states are on the border?
10. Go to the after-christmas sale.	Go to the after-Christmas sale.
11. Search the internet for jobs.	Search the Internet for jobs.
12. Did you contact the Attorney?	Did you contact the attorney?
13. We went to lake Erie on vacation.	We went to Lake Erie on vacation.
14. Make reservations for flight 2375.	Make reservations for Flight 2375.
15. Computer Modems are on sale.	Computer modems are on sale.

Proofread each of the following paragraphs and mark any capitalization errors with the appropriate revision symbols.

Paragraph 1

Jackson Neyland, Assistant Coordinator of the Volunteers for Literacy, is organizing a used book sale to earn money and to promote the need for involvement in the Volunteers for Literacy Program in the greater los angeles area. The event is scheduled for Sunday, November 12. Any Volunteers who would like to assist with this worthwhile project should call Jackson for more information. Book donations can be made at the Chamber of Commerce office at 2334 Howard Street. Funds earned or contributed will be used to provide reading materials for people enrolled in the Program.

Paragraph 2

The Green Thumb Florist, inc., is pleased to announce the grand opening of its new store on Saturday, february 21, in the Tri-City Mall. Mr. Alex Bonsworth, a recent graduate of the University of south dakota, is the store manager. The mall store of The Green Thumb offers customers Worldwide delivery as well as a self-service counter where they can create their own floral arrangements. In addition, Mr. Bonsworth will offer classes in flower arranging during the Spring and Summer months.

Paragraph 3

Ms. Allison Ansley, president of ansley electronics, announced plans for the company to build a new manufacturing plant on the West side of Nashville, tennessee. Ms. Ansley said that the company's rapid growth in the past five years has made the Expansion possible. The new plant will employ approximately 250 people and is scheduled to be completed by september of next year.

SOFTWARE TIPS

Keep in mind that the automatic correction feature in word processing software may not correct all capitalization errors. For example, suppose you typed the following sentence:

WE are issuing a new contract.

Software that is set up to correct two initial capital letters will not make this correction for a two-letter word at the beginning of a sentence. In the above example, the software would not change *WE* to *We*.

Application 3-A

Proofread the following memo. Use appropriate revision symbols to mark corrections in capitalization.

MEMO TO: Abigail Miller—Comptroller

FROM: Robert Billingsly—Office Manager

Date: July 2, <YEAR>

SUBJECT: Annual Audit

As mentioned to you in a conversation earlier today, we will begin our annual auditing procedures at 8 A.M. on Monday, July 8. this audit will be for the FISCAL Year just ended, running from July 1 to june 30.

Mr. Jeff Snyder, cpa, of Snyder, Hilton, and Berstrom, inc., will have ten accountants with him, and he anticipates completing the audit within two weeks. Ms. ellen Lawrence will be working primarily with the Computer part of the process.

Please introduce Mr. Snyder and Ms. Lawrence to all appropriate staff members.

Application 3-B

Proofread the following letter. Use appropriate revision symbols to mark corrections in capitalization. (10 points for each properly marked correction)

Columbia Coastal Savings

14 South Pinehurst Avenue, Columbia, SC 29608-1469 / Tel: 803.555.2272 / colcoastsav.com

August 3, <YEAR>

Ms. Millie Hempstead
Special Accounts Manager
Epic Regency Hotel
3687 East Brentwood Terrace
Columbia, Sc 29602

Dear Ms. hempstead:

On Wednesday, August 15, a group of international students will be arriving in Columbia on their way to various locations throughout the united states. Our company has agreed again this year to pay for their lodging the night they will be in Columbia.

In the past, your hotel has graciously offered a discount to help defray the expenses for lodging international students. Last Fall, in fact, you gave us a discount and provided a special Continental Breakfast for one such group.

Will you help again this year? There will be eight male students and twelve female students, which means that ten double rooms will be sufficient. We have already reserved the rooms.

Thank you for considering this request. please call me as soon as you have reached a decision.

Very Truly Yours,

Anita Burns
Manager

skj

Application 3-C

Your organization is publishing a company cookbook featuring recipes from your associates. The company that is typesetting the cookbook has sent you printed proofs to verify against the original typed copies of the recipes. Compare the original copies of the recipes below with the proof copies on the next page. Use appropriate revision symbols to indicate capitalization errors plus other types of errors.

Original Typed Recipes

Myrna's Potato Casserole

2 pounds frozen hash brown potatoes (thawed)

1 teaspoon salt

½ cup melted margarine

1 small onion (minced)

½ teaspoon black pepper

1 can cream of mushroom soup

1 cup sour cream

2 cups grated cheddar cheese

8 strips of bacon (fried and crumbled)

3 tablespoons minced parsley

Combine all the ingredients in a large mixing bowl. Spread the mixture in a 2½ quart casserole dish. Bake the casserole one hour at 350 degrees.

Sue's Easy Fudge

2 sticks margarine (melted)

½ cup peanut butter

1 teaspoon vanilla flavoring

¼ cup cocoa

1 box confectioner's sugar

Melt the margarine in the microwave. Stir in the peanut butter, vanilla flavoring, and cocoa. Add the confectioner's sugar. Mix the ingredients well with a spoon. Place the mixture in a 10 × 6 inch glass dish. Chill and serve.

Application 3-C (continued)

Printed Proofs

Myrna's Potato Casserole

2 pounds frozen hash brown potatoes
1 tablespoon salt
$1/2$ cup melted margarine
1 small onion (minced)
$1/2$ teaspoon black pepper
1 can cream of mushroom soup

1 cup sour cream
2 cups grated cheddar cheese
8 stripes of bacon
   (fired and crumbled)
3 tablespoons minced parsley

Combine all the ingredients in a large mixing bowl. Spread the mixture in a 2 $1/2$ quart casserole dish. Bake the casserole on hour at 350 degrees.

Sue's Easy Fudge

2 sticks margarine (melted)
$1/2$ cup peanut butter
1 teaspoon vanilla flavoring
$1/4$ cup cocoa
1 Confectioners' sugar

Melt the margarine in the microwave. Stir in the peanut butter, vanilla flavoring, and cocoa. Add the confectioner's sugar. Mix the ingredient will with a spoon. Place the mixture in a 10 x 6 inch glass dish. Chill and serve.

Application 3-D

Use revision symbols to correct capitalization errors plus any other
types of errors in the following memo.

MEMO TO: Jason Goforth

FROM: Natalie Brookes

DATE: September 8, <YEAR>

SUBJECT: Transportation for Amy Cox

Thank you, Jason, for offering to meat Amy Cox's flight this Friday
afternoon, September 10. Her itinerary (including airline, flight
numbers, and hotel accommodations) is enclosed. Please take her
to the Glenwood Hotel at 2794 south Allenwood Drive. We have a
sweet of rooms reserved in her name.

As you no, Amy will be hear to discuss the opening of our branch
office in montreal, which will include a look at staffing issues.

Incidentally, Amy graduated form Duke university about the same
time that you did. This common interest should give you some
thing to chat a bout on your way to the hotel.

Enclosure

CD-ROM Application 3-E

The person who typed the following memo accidentally used the software feature that changed the memo to all lowercase letters. Using your word processor, open the file DPES03E from the CD-ROM. Correct each capitalization error, then run the spell checker. (The software will find some—but not all—of these errors.) Use all-capital letters for the memo guide words. Save the revised memo using your initials in place of the DPES. Proofread the memo on the screen and make any additional corrections. Save and print the corrected memo.

---

memo to: will brown

from: clarence brentworth

date: august 8, <YEAR>

subject: sales meeting on august 13

we are having a special sales meeting on monday, august 13, at 8:30 a.m.; a continental breakfast will be served beginning at 8:15.

drew fields of island cruise lines will be here to showcase his many spring cruises. our contract with island cruise lines offers more potential for profit than our contracts with other cruise lines.

please attend this meeting if at all possible.

CD-ROM Application 3-F

Proofread the following draft of a letter for capitalization errors as well as other types of errors. Using your word processor, open the file DPES03F from the CD-ROM. A copy of the letter is shown here. Make your corrections, then run the spell checker. Save the revised letter using your initials in place of the DPES. Proofread the letter on the screen and make any additional corrections. Save and print the corrected letter.

February 22, <YEAR>

Mr. George Gordon
Post Office Box 38288
Ogden, UT 84409

Dear Mr. Gordon:

This letter confirms the cancellation of your may 20 cruise to the British Virgin islands. Since you notified us tree months in advance, you qualify for a complete refund.

Congratulations on your new position with National Communications, Inc., off New Orleans. Even through you will not be able to take to take your scheduled cruise this Spring because of your move, I sincerely hope that you will treat yourself to and exciting cruise adventure latter in the year.

Enclosed is a refund check for $300, the full a mount of your deposit. I will keep you on our mailing list to receive information on cruises and other special trips. Please send me your new address as soon as it is convenient.

Sincerely Yours,

Nancy Ellington
Travel Consultant

ljk
Enclosure

Plurals, Possessives, and Word Division

After completing this chapter, you should be able to:

1. Apply rules for forming plurals and possessives and dividing words as you proofread.

2. Detect and correct errors in plurals, possessives, and word division.

3. Use appropriate revision symbols to correct errors in plurals, possessives, and word division.

Chapter 4 presents rules for forming plurals and possessives and for dividing words. The rules presented emphasize the types of errors that frequently occur in business writing. You must know the rules before you are able to find errors. The following review of the rules will help refresh your memory and enable you to quickly recognize and correct errors in plurals, possessives, and word division.

PLURALS

Errors can easily occur when you are forming the plurals of nouns. Make sure you understand each of the following ten rules for forming plurals.

Rules for Forming Plurals

1. Most plurals are formed by adding *s* to the singular forms.

laugh + s = laughs	system + s = systems
meeting + s = meetings	technique + s = techniques
tradition + s = traditions	receipt + s = receipts

2. To form the plural of most singular nouns ending in *f*, *ff*, or *fe*, add *s*.

proof + s = proofs	staff + s = staffs
safe + s = safes	

Some nouns of this type change the *f* or *fe* to *ve* and add *s*.

leaf + ves = leaves   shelf + ves = shelves

half + ves = halves   life + ves = lives

3. When a singular noun ends in *s*, *x*, *z*, *ch*, or *sh*, add *es* to form the plural.

business + es = businesses klutz + es = klutzes

Gaddis + es = Gaddises   bench + es = benches

box + es = boxes   speech + es = speeches

Xerox + es = Xeroxes   dish + es = dishes

Hertz + es = Hertzes   dash + es = dashes

4. When a singular noun ends in a vowel plus *y*, add *s* to form the plural.

attorney + s = attorneys   boy + s = boys

journey + s = journeys   highway + s = highways

5. When a singular noun ends in a consonant plus *y*, change the *y* to *i* and add *es* to form the plural.

city + ies = cities   inquiry + ies = inquiries

activity + ies = activities   company + ies = companies

6. To form the plural of a hyphenated or a spaced compound noun, make the main word plural. The plural may be formed by adding *s*, *es*, or *ies*.

Hyphenated Compound:

brother-in-law + s = brothers-in-law

time-saver + s = time-savers

cross-reference + s = cross-references

Spaced Compound:

notary public + ies = notaries public

sales tax + es = sales taxes

bulletin board + s = bulletin boards

7. To form the plural of a hyphenated compound noun that does not contain a noun as one of its elements, make the final element plural.

go-between + s = go-betweens have-not + s = have-nots

drive-in + s = drive-ins   know-it-all + s = know-it-alls

8. When the singular noun ends in *o* preceded by a vowel, add *s* to form the plural.

radio + s = radios   portfolio + s = portfolios

An official for a convention center in a Midwestern city was demoted as the result of overlooking an error in a letter he proofread. The official failed to notice that a football game was mistakenly scheduled for the same date that a convention was to take place. As a result, the convention was moved to another city, resulting in a loss of at least $10 million that convention attendees would have spent. The official who overlooked the error was reassigned to another job and took a 10 percent cut in pay.
Source: St. Louis Post-Dispatch

Some singular nouns ending in *o* preceded by a consonant form their plurals by adding *s*; others add *es*. A dictionary or a wordbook lists the correct plurals.

memo + s = memos	*BUT*	tomato + es = tomatoes
photo + s = photos	*BUT*	hero + es = heroes

9. Form the plurals of personal titles, numbers, and abbreviations by adding *s*.

Singular	*Plural*
Dr.	Drs.
CEO	CEOs
c.o.d.	c.o.d.s
70	70s
1990	1990s

10. For some nouns, there are few useful rules for forming plurals. You should know the irregular plurals of the following commonly used nouns.

Singular	*Plural*
man	men
woman	women
child	children
foot	feet

CHECKUP 4-1

Write the correct plural for each of the following items in the space provided. Use a dictionary or a wordbook if you are uncertain about forming irregular plurals.

Singular	Plural
1. delay	1. _____
2. runner-up	2. _____
3. video	3. _____
4. opportunity	4. _____
5. get-together	5. _____
6. R.N.	6. _____
7. virus	7. _____
8. embargo	8. _____
9. choice	9. _____
10. brush	10. _____
11. policy	11. _____
12. account receivable	12. _____
13. child	13. _____
14. editor-in-chief	14. _____
15. supply	15. _____
16. woman	16. _____
17. bill of lading	17. _____
18. belief	18. _____
19. potato	19. _____
20. CD-ROM	20. _____

Plurals of Foreign Nouns

Plurals of foreign nouns are often used in business writing. For some foreign nouns there are two correct forms—an English plural and a foreign plural. The following table lists some foreign nouns and their plurals. For foreign nouns with two different plural forms, the preferred plural is shown in bold.

PLURALS OF FOREIGN NOUNS

SINGULAR	ENGLISH PLURAL	FOREIGN PLURAL
appendix	**appendixes**	appendices
chaise longue	**chaise longues**	chaises longues
criterion	criterions	**criteria**

PLURALS OF FOREIGN NOUNS

SINGULAR	ENGLISH PLURAL	FOREIGN PLURAL
emphasis		emphases
focus	**focuses**	foci
formula	**formulas**	formulae
memorandum	**memorandums**	memoranda
prospectus	prospectuses	
vertebra	vertebras	**vertebrae**

CHECKUP 4-2   Use a dictionary or a wordbook to look up the plural for each of the following foreign nouns. Then complete the accompanying sentence by writing the plural in the space provided.

1. analysis
   We completed several _____ in order to confirm the test results.

2. crisis
   The government is prepared to handle both domestic and international _____ .

3. hors d'oeuvre
   Several types of _____ will be served at the luncheon.

4. parenthesis
   Use _____ to enclose words within a sentence that give nonessential information.

5. diagnosis
   The doctors gave Jeanette two different _____ for her condition.

6. addendum
   There are two _____ to the contract.

7. erratum
   Make note of all the _____ that should be corrected in the next printing of the book.

8. census
   Review the statistics in the last three _____ and compare the findings.

9. agenda
   Make sure the _____ for all the sales meetings are mailed by June 15.

10. stimulus
    Doctors often test a patient's responses to painful _____ .

POSSESSIVES

Possessives are used to show ownership. As you can see from the following examples, both nouns and pronouns may be used to show possession.

Nouns:	company's plans	reporter's story
Pronouns:	my computer	our health benefits

Although most possessives are easy to form, many of us confuse the spelling of possessives. Learning the following rules will help you form possessives correctly.

Rules for Forming Possessives

Follow these guidelines for forming possessives.

1. For most singular nouns, form the possessive by adding an apostrophe (') plus *s*.

   officer/officer's   brother/brother's

   Phillip/Phillip's   supervisor/supervisor's

2. If the possessive of a singular noun or a proper name ending in *s* would be hard to pronounce with an apostrophe plus *s*, then add only the apostrophe.

   crisis/crisis'   Ms. Cummings/Ms. Cummings'

   thesis/thesis'   Brian Roberts/Brian Roberts'

3. If a singular noun or a proper name ends in *s* or an *s* sound and the possessive is pronounced with an extra syllable, add an apostrophe plus *s*.

   boss/boss's   Thomas/Thomas's

   campus/campus's   Jon Sanchez/Jon Sanchez's

4. Plural nouns or proper names ending in *s* take only an apostrophe to form the possessive.

   officers/officers'   supervisors/supervisors'

   bosses/bosses'   the Adamses/the Adamses'

   the Wellses/the Wellses'

5. Plural nouns that do not end in *s* take an apostrophe plus *s* to form the possessive.

   men/men's   women/women's   children/children's

6. If a compound noun is singular, add an apostrophe plus *s* to the last word in the compound to form the possessive.

   editor-in-chief/editor-in-chief's

   business owner/business owner's

Item listed in the menu for an Illinois restaurant:

"Gaint Cheese Buggers"

Source: Menu Bloopers Web site, R.C. Moschel, contributor

7. If a compound noun is a plural ending in *s*, then add only an apostrophe to form the possessive.

    brigadier generals/brigadier generals'

    sales representatives/sales representatives'

8. If a compound noun is a plural that does not end in *s*, add an apostrophe plus *s* to form the possessive.

    sisters-in-law/sisters-in-law's

    runners-up/runners-up's

9. To indicate separate ownership, make each name possessive. To indicate joint ownership, make only the last name possessive.

    Alice's and Matt's companies (Alice's company and Matt's company—two companies, separate ownership)

    Alice and Matt's company (Company owned by Alice and Matt—one company, joint ownership)

10. Use a possessive form for a noun or pronoun that appears before a gerund and indicates ownership. (A *gerund* is a verb form that ends in *ing* and is used as a noun.)

    Noel's programming is very creative.

    Mr. Swartz complimented Angela on her completing the report early.

    We appreciate your coming to the follow-up session.

Net Link

For additional practice in using plurals and possessives, go to the *Guide to Grammar and Writing* developed by Charles Darling, an English professor at Capital Community-Technical College, **http://webster .commnet.edu/hp /pages/darling**. In the list of Sentence Level topics on the first page, select "Noun Forms" for a review of plurals and possessives. Be sure to complete some of the fun interactive quizzes to test your knowledge.

SOFTWARE TIPS

Spell checkers do not always recognize mistakes in forming possessives. For example, each of the following items should have been typed as a singular possessive; however, the apostrophe was misplaced.

Our supervisors' decision (*should be* supervisor's)

My sisters' house (*should be* sister's)

The departments' new workstations (*should be* department's)

Since there is both a correct singular and plural possessive for each of these words, the spell checker doesn't highlight them as errors. In such cases, it's up to you as the proofreader to make sure that the correct possessive form is used.

In the space provided, write the correct possessive form for each of the following phrases.

1. Mike and Elaine birth certificates
2. both sisters-in-law diplomas
3. Charles and Amber home (one home)
4. both daughters trust funds
5. Ms. Moss presentation
6. annual Nurse Day
7. two witnesses testimonies
8. editor-in-chief brief speech
9. children software
10. Bob computer

1. _____
2. _____
3. _____
4. _____
5. _____
6. _____
7. _____
8. _____
9. _____
10. _____

REVISION SYMBOLS FOR MARKING PLURAL AND POSSESSIVE ERRORS

The following revision symbols are used to mark errors in plurals and possessives. Some of these symbols were introduced in previous chapters.

Revision	Edited Draft	Final Copy
Insert a letter	three patient ˢ	three patients
Delete a letter or word	qualities ~~qualitys~~	qualities
Delete a letter and close up	your memoes	your memos
Insert an apostrophe	Lupes suggestion	Lupe's suggestion
Transpose letters	Dr. Morriss'	Dr. Morris's

Use appropriate revision symbols to correct errors in the use of plurals and possessives in the following sentences.

1. Dr. Valerie Chu insisted on him following her orders.

2. Sally's and Susan's restaurant is the only one open on Sundays.

3. Relief supplies were shipped to Honduras in five large boxs.

4. After the feasibility study's are completed, we will seek construction bids and loans.

5. Stephen and Tasha's supervisors are both retiring this year.

6. Major policies were reviewed by both chiefs of staffs.

7. All the CD-ROMs are in the manufacturers warehouse.

8. Leif Hamrick, our landscaper, planted eight rose bushs near the parking lot.

9. Isaac Muasi, Bill Daviss' employer, plays tennis twice a week.

10. The Rotary Club and two companys sponsored the event.

WORD DIVISION

Dividing words properly at the end of a line is important for your reader. Incorrect word division at the end of a line can cause confusion. Note the following example:

> Despite eyewitness testimony, the defendant could not re-
> collect the incident.

Does the writer mean to use *re-collect*, which means to collect something again, or does the writer mean to use *recollect*, which means to remember? Dividing the word at the end of the line makes the meaning unclear. In general, you should avoid dividing words.

The default setting on most word processors is to avoid hyphenating words. However, in some cases hyphenating words improves the appearance of a document because it makes the line endings more even and it eliminates large amounts of white space.

Compare the following two examples. The first illustrates copy that was typed without hyphenation, and the second shows the same copy with hyphens. Notice how the copy with hyphens is easier to read than the copy with a lot of white space.

Becoming a volunteer is one way to contribute to the well-being of your community. There are several types of volunteer options that may be available. You might assist with a neighborhood blockwatch program that helps protect people and property. Another volunteer effort would be to help clean up the areas along roadways. Volunteers also are needed for literacy programs.

Becoming a volunteer is one way to contribute to the well-being of your community. There are several types of volunteer options that may be available. You might assist with a neighborhood block-watch program that helps protect people and property. Another volunteer effort would be to help clean up the areas along road-ways. Volunteers also are needed for literacy programs.

Rules for Dividing Words

The following rules offer guidelines for dividing words. The authority for word division in this book is *Merriam-Webster's Collegiate Dictionary, Tenth Edition.*

1. Divide words only between syllables.

   en- forced   com- prised   ser- vice

2. Do not divide one-syllable words.

   smooth   praise   merged

3. Do not divide contractions, abbreviations, or numbers expressed as figures.

   wouldn't   mph $236.78

   you're   Sept.   5,280

4. Avoid dividing a word with fewer than six letters.

5. Divide after, not before, a single-letter syllable within the root of a word.

   maxi- mum   *NOT*   max- imum

   bene- fit   *NOT*   ben- efit

   If there are two single-vowel syllables together that are sounded separately, the words should be divided between these two syllables.

   cre- ative   *NOT*   crea- tive

   reli- able   *NOT*   relia- ble

6. Divide between double consonants (unless the double consonants end the root word, as in *drill-ing*, *dress-ing*).

   recom- mend   mid- dle

7. Try to divide a word after a prefix or before a suffix, leaving the root word undivided.

   un- aware   measure- ment

   success- ful   pre- school

8. Divide solid compound words where the two words are joined.

   wrist- watch   tax- payer

   data- base   paper- work

9. Divide hyphenated compound words after the hyphen.

   cross- cultural   start- up   secretary- treasurer

10. Avoid dividing the address for a Web site on the Internet or an e-mail address. If you need to divide a Web site address, break it after the double slash, as in the following example:

    http://   www.glencoe.com

You may also divide a Web site address before a dot, a hyphen, a single slash, or any other punctuation mark.

End of line	Next line
http://www.nws	.noaa.gov/
http://www.ama	-assn.org/

For e-mail addresses, break the address either before the @ symbol or before a dot.

End of line	Next line
nbea	@nbea.org\
listserv@listserv	.law.cornell.edu

TIPS

DIVIDING WEB SITE AND E-MAIL ADDRESSES

When you break a Web site address or an e-mail address at the end of a line, do not insert a hyphen. If you do, the reader will mistakenly think that the hyphen is part of the address.

11. Avoid dividing information that should be read as a unit. Some examples of information that should not be divided include a person's first and last name; a title with a name; the month and the year; the month, day, and year; a number with an abbreviation; a number with a unit of measurement; and a street number and street name.

Harold Chapman	Ms. Carla Santavicca
March 2002	July 4, 2005
25 R.S.V.P.s	15 ft.
936 Gentlewind Avenue	

12. Leave at least two letters on the line with the hyphen, and carry over at least three letters (or two letters plus a punctuation mark).

    al- ready   custom- er.

13. Ending two consecutive lines in hyphens is acceptable. Ending three or more consecutive lines in hyphens is not acceptable.

14. Avoid dividing the first line and the last full line of a paragraph.

15. Do not divide the last word on a page.

When you are in doubt about correct syllabication, check a dictionary. Syllabication is usually listed in the pronunciation that follows the entry word. For example, *Merriam-Webster's Collegiate Dictionary, Tenth Edition*, lists the following entries with their syllabication:

par•tial   \par-tial\

hos•pi•ta•ble   \ho-spi-ta-ble\

In the above entries, the centered dots indicate acceptable end-of-line breaks while the hyphens indicate syllables. Sometimes the syllable breaks and the end-of-line breaks are the same; sometimes they are different.

Completing the following Checkup will test your knowledge of the rules for word division.

CHECKUP 4-5

Using a dictionary or a wordbook as a guide, place a diagonal (/) in the following items to indicate the *preferred* place to divide the item at the end of a typed or printed line. Underline any item that should not be divided.

1. supporting
2. dependable
3. platter
4. o'clock
5. navigate
6. CEO
7. mediocre
8. thirty-first
9. dripped
10. establishment
11. $23,986
12. http://www.uschamber.org
13. lengthwise
14. April 15, 2004
15. wouldn't
16. privilege
17. beginning
18. around
19. preregister
20. dressing

SOFTWARE TIPS

Most word processors have a default setting that does not hyphenate words. If you want to hyphenate words in a document, you must change the setting to one that allows words to be hyphenated at the end of a line.

REVISION SYMBOLS FOR MARKING WORD DIVISION ERRORS

The revision symbols shown on page 90 are also used to correct errors in word division. There is one additional revision symbol that is used with word division—the symbol for inserting a hyphen, as illustrated here.

Revision	Edited Draft	Final Copy
Insert a hyphen	Before students may pre=∧ register for classes, they should meet with their advisors.	Before students may pre-register for classes, they should meet with their advisors.
	We made several modifica=∧ tions to the software.	We made several modifications to the software.

CHECKUP 4-6 Use appropriate revision symbols to correct word division errors in the following sentences.

1. Yesterday morning we received a fax from Johnson B. Drexler, Inc., a-bout our October seminar for CPAs. They want to send seven associates. Please call the hotel and make reservat-ions for seven additional people.

2. Brent and Jason have requested their staff to call immediately an-ytime there is a problem with the automated teller machines.

3. To meet our specific company goals, the programmer will ideal-ly know how to program using Visual C++ and Java.

4. Nancy became vice president of the corporation when she was almost twen-ty-nine. Most of the employees were glad that she was promoted.

Application 4-A

Proofread the following memo. Use appropriate revision symbols to correct errors in plurals, possessives, and word division.

MEMO TO: All Employees

FROM: Jorge Rodriquez, Human Resource Manager

DATE: April 15, <YEAR>

SUBJECT: Parking Lot Regulations

On Monday, April 10, a committee met to finalize regulations that will improve our parking situation. The committee has met diligently for the last six weeks.

The senior managements opinion was that the associates who use the parking facilitys should recommend any changes in regulations. As you will recall, you had several opportunitys to complete surveys indicating preferences and concernes. The most frequently mentioned concern on both the mens and the womens surveys was safety. This issue has been addressed by employing a security guard for each parking facility around the clock.

Enclosed is a pamphlet that lists the revised regulations. The committees goal was to implement regulations that would avoid any crises with regard to parking. Please let me know if you have any suggestions.

eap
Enclosure

Application 4-B

The following flyer will be distributed throughout the city to advertise a benefit to raise money for hurricane victims. Proofread the flyer and correct any errors in plurals, possessives, and word division with the appropriate revision symbols.

Benefit
Yard & Bake Sale

Saturday
September 1, 2001
7:30 a.m. to 7:30 p.m.

for victims of Hurricane William

Graham Industries, Inc.
128 West Jordan Drive, Marietta, Georgia

The associates of Graham Industrys, Inc., are working to raise money for the recent victims of Hurricane William. Our associates have emptied their attics, closets, and garages to provide a variety of furniture, used clothing, and antiques.

Local merchants have donated new products to add to the buying activitys. Homemade cakes, pies, and cookies will also be available.

The associates goal is to raise at least $10,000. Join us on Saturday in this worthwhile humanitarian effort.

Application 4-C

Proofread the following newsletter. Use appropriate revision symbols to correct errors in plurals, possessives, and word division, plus any other types of errors.

LEONARD'S DEPARTMENT STORE NEWS

Volume 2, Issue 11   November 2003

Trexler Acquisition

On October 5, Leonard's Department Store acquired the Trexler Department Stores. This a-cquisition will allow us to expand our customer base tremendously. One of the Trexler stores is located East of Interstate Highway 56, and the other is located West of the Catawba River. We are definitely excited about this acquisition and are pleased that many of Trexlers current associates want to continue working for Leonard's after the acquisition. However, there will be some positions to fill. Please let our Human Resources manager know if you are interested in transferring to either of the locations.

Our Associates

PROMOTIONS—Congratulations to the following associates: **Gail Hemingway** was promoted to sales manager. Gail has been with Leonard's in various sales capacitys for seven years. **Harold Sorrentino**, after passing the CPA exam, was promoted to senior accountant.

NEW ASSOCIATES—**Jan Brick** joined use October 15 in Advertising. She will work as Bob Ramseys assistant. **Angela Smith** started as a payroll accountant on October 25. She recently graduated from Catawba College with a degree in accounting.

Holiday Food Drive

It's time once again to bring in nonperishable food items for our annual Holiday Food Drive. The Salvation Army, which distributes the collected items locally, has requested that we include sum baby food and formula in this year's donations. Your donations should be placed in the metal collection bins at hour Grover Boulevard warehouse by 5:30 p.m. on November 20. Last year, Leonard's associates donated over a ton of food. Let's top that amount this year.

For details about the Holiday Food Drive, contact Gilda Morris, Ext. 3557, in Human Resources.

Community Service News

Thanks to **John Ludlow, Miranda Moore, Cecil Nelson,** and **Roberta Queen,** who have worked diligently on our Adopt-A-Highway efforts. The designated stretch of highway on Interstate Highway 56 is one is one of our citys cleanest.

Application 4-D

You have been asked to design a fax cover sheet for the business where you work. You quickly drafted the following cover sheet yesterday. As you proofread the draft today, you notice different types of errors. Use appropriate revision symbols to correct each error.

J & B Auto Sells and Service, Inc.   John Beckwith, Owner
Specializing in Foriegn Cars   Bill Beckwith, Owner

132 Elizabeth Avenue   **Office:** 803-555-2834
Columbia, Sc 29602   **Fax:**   803-555-8322
                                             E-mail: J&B@web.com

Fax Cover Sheet

Please transmit the accompanying page or pages to:

Name: _____

Telephone #: _____

Fax #: _____

Pages: _____ (total number including cover street)

This fax is form the person specified below:

Name: _____

Telephone #: _____

Fax #: _____

Date: _____ Time: _____ Transmitters Initials: _____

this message is intended for the individual named above. If the reader of this message is not the the intended recipient, the reader is requested to notify us bye telephone and to destroy this message. Faxs are considered the property of the writer.

CD-ROM Application 4-E

Using your word processor, open the file DPES04E from the CD-ROM. A copy of the document is shown here. Correct all errors in plurals, possessives, and word division. Then run the spell checker. Save the revised notice using your initials in place of the DPES. Proofread the notice on the screen and make any additional corrections. Save and print the corrected notice.

NOTICE
Closing of Baxter Decor Company Outlet Store

Effective December 30, Baxter Decor Company is closing its outlet store until further notice. Baxters reason for closing the outlet store is consolidation of its stores at different locationes.

All upholstery and drapery fabrics will be sold below cost. To give our associates first chance at the sale, the outlet store will be open only for our associates on December 15 and 16 from 8:30 a.m. to 8:30 p.m. A company identification card will be required for admission to the sale. After this Saturdays sale, the store will be open to the public.

Thank you for your patronage.

CD-ROM Application 4-F

The following weather forecast will be transmitted over the Internet at 6:30 p.m. the night before the Carolina Panthers football game. Using your word processor, open the file DPES04F from the CD-ROM. A copy of the document is shown here. Correct all errors in plurals, possessives, and word division, plus other types of errors. Then run the spell checker. Save the revised document using your initials in place of the DPES. Proofread the document on the screen and make any additional corrections. Save and print the corrected document.

Official Weather Forecast for the Carolina Panthers Game

Game time is sunday at 1:30 P.M., est, in the pleasant city of Charlotte, North Carolina. Expect moderate to heavy showers with the possibility of some lighting. Rain fall accumulation will be less than one inch.

Temperatures should be in the upper sixties at the beginning of the game but will steadily drop through out the afternoon. By the end of the game, the temperature will be in the lower fifties.

Winds will be from the southeast at 15 to 20 MPH. The winds will shift and will become northwesterly during the game and remain at the same rate. The wind chill factor will be in the mid-fortys by the end of the game.

Your WJWS chief meteorologists recommendation is to dress in layers and to wear warm, water proof clothing.

Comma Usage

OBJECTIVES

After completing this chapter, you should be able to:

1. Apply rules for using commas to separate and set off items.

2. Detect and correct errors in comma usage within sentences and within parts of a letter.

3. Use appropriate revision symbols to correct comma errors.

Proofreading for comma errors is important, because missing or misused commas can change the meaning of a sentence or make a sentence unclear. Read the following example:

Make flight reservations for Laura Beth and Richard.

Without commas, the sentence conveys that two people need flight reservations: Laura Beth and Richard. Notice how, with commas, the sentence conveys that three people need flight reservations: Laura, Beth, and Richard.

Make flight reservations for Laura, Beth, and Richard.

This chapter presents the rules for comma usage that apply most often in business writing. Knowing these rules will help you to recognize and correct errors in comma usage as you proofread.

APPLYING THE RULES

The comma and the period are the two most frequently used punctuation marks, and the comma is the most frequently misused. To make sure that you understand when to use a comma—and when not to use a comma—review the rules in this chapter.

Besides appearing in certain letter parts, commas are also used within sentences. Study the following rules, which explain comma usage in letter parts and comma usage in sentences.

Rules for Commas With Letter Parts

Commas are used with specific letter parts.

1. In the *date line*, the day and the year are separated by a comma.

   October 28, 2003

2. In the *inside address* and the *return address*, the city and state name or abbreviation are always separated by a comma.

Inside Address	Return Address and Date Line
Ms. Margie Bivens	Post Office Box 8248
156 Plains Road	Des Moines, IA 50342
Denver, CO 80214-1476	February 24, 2002

   Note: A return address may appear either at the top of the letter followed by the date line or at the bottom of the letter below the writer's typed name.

3. In the *complimentary closing*, a comma is used at the end of the line when the standard punctuation style is being used. (No comma is used with the open punctuation style.)

   Sincerely yours,   Cordially,

   Ben Abernathy   *Ben Abernathy*

   Ben Abernathy   Ben Abernathy

4. In the *writer's identification line*, a comma is used to separate the writer's name and title when both are on the same line.

   Very truly yours,

   Tracy Caldwell

   Tracy Caldwell, Manager

   However, no comma separates the two when they are typed on two separate lines.

   Very truly yours,

   Tracy Caldwell

   Tracy Caldwell

   Manager

You may want to check Chapter 10 for illustrations that show how Rules 1–4 are applied when formatting letters.

Revision Symbols for Correcting Comma Errors

The following revision symbols show how to insert and delete commas.

Revision	Edited Draft	Final Copy
Insert a comma	We live in Madison Wisconsin.	We live in Madison, Wisconsin.
Delete a comma	Dale, and Teri are the managers.	Dale and Teri are the managers.
Change a period to a comma	After you draft the report. We will review the findings.	After you draft the report, we will review the findings.

CHECKUP 5-1 Each of the following items represents a part of a letter. Use the appropriate revision symbol to insert needed commas or delete unnecessary ones. If a letter part is correct, write *C* for *Correct* to the left of the item number.

1. Return Address and Date Line

   3223 South Ashwood Drive
   Covington KY 41011
   January 14 2002

2. Inside Address

   Mr. Robert Mosely
   1832 Pendleton Court
   High Point, NC 27263-1578

3. Complimentary Closing With Standard Punctuation

   Very truly yours

4. Writer's Name and Title on Two Lines

   Rebecca S. Timmons,
   Vice President

5. Writer's Name and Title on the Same Line

   Amanda Milligan Manager

Rules for Commas That Set Off

Commas are used to set off certain information in a sentence.

5. Within a sentence, use two commas to set off the year when it follows the month and day.

   On July 18, 1998, we expanded our operations into five states.

   What will be the value of my portfolio on December 30, 2015, when I retire?

No commas are used to set off just the month and year.

The next conference will be in April 2002 in Texas.

6. Within a sentence, use two commas to set off the name of a state when it follows the name of a city. Also use commas to set off the name of a province or country from the name of a city.

Tonya changed planes in Atlanta, Georgia, on her last trip to New York City.

Woodson Memorial Hospital will open a clinic in Whitby, Ontario, next year.

7. Commas are used to set off names used in direct address.

Do you agree, Heather, that we should ship the packages early? (Heather is the person spoken to—the name in direct address.)

I would appreciate your feedback, Victor.
(Victor is the person spoken to—the name in direct address.)

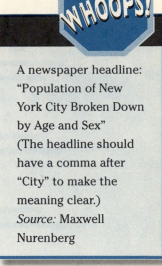

A newspaper headline: "Population of New York City Broken Down by Age and Sex" (The headline should have a comma after "City" to make the meaning clear.)
Source: Maxwell Nurenberg

8. Commas are used to set off words or phrases in apposition.

Ms. Phillips, <u>our accountant</u>, completed our tax returns early.

Mrs. Dennis, <u>the store manager</u>, recommended David for the job.

Our first fund-raiser, <u>a silent auction</u>, was very successful.

The underlined phrases in the above examples are called appositives. *Our accountant* is another way of saying *Ms. Phillips. The store manager* is another way of saying *Mrs. Dennis. A silent auction* is another way of saying *our first fund-raiser*. Appositives are always set off with two commas unless, of course, they appear at the end of a sentence.

Please fax your response by Friday, <u>the last day of the month</u>.

9. Commas are used to set off parenthetical, or nonessential, elements from the rest of the sentence.

We should, in my opinion, purchase the office building and rent it.

Harry Jacobs, who is the head of the city council, will host the banquet.

To determine whether an element is nonessential or essential, read the sentence without the word or words that are set off. If the sentence is clear without the words, then the words are nonessential and commas should be used. If the sentence is not clear without the words, then the words are essential and commas should not be used.

Tom Wilson decided, unfortunately, to postpone his trip.

Tom Wilson decided to postpone his trip.

The sentence is clear without the word *unfortunately*; thus, commas should be used.

CHECKUP 5-2

Use the appropriate revision symbols to insert needed commas in the following sentences.

1. Dr. Sean Miller moved to St. Louis, Missouri after he completed his degree.

2. Susan Washburn my college roommate is now a registered nurse.

3. We have in fact, extended the deadline until the first day of next month.

4. Are you sure that the company is based in Bristol, Tennessee and not Bristol, Virginia?

5. Did you attend the conference in New York City Doris?

6. By November 21, 2020 we will have paid half of what we owe on our home mortgage.

7. Your stock portfolio Tabitha is valued at over $2 million.

8. I moved to California on October 22, 1998 after getting my master's degree in business.

9. Mitchell is in Portland, Oregon until May 1.

10. On Monday, December 9 we will begin staying open 24 hours a day.

11. We should in my opinion close the Atlanta branch by August 1.

12. Matt, a hard-working associate came in two hours early this morning because of the crisis.

13. Thomas Brown, as you probably know. Graduates from Florida State University next spring.

14. Recent high temperatures which have been in the 90s have led to water restrictions.

15. Carolyn Esteban the general manager is also the director of our volunteer program.

Rules for Commas That Separate

Commas are used to separate items within a sentence.

10. Use a comma after each part of an address within a sentence. Note that there is no punctuation between the state abbreviation and the ZIP Code.

    Please write Mr. Dan Seagroves, 1426 West Parker Road, Flushing, New York 11361, to request a copy of the latest regulations.

11. Commas are used to separate three or more items in a series.

    Chris, Don, Frank, and Ralph left for Nicaragua last Sunday.

    Nancy reviewed the facts, made a decision, and took immediate action.

12. Use a comma before the conjunction (*and, or, but, yet, nor*) in a compound sentence. The comma, along with the conjunction, separates the two independent clauses.

    Sarah agreed to assist Darlene, but she was not enthusiastic about the project.

    Malcolm wrote the book, and he also drew the illustrations.

13. Use a comma after an introductory word, phrase, or clause.

    <u>Yes</u>, we will build two houses on the property.

    <u>Incidentally</u>, we have checked all the zoning restrictions.

    <u>In my opinion</u>, we should purchase the office building and rent it.

    <u>Opened in 1992</u>, the museum is celebrating its tenth anniversary.

    <u>Before the remodeling is begun</u>, you must obtain a permit from the city of Shelby.

    <u>When Mr. Jansen calls</u>, please request his e-mail address and his fax number.

INTRODUCTORY DEPENDENT CLAUSES

Look for the following words that often begin introductory dependent clauses at the beginning of a sentence. Use a comma to separate the dependent clause from the rest of the sentence.

after   before   unless
as soon as   if   when
because   though   while

If you decide to travel, leave early.
Before you begin, read the directions.

14. Commas are used to separate two or more consecutive adjectives that modify the same noun.

    The public relations consultant suggested an honest, sensitive response to the victims.

    Denise always writes long, rambling, wordy explanations.

    To determine if a comma is needed to separate two or more consecutive adjectives that modify the same noun, say the word *and* between them. If the sentence makes sense with the word *and*, then the adjectives should be separated by a comma.

    Our medical clinic provides convenient, affordable health services.

    Our medical clinic provides convenient and affordable health services.

    A comma is needed because the sentence makes sense with the word *and* inserted.

As you proofread a document, make sure that you know the reason why each comma is used.

CHECKUP 5-3   Use revision symbols to insert and delete commas in the following sentences. If a sentence is correct, write *C* for *Correct* to the left of the item number.

1. Jaya, Gearish, and Pankaj, have formed a consulting group for people interested in doing business in India.

2. Yes your office will be painted on November 5.

3. We produced, edited, and distributed a documentary film on recycling programs in our state.

4. My new address is 3128 Pleasant Drive Akron, Ohio 44313.

5. While attending a conference in Quebec Denise met with several industry representatives.

6. Elizabeth Berry Thomas joined our company less than six months ago and she has already achieved recognition as top sales agent.

7. Harry's new address is 3642 Rainier Lane, Fredericksburg, VA, 22401.

8. To enter the contest mail a completed entry form to us by April 15.

9. Our company owns valuable, beachfront property.

10. Edwin Jane, and Brenda completed 36 hours of continuing education.

11. Lena's sales are the highest and she definitely will win the award.

12. After your job transfer, you will live in the beautiful scenic mountains of Tennessee.

13. Kelly Walteri sent invitations to all the board members phoned everyone to confirm their reservations and arranged for the hotel accommodations.

14. Manuel will work with the customer service department or he will assist the computer technology group.

15. Most employees would prefer to work in a relaxed less formal setting.

SOFTWARE TIPS

Be cautious in using spell and grammar checkers to check comma usage in a document. These checkers are set up to identify commas that may be used incorrectly; they may or may not highlight places where commas are missing and are needed. For example, the following sentence is missing commas between the items in a series.

The menu included soups salads and appetizers.

The grammar checker in Corel WordPerfect suggests that the words *soups*, *salads*, and *appetizers* might be treated as possessives or as parts of a series that should take commas. The grammar checker in Microsoft Word doesn't highlight any potential comma errors in the sentence.

The commas in the following letter are used correctly. Refer to rules 1–14 in this chapter and, on the line provided, write the rule number that applies to each item.

Rule Number

March 16, <YEAR>

1. _____

Mr. Jeremiah Washburn
3382 Morningview Drive
Utica, MI 48087

2. _____

Dear Mr. Washburn:

Thank you for your interest in the Sea Scape Condominiums. You will enjoy an oceanfront suite designed for relaxation, and you will appreciate being just minutes away from entertainment, seafood restaurants, and shopping malls.

3. _____

Emily Harrelson, our entertainment coordinator, will help you arrange activities for your family. Free golf, tennis, and scuba diving are part of your vacation package. You may choose to take advantage of our modern, well-equipped health spa. You may decide, however, to enjoy a relaxing walk on the beach.

4. _____
5. _____

6. _____
7. _____

You are sure to find vacation fun, Mr. Washburn, when you visit with us in sunny Myrtle Beach, South Carolina, this summer. You were our guest September 15, 2000, and were forced to evacuate during Hurricane Frieda. Yes, your 10 percent Hurricane Frieda discount coupon is still active and will be applied to your vacation package this year.

8. _____
9. _____
10. _____
11. _____

In your letter, you requested the address of Scuba Diving Rentals, Inc. The address is 2238 Ocean Boulevard, Myrtle Beach, South Carolina 29602, which is about two miles from us.

12. _____

Mr. Washburn, please call toll free (1-800-555-3847) to make your reservations soon.

13. _____

Sincerely yours,

14. _____

Bethany Sarratt, Manager

15. _____

When Not to Use Commas

Some writers overuse commas. Using too many commas can be as serious a problem as not using enough commas. The following rules indicate how commas should not be used. The first example in each pair shows incorrect usage; the second example shows the correct usage with the comma omitted.

15. Do *not* use a comma to separate a subject from a predicate that immediately follows. The predicate is the verb plus any of its modifiers.

    Incorrect: The flight attendant, assisted the ill passenger.

    Correct: The flight attendant assisted the ill passenger.

16. Do *not* use a comma to separate a predicate from an object that immediately follows.

    Incorrect: Richard wrote the book, *Surfing the Net.*

    Correct: Richard wrote the book *Surfing the Net.*

17. Do *not* use a comma to separate the parts of a compound subject. A compound subject consists of two or more subjects joined by a conjunction (*and, or*).

    Incorrect: Managers, and their sales staff voted for additional insurance coverage.

    Correct: Managers and their sales staff voted for additional insurance coverage.

18. Do *not* use a comma to separate the parts of a compound predicate.

    Incorrect: Alex just completed the training program, and is currently looking for another job.

    Correct: Alex just completed the training program and is currently looking for another job.

Notice in a church bulletin:

"The choir invites any member of the congregation who enjoys sinning to join the choir."

Source: Web site for *Classic Church Bulletin Bloopers*

TIPS

COMPOUND SENTENCE OR COMPOUND PREDICATE?

If you're not sure if a sentence is a compound sentence or a sentence with a compound predicate, ask yourself if you can break the sentence into two complete sentences. For example:

Pat writes magazine articles and works as a freelance photographer.

If you eliminate *and*, can you make two complete sentences? *Pat writes magazine articles* is a complete sentence; however, *Works as a freelance photographer* is not a complete sentence. Since you cannot make two complete sentences, no comma is needed before the *and*.

The following sentences contain a total of 16 commas, some of which are correctly used. Use the appropriate revision symbol to delete any unneeded commas.

1. Terry Ciccotelli requested, that the new computers have 17-inch monitors.

2. Dr. Anne Jackson, and her nurse were at the plant to give limited health screenings for associates, their spouses, and their children.

3. The person she plans to nominate for employee of the year, is Mildred Poston.

4. Yes, the order you faxed to us was received, and was shipped today.

5. As you know, a qualified applicant, was interviewed by the employee search committee.

6. Ed Harold, called each applicant's references, documented previous employment, and verified college degrees.

7. Darryl trains the new orderlies, and coordinates their work schedules.

8. Anne will develop the bulletin board segment of our Web site, and will monitor the messages posted there.

9. Michael Kaufman, or Doris Tatum will be our candidate for mayor.

10. The results of the survey have not revealed, any new trends.

Application 5-A

Proofread the following draft of a letter. Use appropriate revision symbols to insert and delete commas as needed.

February 18, <YEAR>

Mr. Alfredo Gonzales
4423 Elmhurst Drive
Norman OK 73071

Dear Mr. Gonzales:

Thank you for attending the meeting last week that explained our limited partnership. Thank you also for letting me know that you are interested in investing in this venture.

As you requested I have enclosed a prospectus for the partnership. Also enclosed is a questionnaire that must be completed before we can accept you as an investor.

Please complete sign, and return the questionnaire to us as soon as possible. The questionnaire should be returned to Ms. Glenda Carpenter our attorney at Post Office Box 2843, Norman, OK 73073, by March 1. Once you have been accepted as an investor you will be asked to submit your check for $15,000.

Incidentally we need only three more investors before the project can begin. We hope to have these investors identified by the end of March.

Please call Ms. Carpenter or me if you have questions about the prospectus. I look forward, to hearing from you soon.

Sincerely,

DAVENPORT PARTNERSHIP

Scott Davenport General Partner

slc
Enclosures

Application 5-B

Proofread the following letter for correct comma usage. Use appropriate revision symbols to insert or delete commas as needed.

Big Sky Computers

3245 Nelson Avenue, Missoula, MT 59807
Phone: 406.555.1247 • Fax: 406.555.1298 • bsmt@bigsky.com

July 1, <YEAR>

Ms. Gloria Terazzo
Terazzo Accounting Consultants
Post Office Box 7236
Missoula MT 59807

Dear Ms. Terazzo:

As I mentioned to you on the telephone today I would like to arrange a time for your annual audit of our books. Our fiscal year, as you know ended June 30, and we would like to complete the year-end process as soon as possible.

Mr. Joe Hartwell our new accountant, will be glad to assist you while you complete the audit. He has access to our records our computer system, and our safe.

I have several questions that are too involved for this letter and I would appreciate your meeting with me in my office next week. Would Friday July 8, at 3:30 p.m. suit your schedule? My assistant will telephone you Tuesday to confirm this appointment.

Ms. Terazzo I appreciate the competent meticulous job that your staff always does for us. I look forward to meeting with you next week.

Sincerely,

Olida Loaces

Olida Loaces,
Accounting Manager

ls

Application 5-C

Proofread the following bulletin board notice to be posted throughout your organization's building. Use appropriate revision symbols
to correct comma usage errors plus any other types of errors.

Annual Fall Foliage Excurtion

Saturday, October 25, <YEAR>

Our annual fall foliage excursion has been scheduled for Saturday,
October 25. The trip will take us though the mountains on the scenic
Blue ridge Parkway. We will stop at two apple orchards where you
may purchase several variety's of apples: red delicious and golden
delicious apples for eating and a tart apple for cooking.

As a special treat, Tom Massey has invited us to visit his mother-in-
laws mountain cabin. We will arrive at Mrs. Browns cabin about
10:30 a.m.. You will be served refreshments, and will have the
opportunity for a short hike to a beautiful cool water fall.

Please sign up for the trip by calling 555-2846 as soon as possible.
The bus capacity is 52 people, and the trip will be limited to the to
the first 52 people who sign up. The bus will leave from our parking
lot at 6:30 a.m., and return by 5:30 p.m.

Application 5-D

Proofread the following memo. Use appropriate revision symbols to correct comma usage errors plus any other types of errors.

DATE: July 28, <YEAR>

TO: Patricia Alverex, Human Resource Manager

FROM: Florence Smith-Davis, Marketing Manager

SUBJECT: Telemarketing Seminar

Thank you four organizing the telemarketing seminar for hour entire sails staff. Our marketing representative's have been scheduled to spend one weak each month in the office calling potential customers. I won't them too no how to use their time effectively.

In my opinion two Saturday session should provide the time we need for developing sum knew sales techniques. All off us are looking forward, to learning more a bout telemarketing. Please send me a schedule for the two sessions.

jlc

NAME _____ DATE _____

CD-ROM Application 5-E

Using your word processor, open the file DPES05E from the CD-ROM. Proofread the letter on the screen. Insert needed commas and delete any unnecessary commas. Run the spell checker; then save the revised letter using your initials in place of the DPES. Proofread the letter and make any additional corrections. Save and print the corrected letter.

January 30 <YEAR>

Dr. William J. Jackson
President
Jackson and Jackson Consultants
2814 North Tryon Street
Charlotte NC 28212

Dear Dr. Jackson:

Your seminar on exporting was excellent. Our management team greatly benefited from your session on Saturday January 15. At our last staff meeting we distributed the continuing education certificates that you provided.

It is obvious that you keep up with new exporting regulations, and make seminar participants aware of these. The segment on handling international banking issues will be especially useful to us. Making sure that we receive payment in a timely fashion, is essential when managing a small business.

Please send some information on your seminars to, Ms. Allison Ferguson, ACE Manufacturing Company, 4833 South Ventura Drive Columbia, SC, 29212. She is interested in arranging a seminar in her city.

Thank you for being part of our continuing, staff, development program. We are always pleased with the quality of your seminars.

Sincerely,

Harry Downs Marketing Manager

CD-ROM Application 5-F

Using your word processor, open the file DPES05F from the CD-ROM. Correct all errors in comma usage, plus any other types of errors (assume that the names are spelled correctly). Insert the current year in the date line. Run the spell checker; then save the revised memo using your initials in place of the DPES. Proofread the memo on the screen and make any additional corrections. Save and print the corrected memo.

MEMO TO: Lauren Ellison, Human Resource Director

FROM: Nancy Billingsly, Events Coordinator

DATE: December 19, <YEAR>

SUBJECT: Physical Fitness Program

In a resent survey of our associates over 35 percent requested that we start a physical fitness program. Other company's in our area have already begun similar programs and have seen a decline in absenteeism rates.

After reviewing the services of all local gyms, I have recommended that we initiate a contract with Jack's and Jill's gym that is conveniently located with in two blocks of our building. This gym provides individual fitness evaluations, and plans to help each person move toward specific improvement goals. The owners boast of having the latest best-maintained equipment in the area, and they limit their membership, preventing, as much as possible long waiting lines for equipment use.

Enclosed are several brochures that list services and prices for individual gym memberships. Obviously we would have to negotiate a group rate. I will call you later this week to arrange a time when we can talk about providing a physical fitness program for our associates. Such a program in my opinion would have benefits for the associates and the company.

Other Punctuation

Using correct punctuation makes a business communication easier to understand. It can also make a favorable impression on your reader. Spend the time necessary to write or revise a communication conscientiously; then, spend the time necessary to proofread and correct your communication.

Punctuation errors are easily overlooked. Sometimes these errors are the result of a hectic, time-pressured day. At other times these errors are overlooked because the applicable rule has become a little fuzzy to you. To change fuzzy to clear, check a reference source.

As you review the punctuation rules in this chapter, refer to the discussion in Chapter 1 on spacing used with punctuation.

PERIODS, COLONS, EXCLAMATION POINTS, AND DASHES

Periods and exclamation points are used as end punctuation for sentences. Colons and dashes are used to set off or emphasize material.

Periods

Periods are used to punctuate sentences and abbreviations.

1. Use a period to end a statement or a command. Also use a period to end a polite request—a question where the person spoken to is likely to respond by doing what is requested instead of simply answering the question.

Cultural diversity is an important issue for businesses.
(Statement)

Send the contract to all appropriate parties. (Command)

Will you please fax me your response by Friday morning. (Polite request)

2. Periods are needed in many abbreviations but not all. (Check a comprehensive reference manual to be sure.) Be especially careful of spacing with periods in abbreviations.

a.m.　　　p.m.　　　Inc.

Ph.D.　　　D.D.S.　　　U.S.

Note: If an abbreviation that ends in a period comes at the end of a sentence that takes a period, use only one period to end the sentence.

We awarded the contract to Kisor and Associates, Inc.

3. Customary and metric abbreviations for weights and measurements have no periods. The abbreviation for inches, *in*, may sometimes need a period to avoid confusion with the preposition *in*.

5 lb　　　12 mm　　　132.86 k

32° C　　　13 × 10 ft　　　128 MB RAM

The size of each sample should be precisely as described in the specifications: 3.2 by 4.2 by 4.8 cm.

Two-letter state abbreviations also have no periods.

Bakersfield, CA 93309　　　Fargo, ND 58121

4. Periods are used after numbers or letters that enumerate items in outlines or displayed lists, as in the numbered lists in this chapter. Periods are also used at the end of clauses or long phrases in a list, as in the following example.

We need to:

1. Revise our hiring procedures.
2. Develop a training program.
3. Implement an incentive plan.

Note: The items in the following list do not end with periods because they appear to be a list of inventory items.

These occupations have fast job growth:

a. Systems analysts
b. Desktop publishing specialists
c. Medical assistants

Colons

Colons are used with parts of letters and memos and within sentences.

Statement listed on a résumé:
"Strengths: Ability to meet deadlines while maintaining composer."
Source: Accountemps

1. Use a colon after the salutation in a business letter that uses standard punctuation.

    Dear Mr. Stevens: Dear Ms. Perez:

2. Use a colon after the guide words in a memo typed on plain paper.

    MEMO TO: David Manion

    FROM: Mara Giardino

    DATE: August 8, <YEAR>

    SUBJECT: New Incentive Plan

3. Use a colon after anticipatory expressions such as *the following*, *as follows*, and *listed below* that precede a list.

    You must bring the following items with you:

    - Birth Certificate
    - Driver's License
    - Passport

    The colon is also used after words such as *note* and *remember* that introduce rules or guidelines.

    Note: Everyone must attend the planning conference.

4. Use a colon between a clause that contains an anticipatory expression (*the following*, *as follows*, and *these*) and a series of explanatory words, phrases, or clauses. Anticipatory expressions draw attention to the material that follows.

    These are our main objectives for December: to boost sales, to increase profits, and to decrease inventory.

    Sometimes the anticipatory expression is implied and not stated, as in the following example:

    We have three goals for December: boosting sales, increasing profits, and decreasing inventory.

5. Note that the first word following a colon is capitalized (1) if that word begins a complete sentence that presents a formal rule or statement, (2) if that word follows a short introductory word such as *Note* or *Caution*, or (3) if that word begins on a new line (as, for example, in lists).

    All of us agree with our manager: Tornado drill procedures must be followed explicitly. (Formal statement)

Exclamation Points

The exclamation point is used to show strong feeling or emotion such as surprise, dismay, or enthusiasm.

1. The exclamation point may be used after a complete sentence or after one word or phrase.

    Darron won the race!

    Warning! This product may be hazardous to your health.

2. An exclamation point may be used instead of a question mark when strong feeling is expressed.

What made you do that!

USING EXCLAMATION POINTS

Watch for overuse of the exclamation point in business writing. Using too many exclamation points makes the mark lose its effectiveness.

Dashes

A dash may be used in place of a comma, a semicolon, a colon, or parentheses to provide a more forceful break.

1. One dash separates a strong comment at the end of a sentence from the rest of that sentence. A dash also separates an afterthought or an abrupt change in thought from the rest of the sentence.

   The customer requested that we ship the order immediately— by this afternoon, if possible. (Strong comment)

   We need to fill the position—and quickly! (Afterthought)

   He said he wants to reconsider—do you agree? (Abrupt change in thought)

2. One dash separates a summary statement from the rest of the sentence. A summary statement often begins with words such as *all*, *these*, and *they*.

   Carolyn, Darlene, and Shirley—all were promoted.

3. Two dashes are used to set off nonessential information if the break is in the middle of the sentence.

   Only one person—Lane Wesley, our supervisor—has the combination to the safe.

4. A dash may be used in place of a semicolon to separate two independent clauses that go together.

   Our nurses are key personnel—we could not run the hospital without them.

5. When used in pairs, dashes are very similar to parentheses. However, parentheses *de-emphasize* statements; dashes, on the other hand, *emphasize* them.

   All claims—according to company policy—were processed within six business days. (Dashes emphasize content.)

   All claims (according to company policy) were processed within six business days. (Parentheses de-emphasize content.)

CHECKUP 6-1 If needed, insert a period, a colon, an exclamation point, or a dash in each indicated blank space in the following letter. Leave the space empty if no punctuation is needed. The letter uses standard punctuation.

April 25, <YEAR>

1. Ms__ Ellen Reilly
Office Manager
Staffing Specialists, Inc.
42145 West Allendale Road
2. Hopkins, MN__ 55345

3. Dear Ms. Reilly__

4. Congratulations __ Your purchase of five Tanner computers will
give you an advantage over every other temporary agency in your
5. area __

6. Your new computers will be delivered by May 7 __ sooner if possi-
7. ble. We will provide you with these services __

- Equipment Installation
- Staff Development
- Maintenance

8. Productivity, efficiency, accountability, and profitability__ these are
9. your goals. Your new Tanner computers will help you meet them__
10. Please call us any time when we can help you further__

Sincerely,

Benjamin Rush, Sales Representative

SOFTWARE TIPS

When typing a dash, use two hyphens with no space before, after, or between them. Most word processing software automatically changes the two hyphens (--) to a dash (—) after the space bar is pressed. Note that there is no space before or after the printed dash regardless of the way it is typed. Type the following sentence to see how your software treats two hyphens typed in succession.

The policy specifies prompt action--no exceptions.

Revision Symbols for Marking Punctuation

The following revision symbols are used to mark periods, colons, exclamation points, or dashes.

Revision	Edited Draft	Final Copy
Insert a period	Call today By tomorrow the rates will change.	Call today. By tomorrow the rates will change.
Insert a colon	Complete the following tasks:	Complete the following tasks:
Insert an exclamation point	Fantastic! You will be pleased.	Fantastic! You will be pleased.
Insert a dash	Amy flew the plane he served as navigator.	Amy flew the plane—he served as navigator.
Delete punctuation	Joe is about fifty.	Joe is about fifty.

CHECKUP 6-2 Use appropriate revision symbols to insert periods, colons, exclamation points, and dashes as needed in the following sentences. Delete any unneeded punctuation.

1. Will you call me when the contract is signed

2. Eric, Kellie, and Jason all of them disagreed with the policy.

3. Ingrid's suggestion is best Limit plant tours to persons at least 18 years old.

4. Our plane leaves at 2 pm on Monday.

5. Call Anne Melton she's with Murray Construction Company and request a bid.

6. Revise the following pages in the policy manual pages 32, 78, 134, and 146.

7. Congratulations You deserve the promotion.

8. Amy will receive her P.h.D. in August.

9. November, December, and January all are high-volume sales months.

10. Greta, Lillian, and Tom explained the new procedures to me

TIPS

MARKING PUNCTUATION CORRECTIONS

To make sure you don't overlook corrections, place a check mark in the margin next to each line that has a correction, as shown in the following example. This way you can go through a document and easily locate lines that require corrections.

Make sure all the arrangements are made we want
to avoid surprises.　　　　　　　　　　　✓

CHECKUP 6-3

Proofread the following paragraphs and insert any needed periods, colons, exclamation points, and dashes. *Note*: You may need to delete or change existing punctuation.

If you would like to take a college course but you don't feel you have the time consider taking an online course. An online course involves using the computer, e-mail, and the Internet. Instead of traveling to a campus and attending a class, students can take a course at their convenience they can complete their work at any time and from any location. Students in online courses have a variety of options for communicating with classmates and the instructor e-mail, electronic bulletin boards, and chat rooms.

These are some benefits of enrolling in an online course

1 Flexible hours for completing coursework.
2 More opportunities for contact with the instructor and classmates.
3 Increased knowledge of computer use.

An online course is ideal for a variety of people from those with full-time jobs to retirees. Online courses give these individuals the convenience of a course that fits their busy schedules. People who live far from a college or who lack adequate transportation also find online courses helpful there's little or no traveling involved. Think of the possibilities.

PARENTHESES, HYPHENS, AND SEMICOLONS

Parentheses, hyphens, and semicolons are used to separate material or to set off nonessential material.

Parentheses

Parentheses are used to set off nonessential information.

1. Use parentheses to enclose explanatory words, phrases, clauses, or numbers that are included within a sentence but are independent of the main idea of the sentence.

   The balance of the payment ($250) is due on August 1.

   Mr. Proxmire (our regional vice president) will be interviewed by the press.

   Note: The parentheses are used instead of commas to place less emphasis on the material.

2. Use parentheses to enclose numbers or letters that enumerate items within a sentence.

   All of us agreed to (1) form a task force, (2) investigate new product lines, and (3) increase market share.

3. Use parentheses to enclose references, directions, or dates that add extra information.

   The sexual harassment policy has been revised (see page 104).

   Norman Rockwell (1894–1978) was a famous American illustrator.

4. Parentheses may be used to enclose an interruption within a sentence or to enclose an entire sentence. Note the capital letter for *In* and the period within the parentheses in the second example.

   Please refer to my most recent e-mail message (sent July 15) regarding the revised schedule.

   The present catalog lists the wrong price for life jackets; therefore, we must correct the next printing. (In fact, we should check all the prices before we reprint.)

Note the following examples that show how other punctuation marks are most often used with parentheses.

- A comma, semicolon, colon, or dash goes outside a closing parenthesis.

   Although we completed our construction several months ago (in April), we have not yet had our grand opening and ribbon cutting.

- A period goes outside a closing parenthesis except when it punctuates an abbreviation or a sentence in parentheses.

  Our new CEO is highly respected. (He held key positions at two of our competitors.) Our board of directors unanimously approved his appointment.

- Question marks and exclamation points go outside a closing parenthesis unless the mark belongs with the item in parentheses or punctuates a separate sentence in parentheses.

  Have you met Beth (or is it Elizabeth)?

  Ask Lauren about the new benefits package. (Wasn't she involved in selecting the options?)

Hyphens

The hyphen is most commonly used to join words—or parts of words—together.

1. Use hyphens for all words and compound words that are hyphenated in your dictionary.

   top-notch   air-condition   open-minded   sight-seeing

2. Use hyphens for most compound adjectives—two or more words joined together as a unit to modify a noun.

   Kevin needs an 8-inch pipe to fix the leak. (8 *inches* of pipe)

   Lisa has an office in a 30-story building. (30 *stories* high)

   We bought a low-intensity lamp. (A lamp of *low intensity*)

   Dana signed a five-year contract. (A contract of five *years*)

3. Use hyphens for fractions that stand by themselves (*two-thirds*, *one-half*). Also use hyphens to express compound numbers from *twenty-one* to *ninety-nine* in words.

   Our gas tank is three-fourths full.

   She worked at the college for twenty-five years before retiring.

   We are eagerly awaiting the twenty-first century.

Headline in a newspaper:
"Squad Helps Dog Bite Victim"
(Did the dog have help in biting someone or did someone get bitten by a dog? A hyphen would clarify the compound adjective *Dog-Bite*.)
Source: The World According to Newspaper Headlines

4. Use hyphens to show end-of-line word breaks; follow a dictionary or a wordbook to make sure the breaks are correct.

   According to our new company policy, please discard all junk mail that is delivered to our office. Place it in the appropriate recycling bins.

5. To save space, hyphens may be used with dates (6-9-99) in lists but not in the date line of a letter or memo.

Alexander J. Murphy	003-98-4583	5-10-85
Elizabeth M. Arnold	090-55-0497	8/17/96

6. A hyphen may be used instead of the word *to* when two figures in a sequence are joined. Do not leave any space before or after the hyphen.

   The conference is scheduled for April 17–19.

   Revise pages 242–248 in the policy manual.

Semicolons

Semicolons are used to join items.

1. The most common use of the semicolon is to join two closely related independent clauses that are not joined by a coordinating conjunction (*and*, *but*, *or*, *nor*).

   Shannon took the photographs today; the prints should be ready by tomorrow.

   Alex supported the legislation; his colleagues voted against it.

2. The semicolon is used to join two related independent clauses when the second clause begins with a transitional expression such as *therefore*, *however*, *for example*, *consequently*, or *moreover*.

   Travis was late again this morning; however, he had a legitimate reason this time.

   Bob contributes regularly to his retirement account; consequently, his monthly retirement check will be sufficient.

   Ms. Hoyle refused to increase our advertising budget; she suggested, moreover, that we decrease it by at least $500.

   Note: A comma is used after the transitional expression that joins the two clauses.

3. The semicolon replaces the comma in a series when one or more of the items in the series already includes a comma.

   Cathy will be consulting in Chicago, Illinois; Columbia, South Carolina; St. Louis, Missouri; and Bristol, Tennessee.

   The three semicolons help to separate these four items; commas would merely cause confusion.

Net Link

Punctuation Made Simple, a Web site developed by Gary Olson, gives a helpful overview of the importance of punctuation. Go to the Web site at **http://nmosferatu.cas .usf.edu/JAC/pms/intro .html** and read the overview. Then review the sections on the colon, semicolon, and dash.

Revision Symbols for Marking Punctuation

The following revision symbols are used to mark parentheses, hyphens, or semicolons.

Revision	Edited Draft	Final Copy
Insert parentheses	The findings are described and explained (see page 123	The findings are described and explained (see page 123).

Revision	Edited Draft	Final Copy
Insert a hyphen	We treated thirty̲two patients today.	We treated thirty-two patients today.
Insert a semicolon	He will find out;however, it may be too late.	He will find out; however, it may be too late.
Change a comma to a semicolon	Costs have increased,therefore, changes are needed.	Costs have increased; therefore, changes are needed.

CHECKUP 6-4 Use appropriate revision symbols to insert parentheses, hyphens, and semicolons as needed in the following sentences.

1. Your tasks will include the following: 1 opening the restaurant each morning, 2 making the bank deposit twice daily, and 3 closing the restaurant each evening.

2. Next year is John and Sally's twenty fifth wedding anniversary.

3. My plane was late however, I did not miss my connecting flight.

4. The accounting statements include up to date sales figures.

5. Your deposit wasn't made until 4:45 p.m. today, therefore, it will not be credited to your account until tomorrow.

6. Dennis Patrick he is our accounts receivable associate spends at least six hours per day working at his computer.

7. At least two thirds of the directors must vote in favor of the motion.

8. Candice will demonstrate our products in Tampa, Florida, Raleigh, North Carolina, Denver, Colorado, and Austin, Texas.

9. The principle is explained in Chapter 5 see page 112.

10. Because the land is extremely valuable, Laney demolished the dilapidated three story building.

11. Our newest staff member she's a technology specialist was hired to maintain our Web site.

12. We will be attending a computer technology seminar from April 15 19.

13. Sheila adjusted the temperature in the room Carole still complained of being cold.

14. Our holiday policy is very generous for example, we are allowed three personal days to use at our discretion.

15. The noise pollution at some worksites particularly manufacturing plants can lead to hearing loss.

QUESTION MARKS, QUOTATION MARKS, AND UNDERSCORES

Question marks are used to punctuate words that ask a question, while quotation marks and underscores are used to set off material.

Question Marks

Question marks are used to indicate questions.

1. A question mark may be used at the end of a sentence that asks a direct question.

   Will the feasibility study be completed by February 10?

   Have you submitted the costs for the new Web site?

2. A question mark also may be used at the end of a parenthetical question within a sentence.

   The recommendations in the feasibility study (will it be ready by February 10?) will affect our decision.

Quotation Marks

Quotation marks are used to set off material or to provide emphasis.

1. Use quotation marks to enclose a person's exact words.

   "Our sales figures are good," Joseph said. "In fact, we are exceeding our expectations."

   "You will be amazed at the wealth of data available at our Web site," said Barbara Holden, our business information manager.

2. Use quotation marks to enclose the titles of parts of books, magazines, newspapers, or other published works. These include the titles of chapters, articles, and essays.

   The fifth chapter, "Supervising Difficult People," is the most useful one in the book *Management Challenges*.

   Her article "Capitalizing on E-Commerce" appeared in the *Los Angeles Times*.

   Have you read William Simpson's latest editorial, "That's the Way Technology Works"?

3. Quotation marks are used with special words or phrases that follow the words *marked*, *stamped*, *titled*, and *labeled*.

   Please mark this package "Fragile."

   The CD-ROM is labeled "For individual use only."

   Have the manufacturing personnel stamp the material "Do not remove."

Underscores

Underscores have traditionally been used to provide emphasis in typed materials. However, italic type is more commonly used instead of underscores to emphasize words.

1. Words that represent the actual words are usually underscored but may also appear in italics.

   Throughout this report, the words affect and effect are used incorrectly.

   All employees should understand the term sexual harassment.

2. Titles of books, magazines, newspapers, plays, and other complete works may be underscored. These titles are more often typed in italics or in all-capital letters.

   Three of Alice Hyatt's best-selling books are Healthy Living, Fit for Life, and Food for Fitness.

   Note: Do not underline any punctuation that appears before or after the title.

Revision Symbols for Marking Punctuation

The following revision symbols are used to mark question marks, quotation marks, or underscores.

Revision	Edited Draft	Final Copy
Insert a question mark	Is the project completed ? Laura is concerned.	Is the project completed? Laura is concerned.
Insert quotation marks	He said, "Yes, I will."	He said, "Yes, I will."
Insert an underscore	Her book is titled <u>Enhanced Design</u>.	Her book is titled <u>Enhanced Design</u>.
Transpose punctuation	Ben asked, "Who ordered the pizza"?	Ben asked, "Who ordered the pizza?"

CHECKUP 6-5

Use revision symbols to insert or move question marks, quotation marks, and underscores as needed in the following sentences.

1. The accountant asked, "Will the check be mailed by Friday"?

2. The word problem has a negative connotation.

3. Sean excitedly announced, "I got the job"!

4. The article Exercise for Executives appeared in Business Today, which is a local magazine.

5. We anticipate that additional research will confirm our claims, stated the manager.

6. We agree with your decision, Adam said, but we prefer taking immediate action instead of waiting until Monday.

7. Was the fax marked "Notify Recipient on Arrival?"

8. The attorney asked, Do you agree with the proposed settlement?

9. The menu erroneously listed desert instead of dessert.

10. Can you meet with us on September 10

CHECKUP 6-6

Proofread the following paragraph and insert question marks, quotation marks, and underscores as needed. *Note*: You may need to delete or transpose existing punctuation.

Have you ever traveled to another country. If you have, you may have found yourself a victim of a language barrier. In his book Do's and Taboos of Using English Around the World, Roger E. Axtell discusses the pitfalls of using English in countries where English is not the primary language. In the chapter How to Be Understood, he advises speakers to "Speak slowly and distinctly". Mr. Axtell also recommends avoiding the use of slang, such as using the word cool to refer to something stylish or using the word bad to refer to something good. The best advice is to think before you speak.

Application 6-A

Use appropriate revision symbols to supply the needed parenthe-ses, hyphens, colons, and semicolons in the following memoran-dum. In some cases, you will have to change existing punctuation.

MEMO TO: Lana G. Reynolds

FROM: Jeff Wilson

DATE: April 8, <YEAR>

SUBJECT: Promotions and Transfers

After much review, three employees have been approved for pro-motion. The following criteria see page 172 of the company policy manual were used in selecting the branch managers: (1) qualifica-tions, (2) seniority, and 3 job performance.

The branch managers and their new locations are as follows Victoria Spencer in Danville, Virginia, Dale Ledbetter in Charlotte, North Carolina, and Jackson Fritz in Salem, Oregon. Together these new managers represent forty one years of manufacturing experience.

The managers may assume their new positions as early as July 1 however, they must report by August 1. Nelson Weinberg recently appointed as relocation specialist will help make their moves as smooth as possible.

Each of the new managers will be attending the executive level conference to be held April 26 28 in New York, New York. Conference details will be mailed today.

mc

Application 6-B

Use appropriate revision symbols to insert needed punctuation—dashes, periods, parentheses, question marks, colons, exclamation points, quotation marks, and underscores—in the following memo. You may need to delete or change existing punctuation.

MEMO TO: Terry Blevins, Human Resource Manager

FROM: Anna Roland, Office Manager

DATE: March 10, <YEAR>

SUBJECT: Office Communications

Did you subscribe to the magazine Office Dynamics for our staff Melissa Fredrich, who conducted our last staff development session, said, This magazine should be required reading for all office associates

Attached is an excellent article that I clipped from the magazine. This article, Writing on the Job, emphasizes the importance of correct, effective writing at all levels of the organization. The article gives a humorous slant to the term miscommunication as it relates to the office environment. I would suggest that you use the contents of this article in your preparation for next week's staff meeting Tuesday at 8:30 am on office communications.

I am looking forward to hearing your comments on how important it is for all associates both managers and staff to improve their writing skills. Please emphatically make this point think before you write.

Attachment

Application 6-C

Your company does bulk mailing for various companies. Two of the companies have moved to new locations. Use revision symbols to mark each error in the following postal cards that notify the public of each company's relocation.

We welcome you too join us at our knew location starting November 1, <YEAR>.

Cleveland Neurological Associates
Nancy F. Henderson, M.D., and Brett R. Caskey, MD
234 Mellon Street, Suit 3
Shelby North Carolina 28152
704-555-8323

Bulk Rate
U.S. Postage
PAID

Gastonia Walk In Medical Clinic

Is Moving to a More Convenient Location to Serve You Better

David R. Jessup, M.D., and Tanya S. Kemp, MD.
are pleased to announce the opening of there new offices
Tuesday, November 15, <YEAR>.

G aston Hills Mall
210 South Sharon road, Suite 406
Gastonia, North Carolina 28052
704-555-6831

Thank you for being our patent you helped make our fist year in Gastonia a tremendous success.

We look forward to serving you at our at our new offices.

Bulk Rate
U.S. Postage
PAID

Application 6-D

Use revision symbols to correct errors in punctuation plus any other types of errors in the following letter.

2328 West Marion Street, Atlanta, GA 30359-2328
Telephone: 404-555-2983   FAX: 404-555-2985
www.dtreefashions.com

September 21, <YEAR>

Mrs. Alice J. O'Leary
4829 West Lowell Avenue
Atlanta, GA 30382

Dear Mrs. O'Leary:

Thank you for writing to us about the three blouses that you recently purchased from our outlet store. We are always interested in hearing from our customers.

In your letter, you stated that only one of the there blouses faded and you sent that blouse for our examination. We examined the blouse and noticed that the label specified dry-clean only. The fabric content of this blouse will result in fading if it is washed, therefore, our design team specified that it be dry-cleaned. Because the blouse was washed instead of dry-cleaned, we feel that the treatment of the product caused the fading.

To demonstrate our appreciation for your continued patronage, enclosed is a coupon for a 15 percent discount towards your next purchase at any Doubletree Fashions store 12 locations in all.

Thank you for shopping with use.

Sincerely,

Tom Baxter

Tom Baxter
President

scc
Enclosure

CD-ROM Application 6-E

International Communications, Inc., uses e-mail to circulate its monthly newsletter to all employees. Using your word processor, open the file DPES06E from the CD-ROM. Proofread the newsletter. Add or delete punctuation marks as needed. Then run the spell checker. Save the newsletter using your initials in place of the DPES. Proofread the newsletter on the screen and make any additional corrections. Save and print the corrected newsletter.

NET NEWS

INTERNATIONAL COMMUNICATIONS, INC.

August 1, <YEAR>   Editor: Maya Ling
Volume 6, Number 8

GUEST SPEAKER

Harrison Daniel Renquiste, founder of the Bistro Grilles, will be the guest speaker at the Chicago Chamber of Commerce's annual banquet on Tuesday, September 1, at 6:30 p.m.. Mr. Renquiste is responsible for revitalizing the downtown district by establishing food courts this development has made it a well known place to dine. His motto he is 85 years old is as follows Eat right, sleep well, and work hard.

We have reserved only 30 tickets for the banquet therefore, please call Phyllis Reardon at 555-4549 soon to reserve your ticket.

NEWSMAKERS

Ann Gregg, Beth Dratwa, and Gary Apgar these are the individuals who designed our new company logo. This team recently received a merit award from the International Advertising Association for their design.

Frank Milton, a senior analyst in our Tampa office, made his television debut last month on WKBC-TV as a guest on the evening news. Frank spoke on his recent article, You Can Make a Difference, which was published in the monthly magazine Volunteer. The article described his volunteer work during a recent flood disaster.

Derek Hunt has been named director of European operations effective September 10. Previously an assistant director in the Paris office 1997—2001, Derek will oversee sales and marketing efforts.

CD-ROM Application 6-F

As the manager of Pizza Mania, you have designed the following coupons to be attached to the pizza delivery boxes. Using your word processor, open the file DPES06F from the CD-ROM. Proofread the coupons. Correct punctuation errors plus any other types of errors; then run the spell checker. Change <YEAR> to the current year. Save the coupons using your initials in place of the DPES. Proofread the coupons on the screen and make any additional corrections. Save and print the corrected coupons.

PIZZA MANIA
125 East Fifth Street
Harrisburg PA 17113

COUPON
Two Medium Pizzas
Two Topping
Two 2-Litter Soft Drinks

$14.99

Carryout an Delivery Only
Telephone: 555-8864
FAX: 555-8865

Offer Expires April 30, <YEAR>
Not Valid With Any Other Coupon Offer

- -

PIZZA MANIA
125 East Fifth Street
Harrisburg, PA 17113

KOUPON
Three Small Pizzas
On Toping
Too 2 Liter Soft Drinks

$16.99

Carryout and Delivery Only
Telephone: 555-8864
SAX: 555-8865

Offer Expires April 30, <YEAR>
Not Valid Wit Any Other Coupon Offer

Grammar

OBJECTIVES

After completing this chapter, you should be able to:

1. Recognize and correct errors in subject-verb agreement.

2. Recognize and correct errors in pronoun-antecedent agreement.

3. Recognize and correct errors in the use of nominative-case and objective-case pronouns.

4. Recognize and correct errors in the use of *who* and *whom*.

Knowing how to apply grammar rules correctly is essential in proofreading. Keep in mind that people are often judged by how well they speak and write. For example, employers seek employees with excellent communication skills—just review some of the classified advertisements in your local newspaper or job postings on the Internet.

Chapter 7 stresses the most frequently used and misused grammar rules. Completing this chapter will give you practice in finding and correcting grammatical errors.

SUBJECT-VERB AGREEMENT

Subjects and verbs must agree in number (singular or plural) and gender (feminine, masculine, or neuter).

Singular and Plural Subjects

A singular subject must have a singular verb; a plural subject must have a plural verb.

> My key is in my car. (The subject, *key*, is singular. The verb, *is*, is singular. Because both the subject and the verb are singular, they agree.)

> My keys are in my car. (The subject, *keys*, is plural. The verb, *are*, is plural. Because both are plural, they agree.)

A subject that consists of a phrase or a clause requires a singular verb.

> Proofreading documents is an important task. (The phrase *Proofreading documents* is the subject and takes a singular verb.)

> If you have a suggestion, please share it with us. (The clause *If you have a suggestion* is the subject and takes a singular verb.)

Subjects joined by *and* are plural and require a plural verb.

> Ms. Conroy and Ms. Anders *are* planning to attend. (Plural verb because there are two subjects—both women are planning to attend.)

> The lab technicians and the doctor *are* in the hospital cafeteria. (Use a plural verb because there are two subjects—one plural and one singular.)

Two singular subjects joined by *or, either . . . or, neither . . . nor, not only . . . but also* require a singular verb.

> Ms. Conroy or Ms. Anders *is* planning to attend. (Singular verb because there is only one subject—only one woman is planning to attend.)

> Either the museum or the aquarium *is* closed on Labor Day. (Use a singular verb because there is only one subject—only one place will be closed.)

When a singular and a plural subject are joined by *or, either . . . or, neither . . . nor, not only . . . but also*, make the verb agree with the subject closer to the verb.

> Mr. McCurry or his *assistants have* the disk. (The plural subject is closest to the verb—use a plural verb.)

> The assistants or *Mr. McCurry has* the disk. (The singular subject is closest to the verb—use a singular verb.)

> Not only the manager but also the *associates have* the information. (The plural subject is closest to the verb—use a plural verb.)

A sign seen in a fast-food restaurant: "Be Cool in School! Good Grades Has Its Rewards."

TIPS

PREPOSITIONAL PHRASES

When deciding whether a plural or a singular verb is correct, ignore any prepositional phrase that may come between the subject and the verb.

> The plan for the next two months is aggressive.

> (The subject is *plan*, and the verb is *is*. The prepositional phrase *for the next two months* separates the subject and predicate.)

Look for the following prepositions that often begin prepositional phrases:

at	by	from	into	on	up
before	for	in	of	to	with

Collective Nouns

A *collective noun* is a singular word that represents a group: for example, an audience, committee, company, department, jury, or school. A collective noun used as a subject may be singular or plural depending on whether the members are acting as individuals or as a group.

> The jury *has reached* a decision. (The members are acting as a group—use a singular verb.)

> The jury *have disagreed* on the verdict. (The members are acting as individuals—use a plural verb.)

Indefinite Pronouns

When the indefinite pronouns *each, another, either, neither, one,* and *much* are used as subjects, use a singular verb.

> *Each* of the attendees *is* eligible for tuition reimbursement.

> *Neither* manager *is* available to attend the conference.

When the indefinite pronouns *both, few, several, many,* and *others* are used as subjects, use a plural verb.

> *Both* of the training seminars *are* scheduled for next week.

> *Several* of the presenters *are* scheduled to arrive on Friday.

The indefinite pronouns *some, all, any, none, more,* and *most* may be singular or plural. To determine whether to use a singular or a plural verb, look at the noun the pronoun refers to. The noun usually appears after the pronoun in a phrase that begins with *of,* as in the following example.

> Some of the feedback is negative. (*Some* refers to the singular noun *feedback,* so a singular verb is used.)

> Most of our customers are loyal. (*Most* refers to the plural noun *customers,* so a plural verb is used.)

> All of the manuscript has been written. (*All* refers to the singular noun *manuscript,* so it takes a singular verb.)

> Most of the employees did respond to the survey. (*Most* refers to the plural noun *employees,* so it takes a plural verb.)

The following compound pronouns are singular—they always take a singular verb.

anybody	everybody	nobody	somebody
anyone	everyone	no one	someone
anything	everything	nothing	something

> Everybody is invited to attend the reception.

> No one has left a message.

SOFTWARE TIPS

A grammar checker offers useful information in checking subject-verb agreement. In the illustration in Figure 7-1 below, note how the grammar checker suggests that *have* may be the correct verb for the following sentence:

Most of the spreadsheets has been checked.

Clicking on the question mark button in the bottom left corner of the grammar checker displays sample sentences with subject-verb agreement. Refer to these sample sentences and use your knowledge of subject-verb agreement to help you decide which verb is correct.

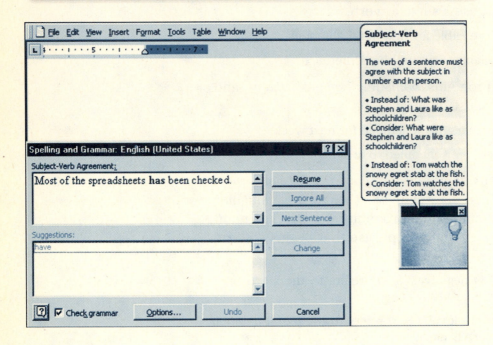

Figure 7-1. Grammar checker for subject-verb agreement.

Subject-verb agreement will be clearer to you after you complete the following exercise.

CHECKUP 7-1 Circle the verb in parentheses that correctly completes each of the following sentences.

1. An invoice for 20 filing cabinets (was, were) received on Monday.

2. Terry and Brenda Blevins (has, have) decided to open a child-care facility.

3. The assistant managers and the manager (was, were) working on the final copy of the report.

4. (Are/Is) Dennis or Nancy conducting the interview?

5. A shipment of apples (was, were) returned to us because they were spoiled.

6. Emily and Howard (are, is) tied for the highest sales award.

7. Neither Irene nor Wesley (has, have) signed the contract.

8. Neither of them (are, is) available for the meeting.

9. The auditors from Austin (are, is) reviewing our accounting procedures.

10. Members of the committee (has, have) voted in favor of the proposal.

11. (Do, Does) Alice realize the opportunity that is available?

12. Both of my parents (sell, sells) real estate.

13. Company policies (applies, apply) to all associates.

14. Most of the administrative assistants (participate, participates) in our volunteer program.

15. Dr. Billingsly or her students (are, is) doing the customer service survey.

16. The board (has, have) selected a new CEO.

17. Several of the trainees (has, have) completed the course.

18. See that everything we discussed (is, are) handled promptly.

19. None of the candidates (has, have) participated in a debate.

20. Either the customer service manager or the service technicians (is, are) responsible for answering customers' questions.

Net Link

Go to the *Guide to Grammar and Writing* Web site at **http://webster.comment.edu/hp/pages/darling** and select the topic "subject-verb agreement." After reviewing the principles of subject-verb agreement, complete the quizzes to test your knowledge. Once you've covered the material on pronoun-antecedent in this chapter, return to the Web site and review the material on this topic.

PRONOUN-ANTECEDENT AGREEMENT

Because pronouns *replace* nouns, pronouns must agree with the nouns that they replace. In other words, they must follow the leader. They must agree in number and in gender with the "leader" noun (antecedent). In the following examples, notice how each italicized pronoun agrees in number and gender with its "leader" noun.

The *man* who delivered the package said *he* wanted to see Mrs. Marceau. (Singular, masculine)

The *woman* who delivered the package said *she* wanted to see Mrs. Marceau. (Singular, feminine)

The *people* who are in the waiting room said *they* want to see Mrs. Marceau. (Plural, neuter)

Either *Brian* or *Bill* will have to give *his* approval. (Singular, masculine)

Either the *Kendricks* or the *Romanos* will give us *their* advice on our new business. (Plural, neuter)

The *Red Cross* will offer *its* assistance after the hurricane. (Singular, neuter)

When an antecedent is a noun that may refer either to a man or a woman, such as *doctor* or *parent*, the pronouns *his or her* and *he or she* are often used to avoid showing gender bias, as in the following example.

An *airline passenger* must show *his or her* picture-identification card to the ticket agent. (Singular subject, *passenger*, and singular pronoun, *his or her*)

While *he or she* and *him or her* avoids showing gender bias, this wording may sound awkward if overused. An alternative to using *he or she* would be to reword the sentence to use a plural noun and pronoun, as in the following example.

Airline passengers must show *their* picture-identification cards to the ticket agent. (Plural subject, *passengers*, and plural pronoun, *their*)

In Figure 7-2, note how the grammar checker in Microsoft Word shows two options for correcting an error in pronoun-antecedent agreement. The first option is to use *his or her*, while the second option is to make the noun and the pronoun plural.

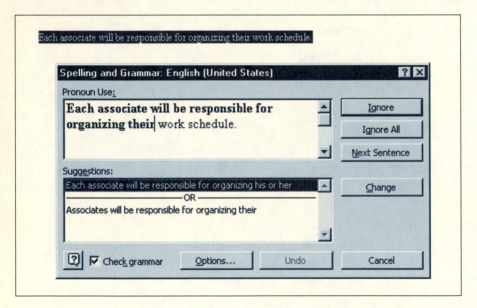

Figure 7-2. Grammar checker for pronoun-antecedent agreement.

Complete the following Checkup to make sure that you have mastered the previous section on pronoun-antecedent agreement.

CHECKUP 7-2   Circle the pronoun in parentheses that correctly completes each sentence.

1. Neither Jonathan nor William wants (his, their) job responsibilities changed.

2. The town council has changed (its, their) recommendations for an exercise facility.

3. All four mechanics will bring (his, their) tools to the competition.

4. Nancy Beason, our fitness coordinator, is selling (her, his) exercise bike.

5. Every voter has been asked to cast (their, his or her) vote in the bond election.

6. The bride who returned the waffle maker said that (he, she) received two of them as wedding gifts.

7. Both visitors presented proper identification before (he, they) were permitted to enter the restricted area.

8. Mr. Trevor, who has worked here about ten years, asked that (he, she) be considered for the accounting position.

9. Each tour participant is responsible for (their, his or her) passport.

10. Each college student can gain valuable experience through an internship program. Later, this experience can be listed on (their, his or her) résumé.

11. Mike wants to increase (her, his) job opportunities by taking coursework that goes beyond what is required.

12. Our accountants completed (his, their) company audit yesterday.

13. Either Bill or Norman will have to move (his, their) computer by Monday.

14. Elaine, along with her friends, is on (her, their) way to the new restaurant.

15. Either the Bonners or the Whites will invite the speaker to (his or her, their) home.

NOMINATIVE AND OBJECTIVE PRONOUN CASES

The form of a pronoun is referred to as its case. Case shows how the pronoun relates to the other words in a sentence. You learned about the possessive pronoun case in Chapter 4. Now you will study the other two pronoun cases, nominative and objective. Review the following table to refresh your memory on nominative and objective cases.

NOMINATIVE CASE		OBJECTIVE CASE	
SINGULAR	PLURAL	SINGULAR	PLURAL
I	we	me	us
you	you	you	you
he, she, it	they	him, her, it	them
who	who	whom	whom
whoever	whoever	whomever	whomever

Nominative-Case Pronouns

Nominative-case pronouns are *I, we, you, he, she, it, they, who*, and *whoever*. Here are two simple rules that will help you use these pronouns correctly. Note the exception that follows the rules.

1. A pronoun that is the subject of a verb must be in the nominative case.

   He will join our firm in October. (*He* is the subject of the verb *will join*.)

   Who is the manager of the store? (*Who* is the subject of the verb *is*.)

   Exception

   A pronoun that is the subject of an infinitive must be in the objective case.

   Kevin wants us to meet him at the airport. (*Us* is the subject of the infinitive *to meet*.)

2. A pronoun that appears after a form of the verb *to be* must be in the nominative case. Such pronouns are *complements*—words that complete the meaning of the being verb. The forms of the verb *to be* are *am, is, are, was,* and *were* and also *be, being*, and *been* used with helping verbs.

   It must have been he on the telephone. (The nominative case *he* is correct after the being verb *must have been*.)

   Possibly it was they who brought the flowers to the hospital. (The nominative case *they* is correct after the being verb *was*.)

   Exception

   One being verb has an exception—the infinitive *to be*. Use the objective case—not the nominative case—as the complement when *to be* is preceded immediately by a noun or pronoun.

   At our office Christmas party, Edward thought Glenn to be me. (The objective case *me* is used because the noun *Glenn* immediately precedes *to be*.)

   The winners seemed to be they. (There is no noun or pronoun immediately preceding *to be*. Thus, the rule—not the exception—applies in this sentence.)

Objective-Case Pronouns

The objective-case pronouns are *me, us, you, him, her, it, them, whom*, and *whomever*. Two rules will help you use objective-case pronouns correctly.

1. Use an objective-case pronoun when the pronoun is a direct or an indirect object. Remember that a *direct object* is the person or thing that receives the action of the verb; an *indirect object* is the person or thing that is indirectly affected by the action of the verb.

   Darryl told me about the new procedures. (*Me* is the object of the verb *told*.)

   Rachel asked him if the proposal had been accepted. (*Him* is the object of the verb *asked*.)

   Steve tossed him the keys. (*Him* is the indirect object of the verb *tossed*; *keys* is the direct object.)

2. Use the objective case for a pronoun that is the object of a preposition or the object of an infinitive.

   Sarah prepared the report for them. (*Them* is the object of the preposition *for*.)

   To whom did Alex address the letter? (*Whom* is the object of the preposition *to*.)

   Has David taken steps to contact her? (*Her* is the object of the infinitive *to contact*.)

CHECKUP 7-3 Circle the pronoun in parentheses that correctly completes each of the following sentences.

1. If you were (I, me) would you apply for the transfer to Denver?

2. Beatrice called (I, me) about the matter.

3. "This is (her, she)," Melinda responded when the telephone caller asked for her by name.

4. Adam mailed the computer disk to (her, she).

5. When Mr. Corey saw Allison in the library, he thought she was (I, me).

6. (Who, Whom) did you speak with yesterday on the telephone?

7. Members of the football team thought that the winner of the award should be (he, him).

8. Jaya wants (I, me) to serve on the committee.

An embarrassed mayor of a major U.S. city demoted his director of youth services after an error-filled, 14-page booklet was printed and released. The brochure, which described city youth programs, contained numerous grammatical errors and misspellings, such as *libary, millenium*, and *nationel*. The writer had apparently failed to proofread or to have someone else review the document. Reprinting the booklet cost taxpayers several thousand dollars.

9. The best candidate for the presidency would be (her, she).

10. Baxter, Inc., shipped (I, me) a computer table.

USING *WHO* AND *WHOM* IN QUESTIONS AND CLAUSES

Using the pronouns *who* and *whom* and *whoever* and *whomever* in questions and clauses can be confusing. Correctly choosing between *who* and *whom* or between *whoever* or *whomever* requires special effort. Remember that the pronoun rules mentioned on pages 146–147 still apply:

- Use the nominative case (*who* or *whoever*) for subjects of verbs and for complements of being verbs.

    Who is handling all of our customer service inquiries?

    Whoever is on duty will work the overtime hours.

- Use the objective case (*whom* or *whomever*) for objects of verbs (direct objects and indirect objects) and for objects of prepositions.

    Whom have you contacted about the bid?

    Whomever you recommend will be our new associate.

Who and *Whom* in Questions

Questions are usually expressed in inverted order, with the verb coming before the subject. Reading the question in the normal order will help you choose between *who* and *whom*.

    (Who, Whom) is the cardiologist treating Gene Haskins? (Inverted order)

    The cardiologist treating Gene Haskins is (who, whom)? (Normal order)

In the second example above, the pronoun follows the being verb *is*, making the nominative form (*who*) correct.

    (Who, Whom) has the professor selected for the internship? (Inverted order)

    The professor has selected (who, whom) for the internship? (Normal order)

In the second example above, the pronoun *whom* is correct because *whom* is used as the direct object of the verb *has selected*. As previously mentioned, direct objects use the objective case.

Who and *Whom* in Clauses

Clauses, like questions, can be in inverted order. The following examples illustrate how to change a sentence from inverted order to normal order to determine the correct pronoun usage.

> We do not know (who, whom) the computer hacker could have been. (Clause in inverted order)

> The computer hacker could have been who. (Clause in normal order)

Try substituting a nominative pronoun for *who* and read the sentence:

> *He* could have been the computer hacker. (Clause in normal order)

CHECKUP 7-4 Circle the pronoun in parentheses that correctly completes each sentence.

1. I do not know (who, whom) the visitor could have been.

2. They plan to select (whoever, whomever) volunteers for the project.

3. We have not yet decided (who, whom) should attend the meeting.

4. Anthony is the one (who, whom) can complete the job on time.

5. (Who, Whom) is the man visiting Don Murphy?

6. (Who, Whom) did you e-mail today?

7. Jim and Ron are the candidates (who, whom) will impress you.

8. (Who, Whom) has the class elected as representatives?

9. The woman to (who, whom) I was talking is Lisa Levy.

10. Donna wants to know (who, whom) you think should get the job.

Proofread the following sentences for errors in subject-verb agreement, pronoun-antecedent agreement, and nominative and objective pronoun case. Write *C* for *Correct* beside the item number of any sentence that is correct. Use appropriate revision symbols to mark each correction, as shown in the following example.

Delores ~~are~~ going to the warehouse.
is

1. Tom, after much argument, gave us her permission.

2. Mail carriers have to work at a steady pace if he or she wants to finish delivering mail on schedule.

3. Relatives who had not seen us in quite some time thought my brother to be I.

4. Whoever signs the letter has the final responsibility for its contents and quality.

5. Each student participating in sports must have their physical examination by September 1.

6. Alice, whom we consider to be our best computer programmer, found the problem immediately.

7. Steven Wirt or Alan Reardon are in charge of closing the restaurant tonight.

8. Do you think that it was her who complained to management?

9. Our renovations process during the last three months were essential.

10. Whom is the owner of the car?

TIPS

MARKING CORRECTIONS

If there is not enough space in the text to mark a correction, place the revision symbol at the appropriate place and write the change in the margin, as shown here.

The new catalog arrived yesterday, and we are pleased with the cover and the design. Please another 10,000 copies as soon as possible. ∧   print

Keep this option in mind as you mark corrections in the following applications.

Application 7-A

Proofread the following draft of a two-page letter. Use appropriate revision symbols to mark errors in subject-verb agreement, pronoun-antecedent agreement, and pronoun case.

March 20, <YEAR>

Mr. Glenn Foxworthy, President
Foxworthy Supply Company
Post Office Box 28448
Wilmington, DE 19808

Dear Mr. Foxworthy:

Thank you for your prompt response to my request for a bid to provide inventory control for our widgets. After reviewing all the bids, I am happy to report that your company have successfully met our requirements for price and delivery.

Widgets plays an essential role in our manufacturing operation. Maintaining and controlling inventory items are costly for us. By signing the enclosed agreement, you are accepting the responsibility for performing weekly audits of our widgets and ordering the sizes that have fallen below the minimum stocking requirements. Under this arrangement, one shipment of widgets are expected each week.

It is important for us to form alliances with vendors whom supply the products and services we need. At the end of the six months, we will evaluate the effectiveness of this method of inventory control. If the inventory control is performed satisfactorily, we will consider contracting with your firm to assume the responsibility for controlling other manufacturing materials.

If you have any questions, please contact Jim Decker. You should consider your contact to be he. Jim has over ten years of experience with us, and she will be eager to help your sales representatives. You may also direct questions to Martha Moore, whom is Jim's assistant. Either Jim or Martha are available to help you.

(continued)

Application 7-A (continued)

Mr. Glenn Foxworthy
Page 2
March 20, <YEAR>

Please sign and return the enclosed agreement by March 25 so that
our new widget inventory control process may start on April 1. We
look forward to your becoming a supplier with who we can enjoy a
pleasant, reliable business relationship.

Sincerely,

Ann B. Taylor, President

scc
Enclosure

Application 7-B

Proofread the following e-mail message and mark corrections in subject-verb agreement, pronoun-antecedent agreement, and nominative- and objective-case pronouns.

To...	Office Staff
Cc...	Richard Fielding, Human Resource Manager
Subject:	Job Sharing

As most of you know, Karen, Steve, and me have been appointed to a task force to examine the possibility of job sharing. Several people in the office have mentioned this option as an attractive alternative to full-time employment in his or her particular situations. With their permission, I have included some specific comments below:

- John and Sally Elliott, whom will become new parents within three months, is considering job sharing as an option to provide child care. They are expecting twin girls, and the twins will require much time from her parents.
- Rosyln Roberts, whom plans to retire within the next year, wants to try job sharing as a way to ease into retirement.
- Dan Taylor would like to share a job with someone during the hours that his children are in school.
- Amelia Wexler is interested in sharing a job upon returning to work after her recent illness and hospitalization. Her and me, as her supervisor, are hoping that job sharing can be implemented to make her recovery easier.

We would like to know whom would be interested in job sharing. Please e-mail Lisa Rowe or I by June 5, with your suggestions, questions, or concerns.

Application 7-C

Proofread the following memo. Use revision symbols to mark corrections in subject-verb and pronoun-antecedent agreement and any errors in pronoun case. Also correct any other types of errors. Remember to mark corrections in the margin if there's not enough space to mark them within the text.

MEMO TO: All Employees

FROM: Anne Wells, Human Resources Manager

DATE: May 5, <YEAR>

SUBJECT: Membership in Cheap Charlie's Discount Club

In response to man requests, I have been successful in negotiating membership for all employees in Cheap Charlie's Discount Club. Most of you probably know that this club offers excellent savings on a variety of items, including groceries, automotive supplys, hardware, toys appliances, and other miscellaneous merchandise. Most discounts are at least one fourth off the regular retail price.

As a benefit to you, the company is paying your membership fee. You may pick up your temporary membership card in Will Duprees office. On your first visit to Cheap Charlie's you will receive your permanent membership card. The card will have your picture on it.

Cheap Charlie's are located on Tryon Street about two miles west of the Interstate 77 exit. Store hours are from 10 a.m. to 10 p.m. every Monday through Saturday, however, store hours is from 1 to 6 p.m. each sunday.

rd

Application 7-D

The following computer-generated slides were developed for a presentation to be given to a company's sales representatives. Notice that errors in a slide show appear more noticeable than those in written documents. Mark all errors in subject-verb agreement, pronoun-antecedent agreement, and pronoun use with appropriate revision symbols.

Sales Letters

1. Attract the readers attention.
2. Establish a close relationship with the reader.
3. Appeal to specific buying motives.
4. Persuade the reader to act.
5. Provide an opportunity to act.

Attracting the Reader's Attention

▌ Introduce the product.
▌ Include the product name: Mighty miracle Cleaner.
▌ List the advantages.
  ▌ Replaces most household cleaners.
  ▌ Packaged as a liquid concentrate.
  ▌ Makes 30 gallons of cleanser.

Establishing a Close Relationship

▌ Empathize with the customer's busy schedule.
▌ Mention the lack of time to clean.
▌ use the customer's name.

(continued)

Application 7-D (continued)

Appealing to Specific Buying Motives

▌ Mention hat the product is biodegradable.

▌ Emphasize the safety of this non-toxic product.

▌ Emphasize that the product is safe for hands--no gloves is required.

▌ State that the product is environmentally friendly.

Persuading the Read to Act

▌ Include testimonials.

▌ Offer him a money-back guaranty.

▌ Stress the ease of use

▌ Emphasize the favorable results.

Providing an Opportunity to Act

▌ Include our tool-free number.

▌ Mention the option of online ordering.

▌ Attack a postage-paid order card.

CD-ROM Application 7-E

The following telephone procedures are part of a company policy manual. Using your word processor, open the file DPES07E from the CD-ROM. Proofread the procedures and correct any errors in subject-verb agreement, pronoun-antecedent agreement, pronoun case, and *who* and *whom*. Save the revised procedures using your initials in place of the DPES. Proofread on the screen and make any additional corrections. Save and print the corrected procedures.

TELEPHONE PROCEDURES

1. Cheerfully answer your telephone and any telephone lines to which you are assigned. Assume that each of the calls received are important.

2. Use a cordial but businesslike tone when answering the telephone.

3. Listen carefully to the caller's message. Even though the call may seem insignificant to you, it is probably very significant to them.

4. If a person ask for you by name, you should respond appropriately by saying, "This is him," or "This is her."

5. If the person requested is unavailable, ask the caller if you may transfer their call to whoever is available.

6. If the caller's response is positive, transfer the call to whomever can help the caller.

7. If the caller prefers to talk only to the person who is originally specified, ask if you can transfer the message to their voice mail or take a message.

8. Use your voice to convey friendliness and helpfulness to the caller.

9. Help the caller if you are able to do so without exceeding your job responsibilities.

10. Permit the caller to end the call. Ending the call, according to courtesy manuals, are the responsibility of the caller.

CD-ROM Application 7-F

Using your word processor, open the file DPES07F from the CD-ROM. Proofread the memo and correct any errors in subject-verb and pronoun-antecedent agreement and nominative and objective pronoun cases. Correct any other types of errors; then run the spell checker. Save the revised memo using your initials in place of the DPES. Proofread on the screen and make any additional corrections. Save and print the corrected memo.

MEMO TO: All Employees

FROM: Betty Westin, President

DATE: June 26, <YEAR>

SUBJECT: Computer Policy Directive

Our company has established a new computer policy that is effective beginning today, Thursday June 26. Thank you for your cooperation in implementing this policy which is stated in the directive that follows. After reading the directive, please sign and date this memo in the spaces provided and return it to my office by Monday, June 30.

DIRECTIVE

Office computers are to be used exclusively for work-related tasks between the hours of 8 A.M. and 5 P.M. At other times, office staff may use computers for personal applications. Personal applications and personal e-mail are bound by legal, moral, and ethical principles.

Susan Harrison and his computer technicians have installed software that will meet your needs. Consider the final authority on computer software to be she. Do not install additional software with out a signed authorization from someone in Susans office.

Computer programs according to Susan, has been installed to monitor work-related usage, Internet browsing, and personal applications. This monitoring system offers the capability of accessing both work-related and personal applications.

Employees whom violate the above policies will be subject to disciplinary action up to and including dismissal, depending on the severity of the infraction.

_____

Employee Signature

_____

Employee Name and Department (Please print.)

_____

Date

Sentence Structure

After completing this chapter, you should be able to:

1. Recognize complete sentences.

2. Find and correct sentence fragments.

3. Find and correct run-on sentences and comma splices.

4. Recognize and correct errors in parallel structure.

5. Recognize and correct dangling and misplaced modifiers.

Writing correctly and effectively is a characteristic of an educated person. Most executives possess this characteristic and expect those working with them to have it also. Being able to construct grammatically correct sentences takes knowledge and practice. Learning to proofread for errors in sentence structure will help you perfect yet another essential element that will make your documents the best that they can be.

Carefully study this chapter on sentence structure in order to prepare yourself to detect and correct sentence structure errors as you proofread.

SENTENCES

A complete sentence has a subject and a predicate and expresses a complete thought. The *subject* is the person or thing that does the action or is spoken about. The *predicate* is the verb that indicates action or a state of being. The predicate may consist of more than one word.

> My assistant bought the computer. (Subject, *assistant*; predicate, *bought*.)

> Jeff and Andy ordered the furniture. (Subjects, *Jeff* and *Andy*; predicate, *ordered*.)

> Please call me tomorrow. (Subject, *you*; predicate, *call*. The subject is understood to be *you*.)

In each of the following sentences, underline the subject once and the predicate twice. If the subject is understood to be *you,* write you in parentheses and underline once.

1. You sold over a million dollars worth of real estate this quarter!

2. Why should we change our policy?

3. They must follow the stated procedures exactly.

4. Ms. Chambers has many talents.

5. Their son was born on August 30.

6. Our project team completed the tasks ahead of schedule.

7. Lock the door before leaving.

8. Shelly is our new department manager.

9. We sold the most products of any sales division!

10. Harry is satisfied that he did a good job.

SENTENCE FRAGMENTS

When either a subject or a predicate (or both) is missing from a group of words that is treated as a sentence, it is known as a *fragment* or an incomplete sentence.

> On the first day of each month was. (Fragment; no subject.)

> After a six-week probationary period, he. (Fragment; no predicate.)

> Early in the morning next Friday. (Fragment; no subject or predicate.)

Some clauses may have a subject and a predicate but still be incomplete. These clauses, called subordinate clauses, do not express complete thoughts.

> When the goal is reached. (Fragment; no complete thought.)

> Because she was elected mayor. (Fragment; no complete thought.)

Note that in each of the preceding examples the clause beginning with the word *When* or *Because* indicates that the reader should expect more information. What will happen "When the goal is reached"? What happened "Because she was elected mayor"? The fragments do not tell us. They express incomplete thoughts. When the expected information is not present, the group of words is not a sentence. Such fragments can be corrected by adding words that complete the thought.

> When the goal is reached, we will celebrate. (This is a sentence, with *we* as the subject and *will celebrate* as the predicate.)

> Because she was elected mayor, she was able to attend the convention. (This is a sentence, with *she* as the subject and *was able* as the predicate.)

Net Link

Go to the *Guide to Grammar and Writing* Web site at **http://webster.comment.edu/hp/pages/darling** for a challenging quiz on repairing sentence fragments.

A grammar checker may recommend more than one option for correcting a sentence fragment. For example, in Figure 8-1 the grammar checker suggests that the fragment "Before we begin the presentation" might be corrected by (1) adding a subject or a verb or (2) combining the text with another sentence. The grammar checker also provides sample sentences to use as a model. You must use your knowledge of grammar to determine which option is best for correcting the fragment.

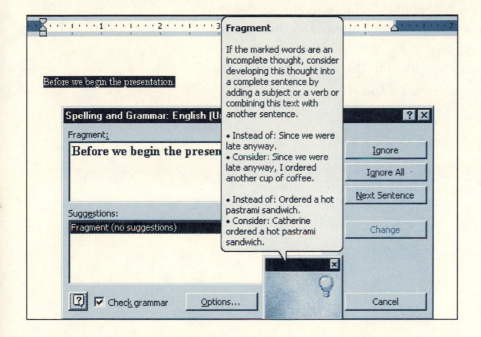

Figure 8-1. Grammar checker suggestions for correcting a sentence fragment.

Completing the following exercise will give you practice in identifying sentence fragments.

CHECKUP 8-2   Each of the following numbered items is either a sentence or a fragment. Circle *S* for each complete sentence and *F* for each fragment.

1. The computer and the software were purchased last week.   S   F

2. Browsing the Internet but not being able to search effectively.   S   F

3. Mark Haywood, who spends much of his time analyzing statistics.   S   F

4. Please fax me the results of his medical tests.   S   F

5. Lillian Austin, who came to work for us last spring.   S   F

One way to correct a sentence fragment is to combine the fragment with a related sentence. Follow these steps:

1. Identify the fragment.

2. Find the related sentence.

3. Join the fragment to the beginning or the end of the related sentence.

4. Revise the capitalization and the punctuation of the fragment and the related sentence as needed.

Note how these steps are used to correct the following fragment.

Our new Web site will be operative. By April 1.

The phrase *By April 1* is a fragment. It relates to the sentence *Our new Web site will be operative*. Join the fragment to the related sentence to form a complete sentence. Do this by changing the capitalization and the punctuation, as shown in the following example.

Our new Web site will be operative. By April 1.

The final copy reads as follows:

Our new Web site will be operative by April 1.

After combining a fragment with a sentence, you may need to revise the sentence punctuation. In the following example, note how the fragment (introductory clause) is joined to the related sentence by using a comma.

As soon as we hear from the contractor, We will be able to schedule a moving date.

The final copy reads as follows:

As soon as we hear from the contractor, we will be able to schedule a moving date.

CHECKUP 8-3 Use revision symbols to mark corrections that would change fragments to complete sentences. (You may need to add words to correct a fragment.) Write *C* for *Correct* beside the number of any item that is a sentence.

1. When the new telephone books arrive. Be sure to recycle the old ones.

2. Because of seniority, Malcolm Lerner has the first choice of available vacation dates.

3. Because of her many, many years of unselfish, devoted service. Madeleine will receive an engraved gold watch.

4. As members of a repair crew. We repaired 25 telephone lines damaged during the tornado.

5. After 24 hours of deliberation. The jury reached a decision.

6. After mailing the report, which was two weeks early.

7. As soon as his pager alerted him.

8. Heather Woodard and Amelia Davidson were transferred to London, England.

9. The sales representatives have laptop computers in their cars.

10. Our pager system, the most up-to-date system on the market.

TIPS

CORRECTING FRAGMENTS

A fragment may be combined with a related sentence by joining it to the beginning, middle, or end of the related sentence. The punctuation and the capitalization will differ depending on where the fragment is added.

> If attendance does not increase. (Fragment) As the producer indicated, the play will be canceled. (Related sentence)

Three ways to correct the fragment:

> *If attendance does not increase*, as the producer indicated, the play will be canceled.

> As the producer indicated, *if attendance does not increase*, the play will be canceled.

> As the producer indicated, the play will be canceled *if attendance does not increase*.

RUN-ON SENTENCES AND COMMA SPLICES

Run-on sentences and comma splices are two frequently made sentence errors that should not escape detection. As you review the examples in the following sections, note that there is usually more than one way to correct a run-on sentence or a comma splice.

Run-On Sentences

A *run-on sentence* consists of two or more independent clauses incorrectly joined either by using no punctuation or by using incorrect punctuation. Keep in mind that an independent clause has a subject and a predicate and can stand alone as a complete sentence.

> Valerie selected the office furniture it will not be delivered until March 15. (*Incorrect*. No punctuation separates the two independent clauses.)

There are four different ways to correct a run-on sentence, as shown in the following examples.

1. Use a comma and a conjunction to join the two independent clauses.

   Valerie selected the office furniture, but it will not be delivered until March 15.

2. Make each independent clause a separate sentence.

   Valerie selected the office furniture. It will not be delivered until March 15.

3. Separate two closely related independent clauses with a semicolon.

   Valerie selected the office furniture; it will not be delivered until March 15.

4. Separate two independent clauses by using a semicolon and a transitional word followed by a comma.

   Valerie selected the office furniture; however, it will not be delivered until March 15.

Net Link

For a humorous, informative review of grammar topics, go to *Big Dog's Grammar* Web site at the URL **http://gabiscott.com /bigdog** and review the section on comma splices and fused (run-on) sentences.

Comma Splices

Two independent clauses incorrectly joined by a comma form a *comma splice*. The comma isn't a strong enough mark of punctuation to separate the two clauses.

   Harold was riding in the company shuttle, he arrived ten minutes late. (*Incorrect*. Comma splice)

If independent clauses are related, they can be joined using a comma and a coordinating conjunction such as *and, but, or*, or *nor*.

   Harold was riding in the company shuttle, but he arrived ten minutes late. (*Correct*. The independent clauses are separated by a comma and a conjunction.)

Two closely related clauses also can be joined with a semicolon.

   He dropped the vase; it broke. (*Correct*.)

CHECKUP 8-4   Identify each item as *C* for *Correct*, *RO* for *run-on sentence*, or *CS* for *comma splice* by circling the appropriate letters. Use revision symbols to mark your corrections. Remember to make changes in capitalization and punctuation as needed.

1. The two companies agreed on a merger, it will be announced January 1.   C   RO   CS

2. College students should take many computer courses they should be very computer literate.   C   RO   CS

3. Completing the physical inventory was time-consuming,   **C   RO   CS**
   however, we feel that we have accurate figures now.

4. Because computers make information more accessible, we   **C   RO   CS**
   should be able to make better use of the data we have available.

5. Please order some paper for the printers, we have only   **C   RO   CS**
   one case left.

PARALLELISM

Parallelism simply means that similar items in a sentence are treated in a similar manner. For example, adjectives should be parallel to adjectives, infinitives to infinitives, gerunds to gerunds, verbs to verbs, and so on. In the following examples, note the words in italics that refer to nonparallel and parallel items.

Not Parallel	**Parallel**
Sam is *intelligent* and has *talent*. (adjectives)	Sam is *intelligent* and *talented*. (adjectives)
Greg's duties are *to analyze* the findings and *writing* the report. (infinitives)	Greg's duties are *to analyze* the findings and *to write* the report. (infinitives)
His hobbies are *reading* and *to sail*. (gerunds)	His hobbies are *reading* and *sailing*. (gerunds)
She will either *design* the Web site herself or *hiring* someone to do it. (verbs)	She will either *design* the Web site herself or *hire* someone to do it. (verbs)

Note that parallel constructions should always be used with the correlative conjunctions *both . . . and, either . . . or, neither . . . nor,* and *not only . . . but also.*

Not Parallel	**Parallel**
Send copies both *to Mr. Pratt* and *Mrs. Wilson*.	Send copies both *to Mr. Pratt* and *to Mrs. Wilson*.
Mr. Evans approved not only *my raise* but also *promoting me*.	Mr. Evans approved not only *my raise* but also *my promotion*.

SOFTWARE TIPS

Most grammar checkers are set up to detect sentences that contain nonparallel items. In Figure 8-2 on page 166, note the explanation of parallelism that the grammar checker provides, as well as the example sentence with the conjunctions *Either . . . or.* You can use the examples given by the grammar checker as guides for correcting the error.

Either they will design the Web site or hire someone to do it.

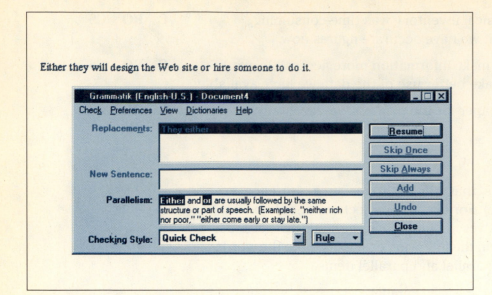

Figure 8-2. Grammar checker suggestions for correcting nonparallel structure.

CHECKUP 8-5 Use appropriate revision symbols to correct errors in parallelism in the following sentences. You may need to insert, delete, or change letters and words. Write *C* for *Correct* to the left of the item number if a sentence has no errors.

1. My goal is to finish college and getting a job.

2. Steven is not only an accomplished musician but also a competent conductor.

3. You may notify him by telephone or sending him an e-mail.

4. Mr. Proxmire consented not only to attend but also addressing the conference.

5. Denice, please send copies of the appeal both to the hospital and the insurance company.

6. At our continuing education conference in Chicago next month, we will attend appropriate meetings, discuss relevant problems, and to enjoy tourist attractions.

7. The new telecommunications equipment is fast, efficient, and will be expensive.

8. Neither Darlene nor Frieda is planning to take a vacation until fall.

9. Volunteer work is rewarding and a challenge.

10. A good manager is not only skilled in talking but also in the ability to listen.

11. The leasing company representative agreed to repair the equipment or replacing it.

12. Mr. O'Leary donated time, money, and equipment to aid hurricane victims.

13. Irella graduating from college, accepted a job, and bought a house.

14. Mike was hired to take photographs, develop film, and repairing cameras.

15. A good proofreader not only spells words correctly but also to punctuate sentences correctly.

DANGLING AND MISPLACED MODIFIERS

Dangling modifiers are words that do not relate to the subject of a sentence. Instead, they are said to dangle, or hang.

In the first sentence of each set of examples below, note how the modifier dangles, or doesn't clearly relate to who does the action.

Driving to work, a deer dashed in front of my car. (*Incorrect*. Was the deer driving to work?)

Driving to work, I saw a deer dash in front of my car. (*Correct*.)

After hiking to the top of the mountain, the beautiful waterfall could be seen and heard. (*Incorrect*. Did the waterfall hike to the top of the mountain?)

After hiking to the top of the mountain, we could see and hear the beautiful waterfall. (*Correct*.)

Misplaced modifiers are phrases that are not properly placed within a sentence. These misplaced modifiers can cause confusion and often result in comical sentences. Following are three examples:

We saw the baboons driving down the unpaved road. (*Confusing*. Who was driving, *we* or the *baboons*?)

As we were driving down the unpaved road, we saw the baboons. (*Clear*.)

Sharon related the amusing incident to the police officer with a slight chuckle. (*Confusing*. Who chuckled, *Sharon* or the *police officer*?)

With a slight chuckle, Sharon related the amusing incident to the police officer. (*Clear*.)

My brother told me how to change the oil in my car on the phone. (*Confusing*. Should the oil be changed over the phone?)

My brother told me on the phone how to change the oil in my car. (*Clear*.)

Seen in an advertisement:

FOR RENT
Apartment for a family with a pool. It includes three bedrooms, two large baths, and a kitchen-den combination.

Who has the pool—the family or the apartment?

The following exercise will give you practice in correcting dangling and misplaced modifiers.

CHECKUP 8-6 In the space provided, rewrite the following sentences to place the modifiers in the correct location. Add words as needed so that the sentence makes sense. If a sentence is correct, write *C* for *Correct* in the space.

1. Playing ball in the park, we saw 24 young children.

   _____

   _____

2. Calling the class roll, each student answered, "Present," when his or her name was called.

   _____

   _____

3. Turning on the siren, the ambulance navigated through the busy rush-hour traffic.

   _____

   _____

4. According to the present poll, the president will be re-elected.

   _____

   _____

5. We purchased the swimming pool from a local sales representative made primarily from concrete.

   _____

   _____

6. The owner had $350 worth of equipment stolen that was parked there in the car.

   _____

   _____

7. Marilyn called the help desk with a question from the Internet about copying files.

   _____

   _____

The following statement appeared in a newspaper article:

Police said witnesses described one of the suspects as a male between 35 and 40 years old with short, straight black hair and a mustache wearing a baseball cap.

Who was wearing the baseball cap?

8. According to the hospital official, the heart transplant by the surgeon was performed successfully.

_____

_____

9. She saw the ambulance while she was driving to work in her rearview mirror.

_____

_____

10. Kathi found a book that explains how to catch really big fish in the library.

_____

_____

Application 8-A

Proofread the following job postings that appear on the Web page for a company. Use appropriate revision symbols to indicate corrections in parallel structure and dangling and misplaced modifiers.

Human Resources Staff Assistant

This individual provides secretarial and clerical support to the human resources staff. The position requires interaction with all levels of employees throughout the organization. Duties include typing correspondence, tracking résumés, making travel arrangements, and to organize and maintain files. The assistant also handles inquiries and requests for information. The work is of an extremely confidential nature. Three years of secretarial/clerical experience is required, along with excellent oral and written skills.

Customer Service Representative

This position is responsible for providing accurate and quickly responses to customers. Responsibilities include researching, resolving, and to reply to inquiries from customers and sales representatives. Other responsibilities include maintaining an open line of communication among accounting, sales, marketing, and customers. The ideal candidate will have good interpersonal and communications skills and knowledge of word processing and database software programs. Energy, enthusiasm, and a customer-oriented attitude are a must!

Administrative Assistant

This individual will provide six-person administrative support to a real estate service department. Duties include typing and tracking real estate documents such as leases, subleases, various legal documents, and invoices. Requirements include excellent written and oral communication skills, good administrative and organizational skills, basic math skills, and knowledge of Windows software programs accurate typing.

Application 8-B

Proofread the following memo. Use revision symbols to correct sentence structure errors such as sentence fragments, faulty parallelism, misplaced or dangling modifiers, comma splices, and run-on sentences.

MEMO TO: The Executive Staff

FROM: Jeanette Lorenzo, President

DATE: December 1, \<YEAR\>

SUBJECT: Retirement Banquet

On Friday, December 15, we will honor 20 employees. Who are retiring from our company. The banquet, to be held in our recreational facilities, is scheduled for 7 p.m.

Each of these employees has 15 or more years of service with our company. We appreciate not only their hard work but also that they were dedicated. A watch will be given to each employee that has been engraved.

Andy and Mary Jean Leonardi will be recognized for their combined total of 60 years with us. Either Dennis Worthy or June Hobbs plans to attend as a representative from our New York office I will let you know later which one is coming.

Please plan to attend the banquet. We have reserved seating for you and a guest, however, please call Gayle Price at extension 3425 if you or your guest is unable to attend.

Application 8-C

Proofread the following copy for a newspaper advertisement for fall tour specials. Use appropriate revision symbols to correct errors in sentence structure plus any other types of errors. Note that this advertisement uses full justification (even right and left margins). Assume that the address, dates, and prices are correct.

DESTINATIONS, INC.

Suite 5000, City Plaza, 5 Plaza Square
Charlotte, NC 28210

Phone: **704-555-1968**
FAX: 704-555-1969   E-mail: destinaincnc.com

FALL BUS TOUR SPECIALS

Pennsylvania Dutch Country

September 3-10 $599

Travel to the beautiful Dutch Country of Pennsylvania. Taste the good food, see the crafts, enjoy the scenery, and to learn about the people.

Fall Mystery Tour

September 15-22 $389

Pack your bags and come along four for days of fun, food, and to relax. Be sure to include a jacket and boots for a brief mountain hike. On the hike, you will fine the clues needed to solve an intriguing mystery, a prize will be awarded to the first "detective" who solves the mystery.

Maritime Provinces and Quebec

October 5-15 $889

If you are searching for the vacation of a lifetime. Canada is your destination. In Nova Scotia, you will tour Cabot Trail and Peggy's Cove. Then travel by boat to Prince Edward Island and New Brunswick. On the mainland, you will visit Montreal and other points of interest in Quebec.

Make your reservations now. All prices is per person and are based on double occupancy. A tour guide, who takes pride in their job, will accompany your group for the entire tour.

Application 8-D

Proofread the following letter. Use appropriate revision symbols to correct errors in sentence structure plus any other types of errors.

NATIONAL BRANCH BANK

9300 Bank Plaza, Duluth, MN 55845-2483
218-555-2348   nationalcenter@duluthcity.net

November 13, <YEAR>

Mr. Frank Panella
Panella's Convenience Store
1326 Harvest Court
Duluth, Mn 55845

Dear Mr. Panella:

Thank you for giving me the opportunity to meet with you about the possibility of installing an ATM machine on your property. As we discussed yesterday. Having an ATM machine will benefit both you and your customers.

Our proposal, used with all our ATM installations, are to lease a small area in your parking lot and installing an ATM that would be accessible from a customers vehicle. Construction would not interrupt the operation of your business.

As mentioned to you, our policy require a five year lease for the property with an option to renew the lease for an addition five years. We propose a lease fee of $300 per month for the first five years. If we request five additional years, the lease fee would be $350 per month.

If the weather cooperates, the ATM should be operational within 60 days from the date that we receive the signed lease from you. Our attorneys are preparing the lease, and anticipate mailing it to you with in a week.

Please telephone or e-mail me if you have any questions. We look forward to working with you in this venture.

Sincerely,

NATIONAL BRANCH BANK

Karen L. Davidson, President

CD-ROM Application 8-E

Using your word processor, open the file DPES08E from the CD-ROM. Proofread the memo and correct sentence fragments, faulty parallelism, misplaced or dangling modifiers, comma splices, and run-on sentences. Save the corrected memo using your initials in place of the DPES. Proofread the memo on the screen and make any additional corrections. Save and print the corrected memo.

MEMO TO: Office Staff

FROM: Joe Hardin, Human Resource Manager

DATE: July 1, <YEAR>

SUBJECT: Changes in Electronic Security System

At a recent staff meeting I mentioned to you that the electronic security system for our building was going to be updated. I received notice today that the changes will be completed and fully operational by next Friday, July 10, the official changeover time will be at 6 p.m. that evening.

Each of you should go to the Plaza Security Office between 2:30 and 5:30 p.m. on Friday, July 10, to exchange your old elevator access card for a new one and getting a new key for the employee entrance. You must take your driver's license and your old elevator access card (or another photo I.D.) with you for identification. You do not need to return your old key.

If you do not go to the Plaza Security Office on Friday. You will not be able to get into our building or use the elevators after 6 p.m. on Friday, however, you can exchange your card and get a new key on Monday morning from 7:30 to 10:30 a.m.

The security guards expressed their appreciation for your cooperation in maintaining security in our building by not loaning your elevator access card or your key to anyone.

Application 8-F

Open the file DPESC08F from the CD-ROM. Proofread the draft of the letter on the screen. Correct sentence structure errors such as fragments, run-on sentences, and dangling modifiers. Also correct any other types of errors. Make the corrections, then run the spell and grammar checkers. Save and print a copy of the corrected draft.

April 5, <YEAR>

Ms. Glenda Harbison
267 Stage Trail Road
South Bend, IN 46628

Dear Ms. Harbinson:

Thank you for submitting your application to our department. According to your résumé, you have the necessary qualifications for our for position of Caseworker I.

According to our standard procedures, you are required to take the state qualifying exam. Qualified applicants with the top five score will be invited to a structured interview to be scheduled at a latter date. You will be notified of an interview appointment if your in the top five applicants.

Your exam time has been scheduled for Monday, April 12, at 2:30 P.M., at the Education Station Center which is in the Rancho Vista Mall. Your exam will last a bout an hour, the Education Station Center will provide all testing materials.

Please call Randy Hayes at 219-555-1212 to confirm your exam appointment. If the appointment is not confirmed by Friday April 9. It will be canceled. Failure to take the exam as scheduled will remove your name from consideration.

Thank you for you interest in our department.

Sincerely,

Jonathan Searcy
Human Resources Manager

Number Style

OBJECTIVES

After completing this chapter, you should be able to:

1. Apply the basic rules for number style.

2. Proofread to find errors in number style.

3. Use appropriate revision symbols to correct errors in number style.

Letters, memos, invoices, medical records, and other business communications often include numbers. Numbers are used for dates, measurements, dollar amounts, quantities, sizes, and so on. It is particularly important to proofread numbers carefully because the reader often has no way of knowing when a number is incorrect. It may be impossible to know, for example, that 756 feet should really be 765 feet or that 34.6 percent should really be 43.6 percent.

Mistakes in numbers may be easily overlooked when you are proofreading a document for content. Therefore, you should proofread numbers and statistical data as a separate step. Each number must be checked carefully to make sure it is accurate.

This chapter will give you practice in applying the rules of number style as you proofread.

STYLE FOR NUMBERS

Proofreading numbers is much simpler when you understand the general rules for number usage in business correspondence. Follow these rules when using numbers:

1. In general, spell out numbers from 1 through 10, and use figures for numbers above 10. However, be consistent in presenting related numbers, whether they are within a sentence, within a paragraph, or within a series of paragraphs.

   All five managers were invited to participate. (Numbers 1 through 10)

   Most of the 20 employees voted to change health insurance coverage. (Number above 10)

Of those surveyed, 1 doctor, 2 nurses, and 15 patients preferred the new plan. (Numbers above and below 10. All figures are used since one of the numbers is above 10.)

Only 2 of the 15 executives had been here for over five years. (Related and unrelated numbers. Figures are used for *2* and *15* because both are related to people. The number of years, *five*, is not related to the number of people and is spelled out because it is below 10.)

2. Spell out a number that begins a sentence as well as any numbers that are related. Reword a sentence if it takes more than two words to spell out a number at the beginning of a sentence.

Fifteen associates were employed during our peak season.

Four nurses and twelve lab assistants completed continuing education courses.

3. Use numerals for the date when listing the month and the day or the month, day, and year.

Our team completed the feasibility study on February 1, 2003. (month, day, year)

Our team completed the feasibility study on February 1. (month and day)

Note: In international correspondence, the day appears before the month and the year, and no commas are used.

Production at the new facility will begin on 8 April 2002.

In formal writing, use an ordinal number (*first, second, third*) for the date when it appears before the month or stands alone.

Our team completed the feasibility study on the first of February.

The report is due on the fifteenth of each month.

4. Use figures and a dollar sign ($) for amounts of money that are exact or approximate. Use figures and the word *cents* for amounts under a dollar. Within a sentence, omit *.00* with whole dollar amounts. However, in columns, add *.00* to a whole dollar amount if any number has cents.

The technician charged $125 for repairing the computer.

Coffee is 50 cents per cup.

The first invoice was for $399.40, and the second invoice was for $200.

$399.40
  200.00
$599.40

5. Use figures for fractions in mixed numbers. Use a space to separate the whole number from the fraction. To construct fractions, use the diagonal (/).

14 ⅝   7 ½

Net Link

For a handy list of ordinal numbers, go to *An On-line English Grammar* at **http://www.edunet .com/english/grammar /sect-2.html#numbers**. Click on the link to "Numbers" that appears on the menu.

Spell out fractions that stand alone. (A fraction that stands alone does not have a whole number preceding it.)

The motion was passed with a two-thirds majority.

We have shipped three-fourths of the order.

6. Use figures for technical measurements and specifications such as dimensions and sizes.

3.6 feet	a 5:1 ratio	11.6 cm
8 MB RAM	16 gigabytes	32°F

7. Spell out ages in nontechnical writing, but use figures when they are technical in nature, such as statistics.

My parents are in their seventies. (nontechnical)

Most college students are between the ages of 18 and 24. (technical)

SOFTWARE TIPS

Most software programs have an autocorrect feature that will automatically format certain items as they are typed. In Figure 9-1, note how the fraction typed as 4 1/4 is automatically formatted as 4 $\frac{1}{4}$ and the ordinal number typed as May 4th is automatically formatted as May 4th.

Figure 9-1 shows a menu with the options for replacing ordinals with superscript numbers and for replacing fractions with a fraction character. You have the option of turning off this feature.

4 1/4 by 5 1/2 by 7 3/4

4 ¼ by 5 ½ by 7 ¾

May 4th

May 4th

AutoCorrect

AutoCorrect | **AutoFormat As You Type** | AutoText | AutoFormat

Apply as you type
- ☐ Headings
- ☑ Borders
- ☑ Tables
- ☑ Automatic bulleted lists
- ☐ Automatic numbered lists

Replace as you type
- ☐ "Straight quotes" with "smart quotes"
- ☑ Ordinals (1st) with superscript
- ☑ Fractions (1/2) with fraction character (½)
- ☐ Symbol characters (--) with symbols (—)
- ☐ *Bold* and _underline_ with real formatting
- ☐ Internet and network paths with hyperlinks

Figure 9-1. The autocorrect feature in Microsoft Word has options for automatically formatting ordinal numbers and fractions.

Complete the following exercise to test your knowledge of the preceding rules for number style.

CHECKUP 9-1 Circle the number style in parentheses that correctly completes each sentence.

1. We need (8, eight) more students to help with the blood donation drive scheduled for Halloween night.

2. (1000, One thousand) copies of the advertising flyer were placed on cars in the parking lot.

3. David began working here on April (10, 10th), 1998.

4. The shelves are (3 1/4, three and one-quarter) inches too long.

5. Nine out of ten employees indicated that they would like to retire by the age of (62, sixty-two).

6. Parcel delivery charges for the contact lenses were ($8, eight dollars).

7. Recreation facilities were built about (15, fifteen) years ago.

8. The basement room width is (32, thirty-two) feet.

9. The purchasing agent bought 15 desks and (5, five) printer stands.

10. Sam said that the floors should be refinished by the (5th, fifth) of May.

The following additional rules will help you use numbers correctly. Study these rules carefully before completing the following exercise.

8. Spell out indefinite numbers and amounts. Such numbers are general in nature—they don't indicate a specific amount.

About a hundred employees received flu shots.

Carlos invested thousands of dollars in his new business.

Over sixty employees volunteer in the community regularly.

9. Use figures to express clock time with the word *o'clock* and with the abbreviations *a.m.* or *p.m.* Omit *:00* for time "on the hour."

Your interview should end by 3 o'clock.

Parcel Shipping, Inc., will deliver the package between 8 and 10 a.m.

The restaurant begins serving breakfast at 6 a.m. and lunch at 10:30 a.m.

In a mailing to taxpayers, the Internal Revenue Service sent preprinted address labels with the wrong barcodes. The labels contained a barcode with the taxpayer's own ZIP Code instead of the one for the IRS. Using the incorrect labels could have resulted in the returns being shipped back to the taxpayers. The IRS said the incorrect labels were due to an error at the printer.
Source: The Washington Post

10. Use figures for percentages, and spell out the word *percent*. Use the percent symbol (%) in statistical or technical writing or in columns where space is restricted.

    82 percent   5.8 percent   15.5%

11. No comma is needed to separate thousands from hundreds in four-digit numbers: *2500*. However, for consistency, use a comma in four-digit numbers when they are used with larger numbers that require commas.

    One computer costs $1,800, but we can buy 12 for $20,000.

12. Use figures with abbreviations and symbols.

    10 p.m.   5.8 cm   8.5% $90

13. Use hyphens or periods to separate the parts of a telephone number.

    555-2848   555.2848

    For a telephone number that includes an area code, use a hyphen, a diagonal, or a period after the area code, or put the area code in parentheses.

    919-555-2848   919/555-2848

    919.555.2848   (919) 555-2848

    For a telephone number with an extension, use the following format:

    614-555-8529, Ext. 7253

14. When two numbers appear next to each other in a sentence and one of the numbers is part of a compound modifier (*a 15-foot room, a 30-year mortgage*), express the first number in words and the second number in figures. Doing so makes the two numbers easier to read.

    The bank financed twelve 30-year loans last week.

    We bought six 2-liter bottles of ginger ale for the punch.

    Cathy gave the bank teller twenty $5 bills.

15. Spell out ordinal numbers (*first, second, third*, and so on) that can be expressed in one or two words. Consider a hyphenated number such as *thirty-two* as one word.)

    Chip and Amber celebrated their seventh anniversary in June.

    Scott's office is on the thirty-second floor.

Northeastern State University planned a promotional giveaway using 20,000 plastic cups with the school's phone number. Trouble was, the phone number was incorrect—it was for a company in Texas. The two numbers were alike except for one digit. The folks at Northeastern had to remove the phone number from all the cups before using them in the giveaway. *Source: The Daily Oklahoman*

CHECKUP 9-2   Circle the number style in parentheses that correctly completes each sentence.

1. Our staff receives about (500, five hundred) e-mails a day.

2. Leasing the building will cost ($35,000, thirty-five thousand dollars) annually.

3. The 14-karat gold bracelet weighed (8.5, eight and one-half) grams.

4. Our records show a (fifteen percent, 15 percent) decrease in returned merchandise for the first quarter.

5. Brunch will be served from (9 a.m., 9:00 a.m.) to 10:45 a.m.

6. Sales for December reached $15,000; however, sales were only ($8500, $8,500) in January.

7. A wedding at (8, 8:00) o'clock in the evening is considered formal.

8. Our profit margin is only (3.5, three and five-tenths) percent of net sales.

9. Shannon's telephone number is (615/555/4827, 615-555-4827).

10. Jeff prepared tea in five (2-gallon, two-gallon) jugs.

REVISION SYMBOLS FOR NUMBER STYLE

The following revision symbols are used to mark corrections in numbers.

Revision	Edited Draft	Final Copy
Spell out a number	④ associates	four associates
	⦅2nd⦆ of April	second of April
Change to figures	12 ~~twelve~~ cell phones	12 cell phones
Change a number	482 ~~582~~ reservations	482 reservations

Revision	Edited Draft	Final Copy
Transpose numbers	689 pounds	698 pounds
Delete a comma and close up a number	1,400 responses	1400 responses
Delete a decimal or a colon and zeros	$10.00 per dozen 8:00 a.m. and 10:00 p.m.	$10 per dozen 8 a.m. and 10 p.m.

CHECKUP 9-3 Use revision symbols to mark the following sentences for correct number style. Write *C* for *Correct* to the left of any item number that has no errors.

1. Both Mr. and Mrs. Parker signed their wills on the 8th of July.

2. 5 members of our association won awards last night.

3. Airline tickets from New York to Hawaii will cost $1,600.

4. Jennifer Nelson is 1 of our most creative designers.

5. The final figure for our storm damage was thirty thousand dollars.

6. A 2/3s majority vote is required to change our bylaws.

7. Give five of the 15 tool kits to Michael Lee.

8. Joseph Vaughan, 65, decided not to retire.

9. Three of our 15 computer operators are taking courses at the community college.

10. Replacing our roof will cost 1000s of dollars.

TIPS

MARKING NUMBER ERRORS

Sometimes there may be more than one way to mark a number error. For example, the following error can be corrected using two different revision symbols:

We bought a small camper for $3,895. (The comma is not needed in four-digit numbers.)

- Delete the comma and close up the number:
  We bought a small camper for $3,895.
- Delete the number and write the correction out:
  We bought a small camper for $3,895. $3895

Either option may be used, but deleting the entire number and writing out the correct number is easier to spot.

Use revision symbols to mark corrections in the following sentences. Write *C* for *Correct* to the left of any item number that has no errors.

1. Last May, I made my 2nd trip to New York.

2. Harry is drinking his third cup of coffee.

3. Sherry's construction company built 3 five-story apartment buildings.

4. If you have any questions, please call me at 419-555-4268.

5. The price of the item is seventy-five dollars.

6. Matt bought the used truck for $8,500; a new one would have cost $21,500.

7. The plumber sent a bill for $1,200.

8. To meet our goals, sales must increase by six percent each month for the next 6 months.

9. Please call me between 8:00 a.m. and 10:00 a.m. tomorrow.

10. Over 1000 people registered for the door prizes.

11. You should strive to pay off your home mortgage when you are in your 50s.

12. The chemicals should be mixed with water in a two-to-one ratio.

13. Almost 1/3 of our tomato plants died from the low temperatures.

14. The walnut desk sells for $789, and the oak desk sells for $499.50.

15. Sally had 95 cents in her desk drawer.

16. Nelson paid $68.00 for his car battery.

17. Our new budget goes into effect on the 1st of July.

18. Demitri was promoted to supervisor on October 1, 1999.

19. Five oak trees and 12 pine trees were damaged by the storm.

20. Each fruit basket has five apples, six bananas, and 12 oranges.

Application 9-A

Proofread the following two e-mail messages. Use appropriate revision symbols to correct errors in number style. If there is not enough room to write a correction above the line, write the correction in the margin next to the line of copy. Use a caret or draw an arrow to show where the corrected copy goes.

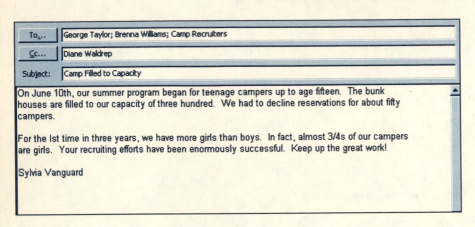

To... George Taylor; Brenna Williams; Camp Recruiters
Cc... Diane Waldrep
Subject: Camp Filled to Capacity

On June 10th, our summer program began for teenage campers up to age fifteen. The bunk houses are filled to our capacity of three hundred. We had to decline reservations for about fifty campers.

For the 1st time in three years, we have more girls than boys. In fact, almost 3/4s of our campers are girls. Your recruiting efforts have been enormously successful. Keep up the great work!

Sylvia Vanguard

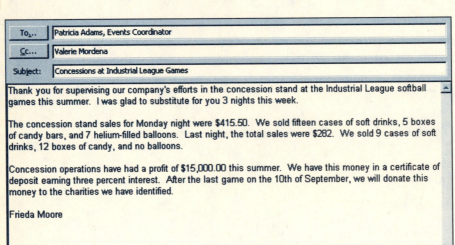

To... Patricia Adams, Events Coordinator
Cc... Valerie Mordena
Subject: Concessions at Industrial League Games

Thank you for supervising our company's efforts in the concession stand at the Industrial League softball games this summer. I was glad to substitute for you 3 nights this week.

The concession stand sales for Monday night were $415.50. We sold fifteen cases of soft drinks, 5 boxes of candy bars, and 7 helium-filled balloons. Last night, the total sales were $282. We sold 9 cases of soft drinks, 12 boxes of candy, and no balloons.

Concession operations have had a profit of $15,000.00 this summer. We have this money in a certificate of deposit earning three percent interest. After the last game on the 10th of September, we will donate this money to the charities we have identified.

Frieda Moore

Application 9-B

Proofread the following letter for correct number style. Use appropriate revision symbols to correct the errors.

JASPER PRINTING AND PACKAGING, INC.

3298 Carson Boulevard, Post Office Box 2843, Wayne, MI 48187
jp&p@mich.net   517-555-2948

March 15, <YEAR>

Mr. Steve Wallenda
Century Sales and Service
1486 Camelot Drive
Wayne, MI 48187

Dear Mr. Wallenda:

Confirming our telephone conversation earlier today, we are quoting you a price of $4295 for printing 500 50-page sales manuals. The pages will be punched for a standard 3-ring binder, which will be furnished by you. The $4,295 total includes scanning the photographs and artwork that you will supply. Itemized costs are as follows:

Scanning Photographs and Artwork	$1,500
Proofreading (8 hours at $15 hour)	120
Design & page layout (10 hours at $80.00 hour)	800
Printing (500 copies at $3.75 per copy)	1,875
Total	$4,295

You will receive a draft to approve approximately two weeks after you send us the needed information and photographs. Your sales manuals will be delivered one week after you approve the draft.

Our price quote is effective for only fifteen days because of an expected price increase in paper. To assure this $4295 price, please order by March 30th. As a new customer, you will receive a ten percent discount if your payment is received within 5 days of the invoice date. Invoice payments are due by the 10th of the month following delivery.

We look forward to working with you on this project.

Sincerely,

Tom Messer

Tom Messer, Sales Representative

Application 9-C

Proofread the following investment proposal. Use appropriate revision symbols to correct errors in number style as well as any other types of errors.

Investment Proposal
for

Mr. and Mrs George Andretti

January 18 <YEAR>

Investment Amount:	$100,000.00
Investment Objective:	Growth and income with moderate to low risk.
	Low expense ratio
	Socially responsible
Asset Allocation:	60.0 percent growth
	40.0 percent income

Diversification:

Equity Portfolio
The sixty percent growth recommendation
will be allocated to 3 families of mutual funds.
In each fund, the investment will be divided
equally between domestic and international
markets.

Mammoth Capital Fund
Jenn Capital Management
Baxter Management

Income Portfolio
The 40 per cent income recommendation will
will be allocated to one mutual fun.

Weyhauser Management Company

Application 9-D

Proofread the following memo. Use appropriate revision symbols to correct errors in number style as well as any other types of errors.

MEMO TO: All Staff

FROM: Estella Perez, Assistant Manager

DATE: March 25, <YEAR>

SUBJECT: Fund-Raiser for Tom and Alice Barton

As most of you know, Tom's and Alice's home was recently destroyed by the tornado that ripped though our community. The rest of us were spared from significant damage.

Many of you have mentioned a fund-raiser to help Tom, Alice, and their 3 children. They lost their home car, and all of their household possessions. A local charity is providing temporary housing for them through the end of may.

To raise funds, we have decided to have a car-wash and a bake sale on Saturday April 1, from 8:00 a.m. until noon in the Walnut Creek Shopping Plaza. We need pies, cakes, cookies, and frozen casseroles. We also need volunteers to wash cars and selling the baked items. All of the funds raised will be given directly to Tom and Alice. Local merchants have offered Tom and Alice a twenty-five percent discount on their purchases.

A sign-up sheet is posted in our break room for you to indicate your preferences in work times. A separate sheet is provided for listing the baked goods that you will bring. These goods should be brought to Walnut Creek Shopping Plaza by 7:45 a.m. on the day of the sell.

Tom and Alice are very appreciative of our efforts.

CD-ROM Application 9-E

Using your word processor, open the file DPES09E from the CD-ROM. Proofread the following notice and correct any errors in number style. Save the revised notice using your initials in place of the DPES. Proofread the procedures on the screen and make any additional corrections. Save and print the corrected notice.

ANNUAL NEW YORK TRIP

This year's trip is a 5-day trip, leaving on May 15 and returning May 20. The cost of the tour package is $999.99 and includes the following:

- Airline ticket
- Hotel accommodations (2 persons per room)
- Dinner 3 evenings (buffet)
- Broadway play tickets for 2 evenings
- One ticket to a television show taping
- Admission to 1 museum
- Ferry to Statue of Liberty
- Financial lectures on Wall Street

Airline and hotel reservations have been made for thirty-two people and will available on a first-come basis. The deadline for reservations is March 10.

Below are some suggestions:

- Bring your driver's license for identification.
- Pack light.
- Bring a jacket for cool evenings.
- Bring 20 $1 bills for tips.
- Expect to spend about $300 on meals.
- Pack medications in carry-on luggage.
- Use credit cards and travelers' checks for large purchases.

Complete the information below and fax it to Barry Hambright at extension 3298. A $399.99 deposit is due by March 10. The $600.00 balance is due by the 1st of April.

Annual New York Trip

Name: _____ Roommate: _____

Home telephone: _____ Office telephone: _____

CD-ROM Application 9-F

Using your word processor, open the file DPES09F from the CD-ROM. Proofread the report and correct any errors in number style plus any other types of errors. Make your corrections; then run the spell checker. Save the revised memo using your initials in place of the DPES. Proofread the report on the screen and make any additional corrections. Save and print the corrected report.

REDUCING OFFICE COSTS

After 3 2-week observations at the Offices of Madison Office Supply Company 4 areas have been targeted for cost reduction. Targeted areas and suggestions for improvement is listed below.

MAIL ROOM

The mail room is operating efficiently with 2 exceptions. First, the postage operators are mailing items lst class that should be mailed 4th class. Second, all parcels are being sent by U.S. mail instead of using a parcel delivery service. Using proper postage procedures and an appropriate delivery service can substantially reduce parcel delivery expenses.

PAYROLL DEPARTMENT

Overtime pay last month was excessive. About $8,000 was paid to fifteen employees. Note that this figure does not include fringe benefit costs. Two administrative assistants, 2 receptionists, 1 switchboard operator, and 10 sales associates worked 1,226 hours in overtime pay. 1 solution to this problem would be to use temporary employees. Office temporaries, Inc., a local company, can provide temporary staffing.

STATIONARY

Expensive engraved letterhead is being used for routine correspondence within the organization. Change to printed letterhead; or better still, use plain paper. Engraved stationary costs $.08 per sheet, printed stationery costs $.03 per sheet.

OFFICE HOURS

The main office is pen from seven a.m. until six p.m. Monday though Friday. Opening 1 hour later and closing 1 hour earlier will mean that a switchboard operator and a and a receptionist will not have to work overtime these two hours each day.

Some of the targeted areas and suggestions may seem minor; however, over a period of 6 months, savings will be significant.

Formatting Memos and Letters

OBJECTIVES

After completing this chapter, you should be able to:

1. Describe the standard and optional parts of memos and letters.

2. Recognize and explain the differences among five letter formats: block, modified-block, modified-block with indented paragraphs, simplified, and personal-business style.

3. Use standard and open punctuation styles correctly in letters.

4. Use appropriate revision symbols to correct formatting errors.

This chapter presents memo and letter formats and the revision symbols used to correct format errors and to make needed changes. A thorough review of memo and letter formats will increase your ability to detect formatting errors.

Format refers to the placement of the parts of a memo or a letter on a page. Proofreading for format errors is important because a document that is formatted correctly makes a favorable impression on the reader. As you proofread memos and letters, pay special attention to the following:

- The spacing used between the various parts

- The alignment of items at the margins

- The placement of special notations

MEMO FORMATS

Memos, also known as *memorandums,* are used for interoffice communication. They are usually informal, providing a quick, easy, and inexpensive method of communicating with one or many employees.

Memos may be formatted on the computer to be printed on plain paper or stationery. Memos also may be prepared using a memo template available with a word processing program.

Parts of a Memo

Note the following details about memos printed on plain paper or stationery as you examine the memos in Figures 10-1 and 10-2 on pages 193 and 194, respectively.

1. When typing a memo on plain paper, leave a 2-inch top margin. Press Enter six times to take you to 1 inch below the default top margin of 1 inch.

2. When typing a memo on plain paper, use the default top, side, and bottom margins in the word processing software. If a memo is running long, use 1-inch top, side, and bottom margins to fit the memo on one page.

SOFTWARE TIPS

In Microsoft Word the default margins are 1-inch top and bottom margins and 1.25-inch side margins. In Corel WordPerfect the default margins are 1 inch for the top, bottom, and side margins. To change the default margins in Microsoft Word, select File from the menu, then choose Page Setup. To change the default margins in Corel WordPerfect, select Format from the menu, then choose Margins.

3. Type the guide words in either all-capital letters and bold *(MEMO TO:, FROM:, DATE:,* and *SUBJECT:)* or in initial capital letters and bold *(To:, From:, Date:,* and *Subject:)*. Use a colon after each guide word. *Note:* Using **MEMO TO** as the first guide word eliminates the need to type the word **MEMORANDUM** or **MEMO** on a separate line above the guide words.

4. Guide words are double-spaced and can be blocked or set in a two-column format. Leave one blank line (press Enter twice) between the last line of the guide words and the first line of the body of the memo.

Blocked Format	*Two-Column Format*	
MEMO TO:	**To:**	**From:**
FROM:	**Subject:**	**Date:**
DATE:		
SUBJECT:		

5. Set a tab two spaces after the longest guide word and begin typing the heading information at this point.

MEMO TO: Gary Anderson

FROM: Marsha Coelo

DATE: October 15, <YEAR>

SUBJECT: Moving Information

6. Use either blocked or indented paragraphs within the memo.

7. Single-space within paragraphs, and double-space between paragraphs.

8. The *writer's initials,* if used, are placed on the second line below the memo body. Type the writer's initials in all-capital letters at the left margin or at the center of the memo.

9. *Reference initials* identify the person who typed the memo. They are typed on the second line below the memo body or on the second line below the writer's initials, if used. Type the reference initials at the left margin in lowercase letters.

10. A *file name notation* is used to indicate the name of the word processing file used for the memo. The file name may be typed on the same line as the reference initials, separated by a diagonal (/) or typed on the line below the reference initials.

trs/order12   trs
                 order12

11. The *enclosure notation* (an indication that something accompanies the memo) is typed on the line below the reference initials, beginning at the left margin. You may use the word *Attachment* if the material is attached directly to the memo.

Enclosure   Attachment   2 Enclosures

12. If the memo is being sent to many people, type the word *Distribution* after the guide word **MEMO TO.** Then on the second line below the reference initials or the enclosure notation, if used, type the word *Distribution* in italics or underlined, followed by a colon. List the names in alphabetical order to avoid listing them by seniority or title. See Figure 10-2 on page 194.

13. A *copy notation* (a list of people getting a copy of the memo) is typed on the line below the enclosure notation, beginning at the left margin. See Figure 10-3 on page 195 for an alternate placement.

MEMO TO: All Staff Members

FROM: Raylene Morrison, Director of Computer Systems

DATE: September 23, <YEAR>

SUBJECT: Company Intranet Directory

The Guthery Manufacturing Company Intranet is a convenient resource for all employees. Since its development two years ago, our Intranet has expanded to include news groups and product information sites for over 30 subsidiaries.

Besides information about our subsidiaries, the Intranet offers helpful applications for submitting travel and expense reports, accessing health and benefits information, and using a search engine to conduct Internet research.

One of the most heavily used sites on our Intranet is the employee directory. We are pleased to announce several upgrades to this directory to make it more convenient to use, including a detailed search option.

RM

jbr
intranetmemo.2

Figure 10-1. Memo on Plain Paper. The message is aligned at the left margin. Paragraphs may be blocked or indented. Note the placement of the writer's initials, reference initials, and file name notation.

INTEROFFICE MEMORANDUM

To: Distribution   **From:** Daniel Monahan

Subject: Research Proposals   **Date:** April 22, <YEAR>

Research proposals for the next calendar year are being accepted through June 1. One bound copy of each proposal should be delivered to each of our five vice presidents. Proposals must completely describe the intended research, including the projected costs. The attached guidelines for proposals provide more detailed information.

Because research funds are limited, we can approve only the two proposals that will best work toward our company goals. The thoroughness and quality of each proposal will be a consideration in granting research funds.

Please encourage the members of your departments to submit proposals for consideration.

jkl
Attachment

Distribution:

J. Brown
D. Gravett
J. Hobbs
J. Land
D. Parker
G. Price
M. Theado

Figure 10-2. Memo With Distribution List. The guide words are typed in a two-column format. Note the use of a Distribution list.

Memo Templates

A memo template contains the formatting for a memo—it has the guide words and the spacing already set up. The user simply tabs from one place to another to fill in the needed information. Note that the memo template in Figure 10-3 below includes the copy notation in the heading.

Company Name Here

Memo

To: [Click **here** and type name]
From: [Click **here** and type name]
CC: [Click **here** and type name]
Date: 11/11/99
Re: [Click **here** and type subject]

How to Use This Memo Template

Select the text you would like to replace, and type your memo. Use styles such as Heading 1-3 and Body Text in the Style control on the Formatting toolbar. To save changes to this template for future use, choose Save As from the File menu. In the Save As Type box, choose Document Template. Next time you want to use it, choose New from the File menu, and then double-click your template.

Figure 10-3. Memo Template. In this memo template from Microsoft Word, note that each guide word is followed by a fill-in where you type the information.

SOFTWARE TIPS

When you use a memo template, the date line has a date field that automatically inserts the current date. Some memo templates have the date field set up to list the date as numbers; for example, *January 7, 2002,* may be listed as *1/7/02.* In the date line, make sure the name of the month is spelled out.

Completing the following exercise will help you learn the correct format for memos. Reread the text and look at the preceding memos to make sure you are answering each question correctly.

Respond to each numbered sentence by circling *T* for *True* or *F* for *False*.

1. Plain paper is acceptable for memos.   T   F

2. Templates with guide words already formatted   T   F
   may be used for memos.

3. Guide words in memos may be single-spaced   T   F
   or double-spaced.

4. Colons should not follow each guide word.   T   F

5. It is correct to omit the colons following all   T   F
   four guide words in memos.

6. Either initial-capital letters or all-capital letters   T   F
   are correct for the guide words in a memo.

7. It is correct to block all paragraphs or to   T   F
   indent all paragraphs within a memo.

8. Lines within paragraphs should be double-spaced.   T   F

9. The reference initials and the copy notation   T   F
   should begin at the center of the memo.

In the space provided, write the word or words that best complete each sentence.

10. The four guide words that usually precede the memo body
    are _____, _____, _____,
    and _____.

11. Memos typed on plain paper usually have left, right, and
    bottom margins that are _____ inch/inches.

12. Use a top margin of _____ inch/inches, except
    for long memos.

13. Writer's initials, when used, may begin at the _____
    and on the second line below the memo body.

14. When a memo is addressed to many individuals, the word
_____ appears after the appropriate guide word
and above the list of recipients.

15. Press Enter _____ times after the last guide
word before typing the body of a memo.

16. Press Enter _____ times to leave one blank line
between paragraphs.

17. The minimum top margin for a memo is _____
inch/inches.

18. The names in a distribution list should be typed in
_____ order.

19. Reference initials are typed in _____ letters.

20. Memos are used for _____ communication.

REVISION SYMBOLS FOR FORMATTING

The following revision symbols are used to mark corrections in formatting in memos and letters as well as other documents. Study each symbol carefully before completing the next exercise.

Revision	Edited Draft	Final Copy
Bold	MEMO TO:	**MEMO TO:**
Italics	Distribution: *ital*	*Distribution:*
Underscore	See Distribution:	<u>See Distribution</u>:
Move to the right	February 5, 2002	February 5, 2002
Move to the left	Sincerely,	Sincerely,
Move as shown	c: Gail Bender Enclosure	Enclosure c: Gail Bender

Revision	Edited Draft	Final Copy
Center line	] TITLE [	TITLE
Single-space	ss ⌈ xxxxxxxxxx ⌊ xxxxxxxxxx	xxxxxxxxxx xxxxxxxxxx
Double-space	ds ⌈ xxxxxxxxxx ⌊ xxxxxxxxxx	xxxxxxxxxx xxxxxxxxxx
Align horizontally	Colleen answered the letter.	Colleen answered the letter.
Align vertically	Colleen answered the letter today. You should receive her response on Monday. $122.30 22.40 $144.70	Colleen answered the letter today. You should receive her response on Monday. $122.30 22.40 $144.70

CHECKUP 10-2 The memo on page 199 has a variety of formatting errors. Use the appropriate revision symbols to mark each change specified in the following list.

1. Use bold for *MEMO TO*.

2. Add a colon after *MEMO TO*.

3. Double-space between the *DATE* line and the *FROM* line.

4. Line up the guide words at the left margin.

5. Double-space before the body of the memo.

6. Single-space the second paragraph.

7. Line up the third paragraph at the left margin.

8. Double-space between the second and third paragraphs.

9. Move the writer's initials to begin at the left margin.

10. Single-space the reference initials, enclosure notation, and the copy notation.

MEMO TO   Glenda Turrbyfield, Human Resources Manager

DATE: May 2, <YEAR>
FROM: John Madison, Marketing Director

SUBJECT: Needed Personnel
My administrative assistant, Eleanor Wray, has resigned to return
to college and finish her accounting degree. She plans to work a
three-week notice, making her last day of employment May 23.

Please initiate your usual hiring procedures to fill this vacancy. I would

like Eleanor's replacement to learn our operation thoroughly before our

summer rush begins the end of June.

   A copy of Myra's job description is enclosed. I would appreciate
seeing any résumés for qualified applicants that you now have on
file. Incidentally, Myra is interested in returning to work for us
when she completes her degree. She should graduate in about two
years. You might want to consider her for an internship next summer. Her employment record here has been impeccable.

                          GT

jks

Enclosure

c: Clyde Galinski

Seen in a memo:
"I do advise a meeting
nad I will be present if
you believe that I
would be of some
help."

LETTER STYLES

There are several letter styles appropriate for business use. The
ones most widely used are illustrated in Figures 10-4 to 10-8 on
pages 204–208. These styles are as follows:

- Block style

- Modified-block style, standard format

- Modified-block style with indented paragraphs

- Simplified style

- Personal-business style

   One variable element of letter style is the alignment of letter
parts. In the block style (Figure 10-4), all lines begin at the left
margin. In the modified-block style, the date line and the closing
lines begin at center, but all other lines begin at the left margin.

Paragraphs may be indented or not indented in the modified-block style (Figures 10-5 and 10-6). In the simplified style, all lines are flush with the left margin and the salutation and complimentary closing are omitted (Figure 10-7). The personal-business style follows the modified-block style but uses a typed or printed return address because it is written on plain stationery (Figure 10-8).

Another variable element of letter style is punctuation. There are two basic punctuation styles: standard and open. Only two lines of the letter—the salutation and the complimentary closing—are affected.

- In *standard punctuation style,* a colon is used after the salutation and a comma after the complimentary closing. Most writers prefer this style, which is shown in the modified-block letter in Figure 10-5 on page 205.

- In *open punctuation style,* the colon after the salutation and the comma after the complimentary closing are omitted, as shown in the block style letter in Figure 10-4 on page 204.

Frequently, businesses adopt one style for all their letters. Some businesses let each writer choose the style, but styles should never be mixed within the same letter.

Parts of a Letter

Letters contain both standard and optional parts. These parts are listed in a certain sequence, as described in the following section.

Standard Letter Parts

Standard letter parts always appear in a letter. These parts include the date line, inside address, salutation, body, complimentary closing, and writer's identification.

- The *date line* includes the month, day, and year. Spell out the name of the month and use figures for the day and the year. Type the date line as the first line of the letter.

  October 29, 2002

  For international business correspondence, the day is typed first, followed by the month and the year. No commas are used in this style.

  29 October 2002

- The *inside address* includes the name and address of the person to whom the letter is addressed. Begin the inside address at the left margin on the fourth line below the date line. To do this, press Enter four times after typing the date.

Ms. Cheryl Kisor
Grant Medical Center
15 Grant Avenue
Riverside, OH 45231

If you are writing to someone at a company and do not know his or her name, use the job title of the person who could help you.

Personnel Manager
Grant Medical Center
15 Grant Avenue
Riverside, OH 45231

For international business correspondence, type the name of the country in all-capital letters on the last line of the address.

Mr. Kevin Lim
2nd Floor, #151 Hson Road
Taipei 110
TAIWAN

- The *salutation,* or greeting, is typed on the second line below the last line of the inside address or below the attention line, if one is used. To do this, press Enter twice after the last line of the inside address or the attention line.

   Dear Mr. Johnson: Dear Ms. Durkee:

If you know the person's name but do not know if the person is a man or a woman, use the person's first and last name instead of a title such as *Mr.* or *Ms.*

   Dear Leslie Camden: Dear B. G. Manoff:

- Begin typing the *body* of the letter on the second line below the salutation or the subject line, if one is used. Single-space the paragraphs, and double-space between paragraphs. Press Enter twice between paragraphs in order to leave a double-space.

- The *complimentary closing* includes a closing thought. Type the complimentary closing on the second line below the last line in the body of the letter. To do this, press Enter twice after the last line in the letter. Capitalize the first word in the closing. The following are some typical closings.

   Sincerely,   Sincerely yours,

   Cordially,   Cordially yours,

- The *writer's identification* includes the writer's typed name. Type the writer's identification on the fourth line below the complimentary closing or the company name, if one is used. To do this, press Enter four times after the complimentary closing or the company name.

Net Link

Go to the Universal Postal Union Web site at **http://www.upu.int/** for information on how to address letters mailed to other countries. Click on the "Postal addresses" link and select a country. The site includes guidelines for addressing mail for a particular country and will provide a sample address to use as a model.

Special Notations

Several notations and special lines are needed to make certain letters complete. (See the letters in Figures 10-4 to 10-8 on the following pages.) These notations and special lines are optional; they are used only when appropriate. Pay particular attention to the following notations on the letters:

- The *attention line* is used to direct a letter to a specific person even though the letter is actually written to the company. Type the attention line as the first line of the inside address or on the second line below the inside address. (See Figure 10-4 on page 204.)

- The *subject line* directs the reader's attention to a specific topic. Type the subject line in all-capital letters or in capital and lowercase letters on the second line below the salutation. (See Figure 10-5.)

- The *company name* below the complimentary closing is usually considered optional. When used, it means that the writer is speaking for the company. Type the company name in all-capital letters on the second line below the complimentary closing. Leave three blank lines below the company name before typing the writer's name. (See Figure 10-5 on page 205.)

- The *writer's title,* when used, can be on the same line as the writer's name, if space permits, with a comma separating the name and title. If the writer's name and title are on two separate lines, align the title on the line below the name, and do not use a comma after the name. (See Figure 10-6 on page 206.)

  Sincerely,   Sincerely,

  Jan Wray, Manager   Janet R. Wray, Ph.D.
                                          Professor of Business
                                          Administration

- The *reference initials* are those of the person who typed the letter. No reference initials are needed if the writer types his or her own letter. Type the reference initials in lowercase letters on the second line below the writer's identification. To do this, press Enter twice. (See Figure 10-6 on page 206.)

- The *file name notation* lists the name of the word processing file that was used to prepare the letter. The file name may be typed on the same line as the reference initials and separated by a diagonal (/) or typed on the line below the reference initials. (See Figure 10-4 on page 204.)

- An *enclosure notation* indicates that something has been included with the letter. Various formats such as the following are correct:

Enclosure	Enclosures:	3 Enclosures
	1. Deed	
Enclosures 3	2. Invoice	

- A *delivery notation* indicates that the letter was delivered in some way other than first-class mail. Type the delivery notation on the line below the enclosure notation or the reference initials, if used. Notations such as the following are used:

  By certified mail   By Express Mail

  By special delivery   By fax

- A *copy notation* records the names of those receiving a copy of the letter. The notations *c* and *cc* are widely used. A colon may or may not follow the copy notation. Type the copy notation on the line below the delivery notation, enclosure notation, or reference initials, whichever appears last. (See Figure 10-5 on page 205.) Various formats such as the following are correct:

c	Laura Abner	c:	James Everhard
	Brian Jackson		Holly Marshall

cc	Elaine Cowen	cc:	Louise Parker
	Michael Gault		Alan Vasquez

  If copies are sent to several persons, list the names in alphabetical order.

  c: Jim Fouts
      Teresa Hawley
      Ken Lawton

- A *postscript* presents an afterthought. Use the letters *P.S.* or *PS* to begin a postscript. Type a postscript as the last item in a letter. Leave one blank line before the postscript. (See Figure 10-5 on page 205.)

  P.S. Place your order by March 5 to receive an additional 10 percent savings.

- The *blind copy notation* is used when the addressee is not intended to know that someone is getting a copy of the letter. This notation appears on the file copy that remains at the writer's company. Type the blind copy notation on the second line below the last line in the letter. (See Figure 10-6 on page 206.) *Note*: Although the blind copy notation should not appear on the original copy of a letter, accidentally placing it there is a common error.

  bc: Jacob Travis

"We maintain travel prifiles for all our corporate clients."

Was *profiles* the word the writer meant to use?

SPEEDY
OFFICE SERVICES
One Baxter Place, Suite C, Shreveport, LA 71106
Phone: 318-555-2941   Fax: 318-555-2949
E-mail: speedy@shreve.net

November 13, <YEAR>

Attention: Office Manager
Neelon Automotive Sales
4452 Bethany Avenue
Shreveport, LA 71106

Dear Neelon Automotive Sales

Thank you for accepting our bid to provide all your stationery and copier supplies.
We appreciate the opportunity to serve you.

As specified in our bid, your orders will be delivered within two business days of our
receiving them. In addition, as a new customer you will receive a 10 percent
discount on all orders for the first six weeks, beginning with the date of this letter.

Best wishes as you begin business in Shreveport. The team at Speedy Office
Services looks forward to handling all your office needs.

Sincerely yours

Patricia Tate

Patricia Tate
Sales Manager

htl
neelon13nov

Figure 10-4. Block Style.   The block style is very consistent. Each line begins at
the left margin; no paragraphs are indented. Open punctuation is illustrated.

COMMUNICATIONS INC.

156 Erikson Avenue, Minneapolis, MN 55416-4076 • 612-555-3943 Telephone • 612-555-3944 Fax • cmmunication@mmin.com

June 15, <YEAR>

Ms. Lydia Barclay
Computer Solutions
394 Wellington Street
Toronto, ON E5K 2S7
CANADA

Dear Ms. Barclay:

Subject: Electronic Equipment Exposition

Thank you for agreeing to participate in our annual electronic equipment exposition. The show will be held in the Wilson Trade Center in Minneapolis from July 20 until July 25.

Please sign and return the enclosed exhibitor contract, along with a check for the $250 registration fee, by July 3. An addressed, stamped envelope has been provided for your convenience. Currently more than 45,000 people have registered to attend the exposition. Last year 38,560 registered visitors attended the exposition and generated over 6 million dollars in revenue for our vendors.

We look forward to your help in making this year's exhibition the most successful ever.

Sincerely yours,

COMMUNICATIONS, INC.

Harry Banar

Harry Banar
Vice President

jkc

2 Enclosures
By certified mail
c: Ms. Lillian Condrey

PS: Remember to return your signed contract by July 3.

Figure 10-5. Modified-Block Style, Standard Punctuation. In this letter format the date line, complimentary closing, and writer's identification all begin at the center. Standard (mixed) punctuation is illustrated. Note the use of a delivery notation and a postscript.

374 Polaris Drive
Flint, Michigan 48507-0874
Telephone: 313-555-0328
Fax: 313-555-0303

E-Mail: flint@pontiac.com

February 25, <YEAR>

Mr. Dennis Funderburk
624 Thomas Street
Brockton, MI 47123

Dear Mr. Funderburk:

Thank you for your recent letter regarding the cellular phone that you purchased from us. Your letter was quite thorough in describing the problems you are experiencing with sending and receiving calls.

Based on the service record of the Model 38X cellular phone, we have determined that the battery pack is not working properly.

To receive a replacement cellular phone, simply take your existing phone to one of our convenient locations in the Flint area. Bring your receipt as proof of purchase, and we will set you up with a new phone in a matter of minutes.

Mr. Funderburk, thank you for selecting Flint Cellular for your cellular needs. Please let me know when I can help you again.

Sincerely,

Francis Boheler

Frances Boheler
Customer Service Manager

pm

bc Suzanne Lemke

Figure 10-6. Modified-Block Style With Indented Paragraphs. This letter format is the same as the standard modified-block style except that the paragraphs are indented five spaces. Standard (mixed) punctuation is illustrated.

CHARLAINE COMMUNITY COLLEGE

Post Office Box 52381, Spokane, WA 99205-3810
Telephone: 509-555-7482   Fax: 509-555-7484

June 15, <YEAR>

Mr. Solomon Davonshire
3492 West Langley Drive
Spokane, WA 99208

PROGRAMMING POSITION

Thank you, Mr. Davonshire, for sending us your application letter and résumé. We will be accepting applications for positions in our Information Systems department through the end of this month. Our selection process will begin at that time.

Your qualifications, as expressed on your résumé, certainly meet our needs. We do, however, need an official college transcript and three references who could attest to your qualifications, experience, and character. We will not contact your references until after your interview, which will take place after July 1. Ms. Shirley Oberon, our staff coordinator, will contact you soon to arrange a mutually convenient time for us to meet.

Thank you for supplying the additional information.

Gilda Harris

GILDA HARRIS - HUMAN RESOURCES MANAGER

lwc

Figure 10-7. Simplified Style. This style omits the salutation and the complimentary closing. A subject line, typed in all-capital letters, is added. The writer's identification (the name and title) is also typed in all-capital letters.

March 3, <small><YEAR></small>

Mrs. Amelia Schenck
Superintendent
Starr Private School System
Post Office Box 2276
Austin, TX 78768

Dear Mrs. Schenck:

  Thank you for the time you and your staff spent with me yesterday when I interviewed for the second grade teaching position with your system. The luncheon added a personal touch and gave me the opportunity for casual conversation with your teachers.

  Visiting at Starr Elementary confirmed my interest in pursuing a teaching position with your organization. While my expertise is in teaching first and second grade, I would accept the challenge of teaching any grade level. It would be an honor to become a member of the Starr teaching staff.

  Thank you for considering my application. I look forward to hearing from you soon.

         Sincerely,

         Karen Trotman

         Karen Trotman
         103 Carson Hills Drive
         Austin, TX 78723

Figure 10-8. Personal-Business Style. This style is similar to the modified-block style with indented paragraphs and is used when there is no letterhead stationery. The writer's address appears at the bottom of the letter, below the writer's name.

In the space provided, write the word or words that best complete each sentence. Try completing the items without looking at the text. Then, check the text for clarification on items you were unable to answer.

1. A (An) _____ notation indicates that something has been sent with a letter.

2. A person typing a letter places his or her _____ initials appropriately at the bottom of the letter.

3. A (An) _____ presents an afterthought.

4. The _____ line directs the letter to a specific topic.

5. The _____ line directs the letter to a specific person even though the letter is actually written to a company collectively.

6. A (An) _____ notation records the names of those receiving a copy of the letter.

7. A (An) _____ notation goes on the copy only. This lets the recipient of the copy know that the addressee is not aware that the recipient has received a copy.

8. A (An) _____ notation indicates that the letter was delivered in some way other than first-class mail, such as certified mail, fax, or Express mail.

9. The _____ indicates that the writer is speaking for the entire firm. When this letter part is used, it is placed on the second line below the complimentary closing.

10. The _____ , when used, can be placed correctly on the same line as the writer's name or on the line below and aligned with the writer's name.

PROOFREADING LETTERS

- When proofreading a letter, make sure that it consistently follows one format style and one punctuation style.

- Always be sure to check that the date line, the salutation, and other standard parts of a letter have not been omitted.

- Make sure that special notations such as the enclosure notation, copy notation, and postscript are listed in the correct order.

Completing the following exercise will help test your knowledge of letter formats. Check the text and the example letters if you are in doubt about any item.

CHECKUP 10-4   Complete the following statements about business letter formats by circling the letter of the correct answer.

1. The letter style shown here is _____.
   a. Block style
   b. Modified-block style with indented paragraphs
   c. Modified-block style with standard format
   d. Simplified style

> Thank you for sending my order so promptly. My check for $123.92 is enclosed.
>
> Sincerely yours,

2. The punctuation style used below is _____.
   a. Closed
   b. Open
   c. Standard (mixed)
   d. Incorrect

   Dear Mrs. Harrison:

3. The punctuation style used below is _____.
   a. Closed
   b. Open
   c. Standard (mixed)
   d. Incorrect

   Dear Mr. Galinski

4. The letter style used below is _____.
   a. Block style
   b. Modified-block style with indented paragraphs
   c. Personal business style
   d. Simplified style

   Your plane will arrive at 3:55 p.m. on Thursday, May 25. Mike Delgado will meet you and take you to your hotel.

   If you have any questions, please contact me at 1-800-555-6825.

   NORMAN S. MANCHESTER - GENERAL MANAGER

   dht

5. The punctuation style used below is _____.
   a. Closed
   b. Open
   c. Standard (mixed)
   d. Incorrect

   Very truly yours

   Anne Payton, Manager

6. The letter style used below is _____.
   a. Block style
   b. Modified-block style with indented paragraphs
   c. Modified-block style with standard format
   d. Personal-business style

   Your check for $123.92 arrived today. Thank you for your prompt payment.

   Sincerely yours,

7. The letter style used in the following example is _____.
   a. Block style
   b. Simplified style
   c. Computer style
   d. Personal-business style

Dr. Fred Yancy
Post Office Box 3218
Knoxville, TN 37916
May 22, <YEAR>

8. The punctuation style used below is _____.
   a. Closed
   b. Open
   c. Standard (mixed)
   d. Incorrect

   Sincerely yours

9. The letter style used below is _____.
   a. Block style
   b. Modified-block style with indented paragraphs
   c. Modified-block style with standard format
   d. Simplified style

   Please send me your comments as soon as you have had
   time to review the proposal. Your opinion is appreciated.

   Cordially,

10. The punctuation style used below is
    _____.

    a. Closed
    b. Open
    c. Standard (mixed)
    d. Incorrect

    Dear Ms. Reston;

SOFTWARE TIPS

Use either the view document feature or the scroll feature of
your word processor to check the format of a document on the
computer screen before printing it.

- The *view document* feature lets you see a reduced version of
  a page on the screen. Use this feature to check the margins
  and the alignment of letter parts at the margin.

- The *scroll* feature allows you to move through a document
  line by line and check the spacing between letter parts.

Before completing this exercise, review the sample letters presented earlier in this chapter, paying special attention to the spacing between the parts of a letter. Then, for the following letter, indicate in the spaces provided how many times you should press the Enter key at each location.

February 21, <YEAR>   1._____

Mr. Philip Lopez
8219 Della Road, SW
Albuquerque, NM 87105   2._____

Dear Mr. Lopez: 3._____

Subject: Accounting Position   4._____

Yesterday we received your résumé and letter requesting an
employment interview. Your background is impressive, and we
would like to talk with you concerning your career plans.   5._____

We plan to increase our accounting staff in June. Since this is
about the time you will be graduated from college, it may be that
you would like to begin your professional career with Carter
Construction Company.   6._____

Please come for an interview on Friday, March 10, at 3 p.m. If this
time is not convenient for you, call me to arrange another time.   7._____

Sincerely yours,

CARTER CONSTRUCTION COMPANY   8._____

R. William Carter   9._____
Vice President   10._____

sh

CONTINUATION PAGES IN LETTERS AND MEMOS

Letters and memos that have a second, or continuation, page require a heading at the top of the second page. In addition, two-page letters and memos have page breaks and paragraph breaks.

Headings

For letters and memos that are longer than one page, you need to type a heading at the top of the second page. This second-page heading contains the name that appears in the inside address, the page number, and the date of the letter or memo.

The heading for a two-page letter or memo begins on the first line below the default top margin, which is usually 1 inch. Use either a one-line format or a multiple-line format for the second-page heading.

One-Line Heading

In the one-line heading, type the person's name at the left margin, type the page number at the center, and align the date at the right margin.

Mr. Joe Bianco	Page 2	October 21, <YEAR>

Multiple-Line Heading

In the multiple-line heading, the name is typed on the first line, the page number on the second line, and the date on the third line. In the following example, the name *Bucyrus Marketing Company* is used since the letter is addressed to the company. Even if a letter is written to the attention of a particular person but is addressed to a company, use the company's name in the second-page heading.

Bucyrus Marketing Company
Page 2
October 21, <YEAR>

Page Breaks

The transition from the first page of a letter or memo to the second page should be visually smooth to avoid confusing the reader. Thus, you should avoid widow and orphan lines.

A *widow* line is the last line of a paragraph that has been carried forward to the top of another page and appears by itself, as shown in the following example.

Ms. Ellen Graham   2   March 15, <YEAR>

Work may begin as soon as we receive your signed copy of the contract.

An *orphan* is the first line of a paragraph that has been left as the last line at the bottom of a page, as in the following example.

The renovation work is slated to begin June 1. As you know, requisitions for

---

In the following example, note how one full and one partial line at the top of the second page keep the continuation copy from being a widow.

Ms. Ellen Graham   2   March 15, <YEAR>

materials must be submitted to our facilities manager no later than April 20 in order to assure delivery by May 25.

REVISION SYMBOLS FOR PAGE BREAKS AND PARAGRAPHING

The revision symbols on the following page are used to mark page breaks and to indicate paragraph breaks. Study the marks carefully, and then complete the exercise that follows.

Revision	Edited Draft	Final Copy
Begin a new page	The order was delivered today by express courier. **pg** We now have all the components needed to begin assembly.	The order was delivered today by express courier. Page 2 We now have all the components needed to begin assembly.
No new page	The order was delivered **no pg** Page 2 today by express courier. We now have all the components. Assembly can begin during the first shift on Monday.	The order was delivered today by express courier. We now have all the components. Assembly can begin during the first shift on Monday.
Begin a new paragraph	The order was delivered today by express courier. **¶** We now have all the components. Assembly can begin during the first shift on Monday.	The order was delivered today by express courier. We now have all the components. Assembly can begin during the first shift on Monday.
No new paragraph	The order was delivered today by express courier. **no ¶** We now have all the components.	The order was delivered today by express courier. We now have all the components.

AVOIDING WIDOW AND ORPHAN LINES

- When continuing a paragraph from one page to the next page, leave at least two lines on the first page.

- When continuing a paragraph from one page to the next page, take at least one full and one partial line of the paragraph to the second page.

- Use the widow/orphan protection feature in your word processing software to format documents so that widow and orphan lines are not allowed.

CHECKUP 10-6 Use appropriate revision symbols to indicate the specified corrections in each numbered item.

1. Begin a new page after the second line.

   The courier personally delivered the package

   to my office to ensure that it arrived today in

   good condition. We now have the information

   needed to make a decision.

2. Do not begin a new page.

   The courier personally brought the package

Page 2

to my office to ensure that it arrived today in

good condition. We now have the information

needed to make a decision.

3. Begin a new paragraph after the second sentence.

. . . My plane was almost three hours

late. The long delay was caused by bad

weather. I was extremely tired and went

directly to the hotel.

4. Don't begin a paragraph after the first sentence.

. . . My plane was almost three hours late.

The long delay was caused by bad weather.

5. Indicate the only appropriate page break in this paragraph.

The sale will begin at 10:30 a.m.

on Saturday, May 8. All merchandise

will be drastically reduced so that we

may close out our inventory.

Application 10-A

Proofread the following memo, and use appropriate revision symbols to correct formatting errors. Assume that the top and side margins on the memo are correct.

MEMO TO: Dennis S. Clark, Human Resources Manager

   FROM: Edith B. Haroldson, Administrative Assistant

DATE: June 23, <YEAR>
SUBJECT: Reimbursement for Educational Expenses

As you know, I am taking evening courses for credit at the local college. During the first session of summer school, I completed a three-hour course in business communications, bringing my total hours to 90.

Enclosed is a copy of my tuition invoice for $185 and a copy of my most recent transcript showing that I satisfactorily completed the course. My expenses are listed below:

Tuition	$185
Parking	25
Book	45
Supplies	15
Total	$270

I would appreciate your approving this amount for reimbursement. If you need any other documentation, please let me know. Thank you for making this educational benefit available.

expenses23jun
Enclosures

Application 10-B

Proofread the following letter. Use revision symbols to correct any formatting errors. The letter should use the block style format with open punctuation.

Travel Consultants, Inc.

132 Elizabeth Avenue, Boiling Springs, NC 28017
Telephone: 704-555-2841 • Fax: 704-555-2844 • travelco.bs.net

July 5, <YEAR>

Mr. Nathan Harbinger, President
Brentwood Industries
424 Industrial Park
Charlotte, NC 28214

Dear Mr. Harbinger

The arrangements for your excursion to see the Charlotte Knights play the Memphis Volunteers are complete. Every effort has been made to ensure that your company's international visitors relax and enjoy the baseball game.

As a theme for your excursion, we will use "An American Afternoon." We will include everything needed for an old-fashioned picnic lunch, including hot dogs, potato salad, and watermelon.

Your visitors will travel to the game in vintage 1957 Chevrolets. They will be escorted to a luxurious air-conditioned sky booth. Prior to the game, several members of both teams will visit the sky booth to sign autographs.

Your visitors will experience the kind of day that creates unforgettable memories. To personally record these memories, each visitor will receive a disposable camera. Additionally, each visitor will receive a baseball autographed by the Charlotte Knights players.

A detailed itinerary is enclosed. Please call me if you have questions about the excursion.

Sincerely,
TRAVEL CONSULTANTS, INC.

Gloria Paterno

Gloria G. Paterno, President

Enclosure
rtc

Application 10-C

Proofread the following memo typed on plain paper. Use appropriate revision symbols to correct formatting errors as well as any other types of errors. Assume that the top and side margins are correct.

MEMO TO: Susan Kline, Office Manager
c: Amy Roland
Dennis Smith

FROM: Brent Donaldson

DATE: July 21, <YEAR>

SUBJECT: Health Screenings

Our local health department well send Nurses to our plant to administer immunizations and routine health screenings on Monday September 8. The nurses will be in the company lounge from 7 a.m. until 10:00 a.m.

Immunizations available are as follows: influenza, tetanus, and hepatitis B. Be sure to bring your immunization record with you.

Several routine health screenings will be available. You may request tests for diabetes, cholesterol vision, and bloodpressure. The nurses will record your height and weight. You also will have the opportunity to complete a depression screening.

These immunizations and screenings is available for all employees.

Please take advantage of those that are appropriate for you. If have questions, please call me at extension 4382.

Application 10-D

Use appropriate revision symbols to correct formatting errors as well as any other types of errors in the following two-page letter. Assume that the top and side margins are correct. The letter should use the modified-block style with indented paragraphs and standard punctuation.

Travel Consultants, Inc.

132 Elizabeth Avenue, Boiling Springs, NC 28017
Telephone: 704-555-2841 • Fax: 704-555-2844 • travelco.bs.net

July 20, <YEAR>

Mr. and Mrs. Derek Melco
2381 Park Lane
Charlotte, NC 28213

Dear Mr. and Mrs. Melco:

You must be getting excited with your trip to Alaska only two weeks away. All of your travel arrangements have been finalized, and your plane tickets are enclosed. Your flights are are listed below:

Saturday	Leave Charlotte	8:40 a.m.	AM Air 880
August 3	Arrive Seattle	11:42 a.m.	
	Leave Seattle	2:30 p.m.	Alaska 281
	Arrive Juneau	3:45 p.m.	
	Snack		
Saturday	Leave Juneau	2:05 p.m.	Alaska 283
August 10	Arrive Seattle	3:20 p.m.	
	Snack		
	Leave Seattle	10:45 p.m.	AM Air 882
	Arrive Charlotte	1:55 a.m.	
	Snack		

Also enclosed is a copy of your hotel confirmation for five nights (August 3-7) at the Glacier View Hotel in Juneau and for two nights (August 8-9) at the Big Catch Fishing Lodge. Your reservations at both accommodations are guaranteed for late arrival. Both of these hotels come very highly recommended.

As you requested, no activities have been scheduled for Sunday. I think this is very wise; most people try to do too much on a trip like yours.

Thomas Bradley, the concierge at Glacier View Hotel, will have your prepaid admission coupons for the activities listed here. In each instance, you should meet your

Application 10-D (continued)

Mr. and Mrs. Derek Melco	2	July 20, <YEAR>

tour guide in the hotel lobby at the specified time.

Monday August 5	Cruise to Glacier Bay	8:00 a.m.
	Prospecting tour with dinner at the Prospector's Cabin Restaurant	4:30 p.m.
Tuesday August 6	Icy Straits wildlife cruise to view whales, otters, and sea lions	8:00 a.m.
	Dinner at the Salmon House	6:30 p.m.
Wendesday August 7	Helicopter tour to view Mendenhall Glacier	7:45 a.m.
	Dinner at the Fish House	6:30 p.m.

On Tuesday morning at 7:30, you will leave by private plane for you fishing excursion at Icy Straits. The concierge will arrange for transportation to and from the airport. You should have a traveler's check for $100 ($50 per person) to give to the pilot.

You are prepaid at the Big Catch Fishing Lodge for meals, lodging, and fishing guide (including boat, equipment, and bait). Also included is the cost of cleaning, shrink-wrapping, and quick-freezing up to 200 pounds of fish for shipment home.

Big Catch Fishing Lodge will provide transportation to the airport Saturday morning. You will depart by private plane and should have another traveler's check for $100 to give to the pilot for this return flight to Juneau.

By negotiating rates, we were able to save you a total of $2000 off the cost of purchasing each segment of the trip separately. Should you have questions during your trip, please call me toll-free at 1-800-555-8264.

Thank you for letting us makeyour travel arrangements. Have a great vacation!

Sincerely yours,

David C. Wentz, Travel Consultant
Enclosures

CD-ROM Application 10-E

Using your word processor, open the file DPES10E from the CD-ROM. Proofread the personal-business letter; then correct any formatting errors. (The letter should use the modified-block style and standard punctuation.) Save the revised letter using your initials in place of the DPES. Proofread the letter on the screen and make any additional corrections. Save and print the corrected letter.

1525 Springdale Court
Garfield, NC 28120
March 30, <YEAR>

Dr. Jack Custer
Superintendent of Schools
Garfield City Schools
124 Indiana Avenue
Charlotte, NC 28210

Dear Dr. Custer

As a lifelong resident of Garfield, I have supported numerous school levy initiatives for the Garfield City Schools.

I understand the importance of maintaining safe and comfortable environments at out schools. However, I question the school board's recent proposal to use the money from the latest operating levy to purchase temporary classrooms for the high school. A much more effective solution would be to use the funds to begin an expansion of the current high school.

As the spokesperson for the Garfield PTA, I strongly urge you and the school board to reconsider the plans to purchase temporary classrooms. This decision would provide only a temporary solution to what will be a long-term problem.

Sincerely,

Myra B. Weston

CD-ROM Application 10-F

Using your word processor, open the file DPES10F from the CD-ROM. Proofread the letter and correct any formatting errors as well as any other types of errors. The letter should be in the simplified style format. Run the spell and grammar checkers; then save the revised letter using your initials in place of the DPES. Proofread the letter on the screen and make any additional corrections. Save and print the corrected letter.

April 8, <YEAR>

Mr. Shawn Bennett
Spotless Cleaning Company
3829 Graham Boulevard
Charlotte, NC 28210

MAINTENANCE CONTRACT

This letter is to confirm our telephone conversation of the 5th of April concerning the maintenance contract for our quarterly office cleaning. As we agreed, you will clean all of our carpeted areas and the windows (inside and out) and all the painted and paneled wall surfaces. You also agreed to pressure-wash the parking lot and the drive-way.

I have made arrangements with our security personal to give you access to the building on the scheduled dates from 6:00 A.M. until the job is completed. Your compensation for performing each quarterly cleaning will be $900.00.

Thank you for scheduling this cleaning at times that is convenience for us. I know you will do your usual superb job.

ALAN J. SIMMONS, ASSISTANT MANAGER
COMMUNITY ACCOUNTING, INC.

Proofreading Reports and Other Multiple-Page Documents

CHAPTER

11

OBJECTIVES

After completing this chapter, you should be able to:

1. Detect and correct formatting errors in memo reports.

2. Detect and correct formatting errors in both business and academic formal reports.

3. Detect and correct formatting errors in meeting minutes and manuscripts.

Organizations use various report documents—memo reports, formal reports, meeting minutes, manuscripts, and so on—to present information that is used to make decisions and to conduct business. Beside the reports that organizations prepare, there are academic reports that students prepare to demonstrate their knowledge of a subject.

Proofreading reports and other multiple-page documents will involve all the skills you have learned in the previous chapters. Reports offer a particular challenge to the proofreader mainly because of the length of the task. You must proofread carefully to ensure that the content is accurate and that the report follows consistent formatting guidelines for headings, spacing, and page numbers.

MEMO REPORTS

Memo reports, typically internal documents, may range from two to several pages in length. Businesses use memo reports to present information in an organized manner similar to a formal report. The memo report may require headings to present the information logically. In addition to the usual proofreading procedures for regular memos, the memo report challenges the proofreader to pay particular attention to heading alignments and formatting.

Parts of a Memo Report

Guide words (*MEMO TO, FROM, DATE,* and *SUBJECT*) indicate the recipient(s) of the memo report, identify the writer, and give the date the report was prepared. The title of the memo report appears as the subject line. Depending on the format and the purpose, memo reports may contain an introduction, body, summary, and sometimes conclusions, recommendations, and/or findings. See the sample memo report in Figure 11-1 on page 233.

Format for a Memo Report

The guide words in a memo report are formatted the same as in a regular interoffice memorandum. (Refer to Chapter 10 for a discussion of memo formats.)

A memo report may require headings within the body to help pinpoint specific information and to guide the reader through the report. Heading styles used in the body of a memo report include centered, side, and paragraph headings.

- **Centered heading**—Center the heading horizontally on a line by itself, and type the heading in all-capital letters and bold. Leave one blank line before and after the heading.

- **Side heading**—Begin the heading at the left margin. Type the heading in all-capital letters and bold or initial-capital and small letters and bold. Leave one blank line before and after the heading.

- **Paragraph heading**—Leave a blank line between the preceding paragraph and the heading. Indent the heading 0.5 inch from the left margin. Type the heading in initial-capital and small letters and bold. Put a period at the end of the heading and space 1 or 2 spaces to begin typing text after the heading.

Memo reports require a header on all pages after the first page. The header identifies the recipient(s) of the memo report, the page number, and the date the report was submitted. The header copy should begin at the 1-inch top margin. Two header styles may be used—block and horizontal. Refer to Chapter 10 and the discussion of headers on continuation pages of letters and memos. The same header formats used for continuation pages in letters and memos also apply to continuation pages in reports. Note the two examples of header styles shown on the next page.

Block Style Header

Ms. Sondra R. King
Page 4
November 3, <YEAR>

Horizontal Style Header

Mr. E. L. Long   3   July 31, <YEAR>

SOFTWARE TIPS

Most word processing software has a header/footer feature that automatically places text and/or page numbers at the top (header) or bottom (footer) of the page. To avoid having the header or footer copy appear on the first page, select the option that allows you to suppress, or eliminate, the header or footer from the first page.

CHECKUP 11-1
Use appropriate revision symbols to correct errors in the following parts from memo reports. (Refer to the chart of revision symbols on the inside front cover.)

1. Centered heading.

Heading

Xxxx xxxxxxx xxxxxx xxxxxxxxx x xxxxxxxxxxx xxxxxxx xxxxx

xxxxxxx xxxxxxx xxxxxxxx xxxxxxxxxxxx xxxxxx.

2. Paragraph heading.

Heading. Xxxx xxxxxx xxxxxxxxx xxxxxxxxx xxxxxxxxxx

xxxxxxxxx xxxxxxxxxx xxx x xxxxxx xxxxxxxxx xxxxx xxxxxxx

xxxxxx xxxxxxxxx xxxxxxxx xx xx xxxxxx xxx.

3. Side heading.

HEADING

Xxxxxx xxxxxxxx xxxxxxxxxxxxx xxxxxxxxxx xxxxxxxxxxx

xxxxxxxxx xxxxxxxxx xxx x xxxxxx xxxxxxxxx xxxxxx xxxxxxx.

4. Block style header.

Mr. Joseph Serrano
  January 5, <YEAR>
Page 2

5. Horizontal style header.

Mr. Joseph Serrano   2   January 5, <YEAR>

FORMAL REPORTS

Formal reports are usually prepared for distribution outside the organization. Such reports also may be used within an organization to discuss complex issues for which a memo report would not be adequate. These reports may range from a few pages to many pages.

Formal reports are used in both business and academic settings; they often require research and the documentation of sources of information.

Parts of a Formal Report

A formal report may include some or all of the following parts depending on the type of report being prepared. These parts represent front matter pages, the report itself, and back matter pages. Illustrations of some of these parts of a formal report appear in the figures on pages 233 and 234.

Front Matter in a Formal Report

The front matter pages in a formal report provide an overview of the material in the report.

Title page. The title page in a formal business report includes the title, the subtitle (if one is used), the writer's name, the name of the person for whom the report was prepared, and the date the report was submitted. No title page is used for a formal academic report. Instead, the writer's name, the instructor's name, the title of the course, and the date submitted appear at the top of the first page of the report.

Letter or Memo of Transmittal. The transmittal may be written as a memo for internal use or as a letter for sending the report outside the company. The transmittal acts as a cover document; it summarizes the main points of the report and sometimes offers conclusions or findings. The letter or memo of transmittal may be attached to the front of the report or placed immediately before the title page.

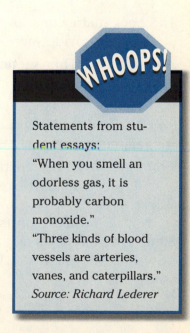

Statements from student essays:
"When you smell an odorless gas, it is probably carbon monoxide."
"Three kinds of blood vessels are arteries, vanes, and caterpillars."
Source: Richard Lederer

Table of Contents. The table of contents lists the titles of each part of the report and the headings in the body of the report, along with the page number where each part begins.

List of Tables or Illustrations. This optional section lists the titles of any tables or illustrations and the page numbers where they appear.

Preface and/or Foreword. These optional sections contain the writer's comments (preface) or comments from another person (foreword).

Executive Summary. The executive summary abstracts, or summarizes, the findings, conclusions, and recommendations in the report. The executive summary is usually one page.

Body of a Formal Report

The body of a formal report includes the introduction, main discussion, and conclusions and recommendations.

Introduction. This first part of the report introduces the main discussion and gives background information on the purpose and scope of the report.

Main Discussion. In this section the writer presents the points under discussion in a logical paragraph format. The main discussion may include tables as well as quotations from outside sources.

Conclusions and Recommendations. This section summarizes the main points of the report. In a persuasive report, recommendations may be treated as a separate section.

Back Matter in a Formal Report

The back matter in a formal report may include one or more elements that provide supplementary information.

Appendixes. This section may include questionnaires, tables, graphics, glossaries, or any other information that supports the research in the report.

Works Cited or References. This section lists information about the reference works that were cited within the body of the report.

Bibliography. The bibliography lists all sources that were consulted in compiling the report, including the sources listed in the Works Cited.

Not all formal reports require all of the sections listed here. Some formal reports may require additional specialized parts that describe the research techniques used, explain the purpose of the study, and so on.

From a public notice that appeared in *U.S.A Today:* The state board of fisheries is considering whether to impose seasonal catch limits on tourists. Who's being caught—fish or tourists?
Source: Reader's Digest

Format for a Formal Report

The format of a formal report varies depending on the nature of the report. Generally, formal reports are double-spaced and have default side (1.25 inch or 1 inch) and bottom (1 inch) margins. A report placed in a binder needs an extra 0.5-inch left margin to allow room for the three-hole punch. Use an approximate 2- inch top margin for front matter pages, the first page of the body of the report, and the first page of each section in the back matter. Use a 1-inch top margin for continuation pages in the body of the report.

Use small roman numerals (i, ii, iii) for page numbers on the front matter pages that appear after the table of contents. Center the page numbers at the bottom margin. The page numbers in the body and the back matter appear in arabic numbers (1, 2, 3). Typically, a page number does not appear on the first page of the report. On the second, third, and consecutive pages of the report and the back matter pages, the page number appears at the upper right corner.

On the title page the copy should be centered horizontally and vertically on the page. Type the title in all-capital letters and bold. If a subtitle is used, type it in initial-capital letters a double-space below the title. Press Enter 12 times below the title or subtitle, whichever is last. Type the words *Prepared by,* leave a blank line, and type the writer's name and identification on separate lines, single-spaced. Press Enter 12 times and type *Submitted to,* leave a blank line, then type the name of the person or persons who requested the report. Double-space and type the date. A sample title page appears in Figure 11-2 on page 233.

The letter or memo of transmittal follows the format for a business letter or an interoffice memorandum. (See Chapter 10.)

For the table of contents, center and type *CONTENTS* or *TABLE OF CONTENTS* in all-capital letters and bold at the 2-inch top margin. Double-space and begin typing the entries in the table of contents. Type the titles of the front matter pages, the headings in the report, and the titles of the back matter pages in all-capital letters at the left margin. Double-space before and after each main heading. Indent 0.5-inch and type subheads in initial-capital and lowercase letters and single-spaced. Align all page numbers at the right margin. Use dot leaders (a series of dots) to align the entries with the page numbers. See Figure 11-3 on page 233. The list of tables and illustrations, if included, follows the guidelines for the table of contents.

The preface or foreword pages and the executive summary all use a similar style. Type the title in all-capital letters and bold, centered at the 2-inch top margin. Begin typing the text a double space below the title, and indent the paragraphs. See the sample executive summary in Figure 11-4 on page 233.

The introduction, main discussion, and conclusions and recommendations all follow the same general guidelines. On the first page, type the title in all-capital letters and bold at the 2-inch top margin, the same as the front matter pages. On the second and subsequent pages, begin typing the text at the 1-inch top margin. Double-space the text.

Paragraphs are indented 0.5-inch for double-spaced reports. If a report is single-spaced, do not use paragraph indents; instead, leave one blank line between paragraphs. For bulleted or numbered lists, align the bullets and the numbers at the left margin. Quotations of four or more lines are single-spaced and indented 0.5 inch from both side margins.

The same types of headings used in memo reports are also used in formal reports. Refer to the discussion of headings on page 227.

The titles of the back matter parts of the report (works cited, bibliography, appendixes, and so on) begin at the 2-inch top margin. The actual supporting documents (glossaries, maps, questionnaires) may be labeled *APPENDIX A, APPENDIX B,* and so on. See the sample bibliography in Figure 11-5 on page 234.

TIPS

CHECKING A FORMAL REPORT

- Title page—Verify the spelling of all names and check the dates. Make sure there is an equal amount of space between elements.

- Table of contents—Check the table of contents against the report itself to make sure the headings and the page numbers match.

- Front matter—Make sure the page numbers are in roman numerals.

- Body of the report—Scan the report and concentrate on the headings to make sure each type of heading is formatted consistently in terms of the alignment and the use of bold or italics.

- Back matter—Make sure the back matter pages have the same top margin as the preliminary pages.

Figure 11-1 (Memo Report)

MEMO TO: Brad Callahan

FROM: Kathryn Lazos

DATE: January 17, <YEAR>

SUBJECT: Copy Center Study

As you requested, I have researched the need for a copy center at our facility.

RECOMMENDATIONS

Based on a review of current copier use plus the need for special copying services, I recommend establishing a full-service copy center at our facility. The copy center would handle large copy jobs as well as monitor the use of self-service copiers.

Full-Service Copying
• Handle production work for sample sales packages and flyers.
• Pick up copy jobs on each floor at established times throughout the day.
• Offer an assortment of binding and finishing options.
• Prepare mailings for large copy orders.

Self-Service Copying
• Restock paper and copier supplies for self-service copiers located on each floor.
• Perform routine software upgrades on self-service copiers.
• Troubleshoot problems with self-service copiers.

I recommend that we request bids from outside vendors on the costs for establishing and maintaining a a full-service copy center. Two potential vendors have been identified—Micro Copy and Impact Copies. The next step would be to request bids from these vendors.

FINDINGS

A review of copier use for the last three months indicates that employees make a combined total of 175,000 copies per week using the current copiers. Several departments, such as marketing and sales, currently send large copy jobs to off-site local copier shops that charge anywhere from 7 to 25 cents a sheet depending on the use of graphics, color, color paper, and special bindings.

Figure 11-1. Memo Report

Figure 11-2 (Title Page)

PROPOSAL FOR A NEW TRANSCRIPTION/DICTATION SYSTEM

FOR

COUNTY GENERAL HOSPITAL

AND AFFILIATES

PREPARED BY

BUSINESS SYSTEMS GROUP

PREPARED FOR

COUNTY GENERAL BOARD OF DIRECTORS

JANUARY 15, <YEAR>

Figure 11-2. Title Page

Figure 11-3 (Table of Contents)

TABLE OF CONTENTS

Figure 11-3. Table of Contents

Figure 11-4 (Executive Summary)

EXECUTIVE SUMMARY

PURPOSE OF THE REPORT

The purpose of this report is to examine the existing dictation/transcription system at County General Hospital and to research voice-recognition alternatives to the current system.

CONCLUSIONS

The current dictation/transcription department at County General Hospital utilizes four separate dictation systems and two separate transcription systems from different manufacturers. Adopting one of the voice-recognition systems researched in this report will streamline the dictation/transcription equipment needed, decrease the transcription time for preparing physicians' reports, and improve the accuracy of the dictation. In addition, the use of a voice-recognition digital dictation system will eliminate the use of costly cassette tapes and digital media.

RECOMMENDATIONS

The following is a summary of the recommendations in this report:

• Purchase Med-Cruiser hand-held dictation units for all physicians at County General Hospital.

• Equip the dictation/transcription department with a voice-recognition digital dictation system.

Figure 11-4. Executive Summary

BIBLIOGRAPHY

"Doctors Without Keyboards: IBM ViaVoice Comes to Assist Medicine." IBM

ViaVoice News. http://www-4.ibm.com/software/speech/news/pr-soluzioni.html.

Accessed 1/25/02.

"Speech Recognition for Medicine" Computer Voice Dictation Solutions, Inc.

http://www.cvds.com/inex2.htm. Accessed 1/14/02.

"Let's Talk!" *Business Week,* February 23, 1998, pp. 60-80.

Figure 11-5. Bibliography

MANUFACTURING DEPARTMENT

Minutes of the Meeting

January 15, <YEAR>

9 a.m. to 10:30 a.m., Conference Room B

PURPOSE	Review status of current projects.
ATTENDANCE	Harold Russell, Janet Hoover, Marcus Dykes, Anna Leland, and Richard DeSantis.
OLD BUSINESS	Harold reported that 86 percent of current projects will meet their scheduled completion dates.
NEW BUSINESS	Discussed the creation of a vendor tracking system. Marcus motioned that a feasibility study be conducted by our business systems group. Anna seconded the motion. We also reviewed the preliminary version of the new purchase order software and compiled written feedback for the programmers.
ADJOURNMENT	The meeting was adjourned at 10:45 a.m. The next meeting is scheduled for February 14 in Conference Room A.

Respectfully submitted,

Janet Hoover, Secretary

Figure 11-6. Meeting Minutes

SOFTWARE TIPS

Although the widow/orphan feature of your software adjusts text to keep single lines from appearing at the top or bottom of a page, this feature will not detect side or paragraph headings in a report that should stay with a particular paragraph. These headings must be moved manually or block protected.

CHECKUP 11-2 Proofread the following table of contents and the first page of the main discussion in a formal report. Use appropriate revision symbols to correct any formatting errors. Pay particular attention to the sequence of items. Assume that the top, side, and bottom margins are correct.

TABLE OF CONTENTS

3

INTRODUCTION

Xxxxxxxxxxxxxxxxxxxxxxxxxxxxxxxxxxxxxxxxxxxxxxxxxxxxxxxxxxxx

xxx xxxxxxxxxxxxxxxxxxxxxxxxxxxxxxxxxxxxxxxxxxxxxxxxxxxxxxx xxxx

xxx xxx xxxxxxxxxxxxxxx.

Xxxxxxxxxxxxxxxxxxxxxxxxxxxxxxx xxxxxxxxxxxxxx xxxxxxxx xxxx
xx xxxxxxxxxxxxxxxxxxxxxxxxxxxxxxxxxxxxxxx xxxxxxxxxxxxxx
xxxxxxxxxxxx xx.

FIRST MAIN HEADING

Xxxxxxxxxxxxxxxxxxxxxxxx xxxxxxxxxxxxxxxxxxxxxxx xxxxxxxxx xxxxxx

xxxxxxxxxxxxxxxxxxxxxxxxxxxxxxxxxxxxxxxxxxxxxxxxxxxxxxxxxxx xxxx

xxxxx xxxxxxxxxxxxxxxxxxxxxxxxxxxxxxxxxxxxxxxxxxxxxxxxxxx.

Side HEADING

Xxxxxxxxxxxxxxxxxxxxxxxxx xxxxxxxxxxx xxxxxxxxxxxxxxx xxxx xxx xx

xxxxxxxxxxxxxxxxxxxxx xxxxxxxxxxx xxxxxxxxxxx xxxxxxxxxxxx

Paragraph Heading. Xxxxxxxxxxxxxxxxxxxxxxxxxxxxxxxxxxxxxxxxxxx

xxxxxxxxxxxxxxxxxxxxxxxxxxxxxxxxxxxxx.

Paragraph Heading Xxxxxxxxxxxxxxxxxxxxxxxxxxxxxxxxxxxxxxxxx

xxxxx xxxxxxxxxxxxxxxxxxxxxxxxxx. Xxxxxxxxxxxxxxxx xxxxxxxxxxxxxxx

xxxx xxxxxxx xxxxxx x xxxxxxxxxxxxxx. Xxxxxxxx xxxxxxxxx xx

xxxxxxxxxx xxxxxxx xx xxxxxxxx.

i

Styles for Citing References

References cited and the bibliography contain basic components—author(s), title, date published, page numbers, and publication information.

The report writer may use one of several citation styles—MLA (Modern Language Association), APA (American Psychological Association), Chicago (*The Chicago Manual of Style*), or another documented style. It's important to use the same style consistently throughout the report. Manuals for each of these styles may be purchased or borrowed from a library. Sample entries formatted in the MLA, APA, and Chicago styles are shown here.

MLA Style. The Modern Language Association (MLA) style for citations follows these general guidelines:

A citation within a report lists the author's last name and the page number in parentheses.

> "Many times, the statistical information does not reflect the over-all impact of the technological changes we face today" (Billings 311).

Entries in the Works Cited at the end of the report are listed alphabetically according to the author's last name. Each entry includes the author's name, the title of the work, and publication information. The first line of each entry begins at the left margin; the second and succeeding lines are indented 0.5 inch. Double-space the entries.

> Alwang, Gregg. "Speech: Ready for Prime Time?" <u>PC Magazine</u> 19 Jan. 1999: 80.

> Billings, James T. <u>How Technology Affects Us Today</u>. Houston: Bethany Publishing Co., 1999.

APA Style. The American Psychological Association (APA) style for citations follows these general guidelines:

Citations within a report include the author's last name and the year of publication in parentheses. A page number is given if a quotation is being cited.

> "Many times, the statistical information does not reflect the over-all impact of the technological changes we face today" (Billings, 1999, p. 31).

Net Link

For information on the MLA, APA, and Chicago styles for citations, go to the Web site for each organization using the URLs listed here.
<u>MLA:</u> **http://www.mla .org/main_stl.htm**
<u>APA:</u> **http://www.apa .org/journals/faq.html**
<u>Chicago:</u> **http://www .press.uchicago.edu /Misc/Chicago /cmosfaq.html**
To locate additional information on citation styles, use a search engine and the key-words "citing sources," "online citations," or "documenting sources."

Entries in the Reference List of sources actually cited are listed alphabetically by author's last name. Include the author's name, the title of the work, and publication information for each entry. Begin the first line of each entry at the left margin; the second and succeeding lines are indented 0.5 inch. Double-space the entries.

Alwang, Gregg. (1999, January 19). Speech: Ready for Prime Time? PC Magazine, 80.

Billings, James T. (1999). How Technology Affects Us Today. Houston: Bethany Publishing Co.

Chicago Style. The Chicago style for citations, developed by the University of Chicago Press, follows these general guidelines:

A citation within a report may be indicated by a superscript number that refers to an entry in the Endnotes with the same number.

"Many times, the statistical information does not reflect the overall impact of the technological changes we face today."[2]

Endnotes or Notes at the end of a report are listed alphabetically by the author's last name and include the title of the work and publication information. Indent the second and succeeding lines of an entry 0.5 inch and double-space the entries.

[1]Alwang, Gregg. 1999. Speech: Ready for Prime Time? *PC Magazine*, 19 January, 80.

[2]Billings, James T. *How Technology Affects Us Today* (Houston: Bethany Publishing Co., 1999), 311.

Online Citations. Online citations are used to cite material taken from electronic sources such as Web sites on the Internet as well as e-mail messages. When listing source information for an online citation, be sure to include the following basic parts:

- author's name

- title of the document

- title of the complete work

- date the document was posted

- the complete URL (the address for a particular Web site) or the e-mail address, enclosed in angle brackets: < >

- the date the source was accessed

Sample entry for a book published online:

> Billings, James T. *How Technology Affects Us Today*. Online.
>
> Bethany Publishing. 14 Oct. 1999,
>
> <http://www.bethany.com/billings
>
> /tech/~23.

For more information on citing references taken from online sources, consult a reference manual such as the ninth edition of *The Gregg Reference Manual* by William A. Sabin, Glencoe/McGraw-Hill.

TIPS

PROOFREADING WORKS CITED AND REFERENCES

- Pay attention to the style used for citing references; make sure the style is used consistently.

- Check each entry to make sure it includes all the necessary elements (author's name, title of the work, and so on).

- Check the information in each citation against the original source document.

CHECKUP 11-3 Proofread the following *Chicago Manual of Style* endnotes. In the space provided, indicate the one item that is missing or incorrect in each.

1. Laura Cummings, What a Wonderful Way to Go! (New York: EKS Book Co., 1997), 255.

   _____

2. Gunnell, George B. "Working Out," *Body by George* (Lord Printing, 1995), 152.

   _____

3. Hayes, N. Barbara, *Technology: A Way of Life in Year 2000* Salem: Hudson & Co., 1996, 95.

   _____

Proofread the following entries from an MLA Works Cited list or APA Reference List. In the space provided, indicate the one item that is missing or incorrect in each.

4. Johnson, Ralph - *Teaching Your Child at Home.* Detroit: Lyons
    Publishing House, 1999.

---

5. Mathes, Rhonda. (1999). *How to Ensure a Profitable Home
    Business.* Los Angeles, CA: Leeds Books

OTHER MULTIPLE-PAGE DOCUMENTS

In addition to memo reports and formal reports, other multiple-page documents you might proofread include meeting minutes and manuscripts.

Meeting Minutes

Minutes of a meeting reflect the proceedings and decisions made during a meeting. Minutes may be single or double spaced with the title of the meeting appearing at the 1.5- to 2-inch top margin.

Meeting minutes contain an introduction, body, and conclusion—just like a report. The introduction gives background information, such as the day, date, time, and location of the meeting and the names of the people absent and present. The body includes a description of what happened at the meeting. The conclusion describes the actions and decisions to be discussed at the next meeting.

Meeting minutes may use an informal format, where the minutes are typed as a memo, or they may use a formal format, such as the one illustrated in Figure 11-6 on page 234.

Manuscripts

Manuscripts are documents prepared for submission to a publisher. Manuscripts generally follow guidelines similar to the report format. The title on the first page appears at the 2-inch top margin. Subsequent pages begin at the 1-inch top margin. Side and bottom margins are generally 1 inch. Normally, manuscripts require double spacing and indented paragraphs. Headings are used to identify sections within the book, chapter, or article being prepared. Manuscripts are formatted according to the publisher's guidelines. When proofreading manuscripts, look for consistency in how headings are formatted as well as consistency in aligning copy at the margins.

Application 11-A

Use appropriate revision symbols to correct formatting errors in the following two-page memo report. The report uses side and paragraph headings.

MEMO TO: Mr. Calvin Rains, President

FORM: L. Linda Cooper, Maintenance Supervisor

DATE: August 24, <YEAR>

SUBJECT: Annual Facilities Study

The Maintenance Department has concluded its facilities study of our entire complex. The following discussion documents our findings and presents our recommendations for updating and/or repairing the existing facilities.

ADMINISTRATION BUILDING

Carpeting. The carpeting, installed in 1995, shows signs of wear. A high-traffic area such as this requires that carpeting be replaced every 3–4 years. Recommendation: Replace with a high-grade commercial carpet. Cost estimate: 5,000 sq. ft. at $23 = $115,000.

Windows. The original windows, circa 1985, continue to waste valuable electricity. A 1995 study determined that escaping air conditioning and heating cost more than $10,000 per year. Recommendation: Replace the 75 windows with DuraWindows. Cost estimate: $15,000. (Cost recovery period would be less than two years.)

Furnishings. The seating areas in the lobby appear worn and dated. The last refurbishing of the sofas, chairs, desks, and tables occurred in 1994. Recommendation: Purchase new furnishings for the seating areas. Cost estimate with trade-in on old furnishings: $21,000.

Application 11-A (continued)

Mr. Calvin Rains   2   August 24, <YEAR>

MANUFACTURING Building
Flooring. The tile has become unsightly and dangerous due to excessive chipping and peeling. Recommendation: After several attempts to repair the danger spots, it appears to be more economical to replace the flooring. Cost estimate: 12,000 sq. ft. at $20 = $240,000.

Doors. The two overhead doors on the west side of the building have warped; therefore, workers have difficulty opening and closing them each day. Repair estimates rival the cost of replacement. Recommendation: Replace the doors. Cost estimate: $2,400.

Restroom Facilities. Although the ADA (American Disabilities Act) required updating these facilities in 1995, employees have indicated a need for additional lavatories. Recommendation: Install three additional lavatories. Estimated architectural and plumbing installation costs: $15,000.

Supply Room. A recent OSHA inspection revealed a safety hazard

in the supply room that must be repaired. Estimated Cost: $500.

RECREATION BUILDING
Exercise Equipment. The treadmills and stationary bicycles, purchased in 1993, have become unusable. Recommendation: Replace three treadmills and five stationary bicycles. Cost Estimate: $5,200.

bk

Application 11-B

Proofread the following manuscript for a newsletter article. Use appropriate revision symbols to correct formatting errors. The manuscript should be double-spaced.

HOW TO BECOME A SOUGHT-AFTER
(AND HIGHLY PAID)
ADMINISTRATIVE ASSISTANT

So now you have finished your college training and accepted that dream position. How do you keep the momentum going and get those raises and promotions? Here's how:

Act Like a Professional

Be that person who never takes supplies home. **Be ethical!** Be that person who never says anything bad about anybody. **Refuse to gossip!** Be that person who always wears a smile and never complains. **Be pleasant!** Be that person who minds his or her own business. **Respect others' privacy!**

Look Like a Professional

Wear that good quality suit, those polished shoes, that tasteful hairstyle. Women, be sure your jewelry and other accessories are appropriate. Men, leave out the earrings until you find out if they are acceptable to wear in the office.

Work Like a Professional

Be pleasant, be prepared, and one more BIG thing: do your work efficiently and correctly.

Your Workspace. Keep only the essentials (telephone, legal pad, pen and pencil, and the current work) on your desk. Leave files and projects in your desk drawer or filing cabinet until you need them. When you leave your workstation, push your chair under the desk.

The MAIL. Open and distribute the mail as soon as it arrives. If you open mail for others, place the mail in order of importance with the most important pieces on top.

Your Documents. Develop your own trademark style (but nothing too flashy!). Attractively formatted documents say that you care about your work—that you are a professional who takes pride in what you do.

Application 11-B (continued)

2

Learn to compose e-mail messages that are both brief and well-written. A sloppy or error-filled e-mail message says that you didn't take the time or pride in your work to think the message out before writing it.

Your Phone Manners. Have you ever been "turned off" to a company because of a rude representative of that company? Do just the opposite. Be polite, be patient, and smile when you answer the phone in order to convey a pleasant tone.

It is just as important to be professional with your voice mail. When you leave a message on someone's voice mail, **speak clearly and say your phone number slowly.** If someone cannot identify your name or phone number, your message is useless.

Your Proofreading. Proofreading can make or break a million-dollar deal. If you want to make an impression with your company, always produce **accurate documents.** Sure, we all make an error now and then, but that's just it—it should be only now and then.

Personal Matters. Refrain from sending cute little sayings or chain messages as e-mail—such messages aren't part of the company's business. If you avoid such gimmicks, you will be taken more seriously.

Arrive at work on time, and put in a full day's work! Don't make a habit of leaving early each work day. **Reliability counts!**

Do what you say you will do by the time or date you promised. **Dependability counts!**

Pitch in—never say, "It's not my job." It takes everyone to get the job done. **Teamwork counts!**

Application 11-C

Proofread the following meeting minutes. Use appropriate revision symbols to correct formatting errors as well as any other types of errors. Refer to Figure 11-6 on page 234 as a guide.

ADVISORY COMMITTEE MEETING

January 27, <YEAR>

Present: Janie Williams, CPS; Patricia Stevenson, Aaron Industries; Jim Andrews, JA Enterprises; D. H. Perkins, White Corporation; Alice Weber, Graphics Plus; and Milton Berry, R & I, Inc.

Absent: Tessa O'Brien, Andrew Company.

Janie Williams called the meeting to order at 1 p.m.. The committee discussed the following agenda items.

MINUTES

The committee reviewed the minutes from the last meeting. Patricia *Stevenson* noted that her name appeared incorrectly as *Stephenson*. The committee noted the change and approved the minutes as corrected.

SOFTWARE UPDATE

The committee recommended that the Data-Visions Technology Center update its software to better prepare students entering the workforce. Jim Andrews agreed to study the software market and to present his findings at the next meeting. D. H. Perkin's agreed to study employment needs and to bring that report to the next meeting.

HARDWARE UP DATE

After much discussion, the committee agreed that the Data-Visions Technology Center would be able to use its existing equipment for at least one or too more budget cycles. Everyone believed that the hardware would support any new software upgrades.

CURRICULUM

Application 11-C (continued)

Advisory Meeting Minutes   Page 2

Several committee members expressed concern whether the existing curriculum reflected today's needs. Do we provide graduates with the necessary job skills? Patricia Stevenson mentioned spelling, proofreading, and grammar skills as weaknesses in producing documents. Millie Berry also noted that some of the graduates exhibited an inability to get to work on time. Milton reminded the committee that punctuality and absenteeism represent the main reasons people loose their jobs. Janie Williams suggested adding a course to the curriculum that would encompass behavioral skills associated with getting and keeping a job. Janie offered the following course topics: punctuality, absenteeism, office politics, and oral and written communication skills. Alice Weber and Jim Andrews agreed to draft a course outline to present at the next meeting.

OTHER

Alice asked about current enrollment figures. Janie responded that she would investigate.

With no further discussion, the meeting adjourned at 3:15 p. m.

Respectfully submitted,

_____
D. H. Perkins, Recording Secretary

Application 11-D

Proofread the following academic report. Use appropriate revision symbols to correct formatting errors as any well as other types of errors.

Thomasson 1

Shelby R. Thomasson

Professor B. Massengale

Government 1312

December 3, <YEAR>

VOTER PARTICIPATION IN

HOUSTON TEXAS

In the past 20 years, voter turnout has never been higher than 50 percent in Houston, Texas. Why do so few people vote? Could it be "political socialization", a persons beliefs about politics? According to Councilman Pete Erickson "People just do not care what goes on." (97)

In past years high numbers of minorities did not go to the polls. However, in the recent mayoral election the minority vote accounted for more than 35 percent of the total turnout. This surprised and pleased local politicians. According to a recent news article, Mayor Hortense Platt said, "It's wonderful since large numbers of minorities in Houston have never shown much interest in our elections. Traditionally, only about 10 percent of minorities have voted." (Jeter 5

In order to encourage more people to participate, local politicians have proposed the following changes

- Expansion of voting by mail
- Community involvement

Application 11-D (continued)

- Tax credits

- Corporate assistance

According to an editorial in the *Houston Times Tribune*, the vote by mail program should be expanded:

> Voting by mail would benefit people in many ways. It would be less inconvenient. Instead of standing in long lines at the poll, working people could vote in the comfort of their own homes. It would also spare the handicapped people the inconvenience of having to get out of the house and allow more handicapped people the opportunity to get involved. (Kirkpatrick 1)

More community involvement would also help to increase voter participation. Dr F. A. Waller of Houston International College wrote:

> The people in the community need to feel that they contribute to the community. If they participate in campaigns and other political functions, they will more likely vote. For example, inspiring the community to support interest in the candidates will create friendly battles between political factions. More people would become aware of candidates that they might not have known existed. They would have a sense of what's going on through their neighbors and friends. It follows, then, that many of the newly educated people will in turn cast a vote. (Waller 159)

Another suggestion for increasing voter participation is to give tax credits to those who vote. As Bertha L. Lampkins so bluntly wrote, "Who wants to pay high taxes? If the government will give me something for free, or just for voting, heck, I'll do it!" (Lampkins 25)

In order for a taxpayer to prove that he or she voted, a simple receipt or other proof of vote would be available when the voter's ballot is recorded.

Application 11-D (continued)

Local corporations could also help in raising the voter participation numbers. Businesses could offer every person who votes an incentive—a 10% off voucher to any retail store or a substantial discount of its own products. This would encourage voter participation in all age groups. The Local Coalition of Businesses (TLCOB) has not yet given its approval to this idea: "TLCOB plans to survey the business community to get their reaction to this idea." (Sharp 8)

One local politician advocates fining citizens who do not vote. He writes:

> The law should read: "It is every persons [sic] duty
> as a citizen to register and vote if eligible. If a citizen
> chooses not to obey the law, then measures should
> be taken. Fining people who do not vote would be a
> good step in protecting this law."

(*Youngblood*)

Although considered a bizarre idea by some, the idea seems to be gaining in popularity among several factions of the political community.

Voter participation in Houston remains low compared to the number of eligible voters. Politicians and citizens should develop tactics to increase voter participation. If people get educated, they will get involved. If people see some incentive for voting, they will be involved.

Thomasson 3

Application 11-D (continued)

WORKS CITED

Erickson, Peter Lawrence. *Caring No More: Local Politics*, Houston:

Bayou Publishing, 1999

Jeter, Dan F. "Local Turnout Excellent." *The Houston Times*, Weekly

Edition, 4 Nov. 1999, weekly ed.: Metropolitan 5.

Kirkpatrick, Larry. "Voting by Mail?," *Houston Times Tribune*, 20

March 1999, Local News Section.

Lampkins, Bertha L. **The Texas Political Scene.** Austin: Texas

Publishing, 1999.

Landon P. Sharp "Giving the Local Voters Incentive," *The Local*

Coalition of Businesses Review, Vol. 23, No. 3, September–

October 1999.

Waller, F. A. "The Socialization of the Voter." New Orleans: Pharaoh

Printing Company, 1998.

Youngblood, Rodney D. "Throw 'Em in Jail if They Don't Vote."

Underground Citizens Online. Internet. 24 March 1999.

Available http://www.undergroundcit.org.

CD-ROM Application 11-E

This application contains the title page, letter of transmittal, table of contents, and executive summary for a formal report. Open the file DPES11E from the CD-ROM. Assume that the page numbers in the table of contents on the CD-ROM are correct. Scan the pages for any formatting errors. Make your corrections; then save and print a copy of the corrected document. The remainder of this report appears in CD-ROM Application 11-F.

**INTERNATIONAL EXPANSION
A FEASIBILITY STUDY**

**Prepared by
L. Brenda Goss
Vice President, Marketing
INTERNATIONAL CONSULTANTS INC.**

Submitted to

**Mr. Edward F. Baliff
Chairman of the Board
AMERICAN TRAINING INCORPORATED**

March 25, <YEAR>

CD-ROM Application 11-E (continued)

The following letter of transmittal should be formatted in the block style with standard punctuation.

_____

March 25, <YEAR>

Mr. Edward F. Baliff
Chairman of the Board
American Training Incorporated
1414 South Lake Avenue
San Antonio, TX 78258

Dear Mr. Baliff

The enclosed report on the feasibility of expanding American Training Incorporated's business operations internationally concludes my team's six-month investigation.

We have performed a comprehensive study of the international situation as relates to your company's goals. We appreciate the opportunity to work with ATI in such an exciting endeavor.

When you have had a chance to read the report, we will be glad to arrange a meeting to discuss how to proceed.

Sincerely,

L. Brenda Goss

Vice President, Marketing

bk

CD-ROM Application 11-F

This application contains the body and back matter pages for the report begun in CD-ROM Application 11-E. (The first two pages of the report are shown here.) Open the file DPES11F from the CD-ROM. Scan the pages for any formatting errors; then carefully proofread for other types of errors. Make your corrections; then run the spell and grammar checkers. Save and print a corrected copy of the report.

INTERNATIONAL EXPANSION: A FEASIBILITY STUDY

INTRODUCTION

The marketing team of International Consultants Inc. (ICI) began an analysis of the feasibility of expanding the sales of American Training Incorporated (ATI) products into international markets. Mexico and Canada appeared to be the logical initial markets; however, the studies showed that other Latin American countries should also be considered further

The marketing team determined strategies and media for advertising the products in each of the prospective countries, as well as locations of sales. The team also made a thorough study of workforce availability.

ICI's Legal Department supported the research and investigated all aspects of international law as pertinent to this business proposal.

FINDINGS AND ANALYSIS

Markets and Stability

Potential markets considered for expansion fit into five general areas: Latin America, Canada, Western Europe, Japan, and China. The marketing team, along with Legal counsel, immediately disqualified other areas of Europe and Asia due to political instability. The following table lists the eligible countries, with political and economic stability ratings from Jones-Dillard Rating Service:

CD-ROM Application 11-F (continued)

TABLE 1.1		
COUNTRY	POLITICAL STABILITY	ECONOMIC STABILITY
Canada (all provinces)	superior	excellent
China	excellent	good
Columbia	volatile	fair
Finland	good	good
France	fair	good
Germany	good	good
Great Britain	excellent	excellent
Guatemala	fair	fair
Ireland	good	good
Japan	fair	fair
Mexico	good	good
Panama	fair	fair
Scotland	good	good
Switzerland	excellent	excellent

Because of the proximity of Mexico and Canada to the U.S. and their acceptable ratings, the team determined that international expansion should begin with these two countries. A discussion of the investigation of each country follows.

Mexico. Although political turmoil and economic disaster have occurred in Mexico in the past, the current outlook seems excellent. Political leaders encourage American business by allowing a tax rebate of 3 percent on every sales dollar.   The ratio of the dollar to the peso remains favorable. In addition, the construction of the Trans-Mexican highway will be completed next year.

Canada The U.S. enjoys excellent relations with the current Canadian administration. The economic advisors to the prime minister have expressed a desire to work with the company in this endeavor. Construction on the Trans-Canadian highway appears to be nearing completion.

Proofreading Statistical and Technical Documents

OBJECTIVES

After completing this chapter, you should be able to:

1. Detect errors in special number formats such as percentages, calculations, and measurements.

2. Proofread tables, spreadsheets, and databases to ensure accuracy.

3. Proofread specialized forms such as invoices and purchase orders to ensure accuracy.

Chapter 12 discusses the types of errors commonly found in statistical and technical documents. Spreadsheets, databases, invoices, and other detailed documents must be accurate to avoid costly and embarrassing mistakes. Finding errors in such complicated material proves especially challenging.

This chapter will alert you to the types of errors that may occur in statistical and technical documents—from using the incorrect technical term to making a mistake in a calculation. Learning what types of errors to look for will fine-tune your ability to detect errors in these types of documents.

PROOFREADING FOR ACCURACY

Technical material involves numbers and statistics—information that is critical to making business decisions. An error on an invoice, spreadsheet, or database can cost a company profits and goodwill. A decimal out of place, a missing or additional figure, or a transposed figure could make a significant difference. For example, a number on a bid proposal intended to be $3500 but typed as $350 would cost the company $3150.

Many times the information in statistical and technical documents is taken from an original, or source, document. An example of this would be taking sales figures from individual reports and compiling the data in a spreadsheet. Proofreading the material would involve comparing the figures in the spreadsheet with the original data.

Some documents combine text, numbers, and specialized terms that are technical or statistical in nature. To confirm the accuracy of such information, use the following proofreading methods:

- Verify factual information by checking an appropriate source. Some examples of factual information are names, dates, units of measurement, and symbols for chemical elements. For example,

    Should the symbol for water be H^2O or H_2O?

- Check to make sure specialized terms are used correctly. Look up the meaning of such terms in a dictionary or other appropriate reference book. For example,

    We need to determine the *liquidity* of our assets.

- Proofread each part of a document—text, numbers, and technical terms—as a separate step. Read through the text, check the statistics, and then verify the technical terms. For example, proofreading the following table would involve checking the part number first, then the part name, and then the function.

Net Link

A variety of Web sites offer information on specialized terms. For example, you can find out the meaning of legal terms using Nolo's Law Dictionary at **www.nolo.com /dictionary/wordindex .cfm.**

PART NO.	PART NAME	FUNCTION
XR7-8261	Intake manifold	Channels flow of fuel and air to combustion chamber
PS2908	Harmonic balancer	Balances the engine crank for optimal engine performance
EL4831	Solenoid	Controls operation of electrical devices

- Be aware of the number of digits in particular types of numbers. For example, Social Security numbers have 9 digits: 000-00-0000; post office box numbers usually have 5 digits: 00000. Count the number of characters (letters and/or numbers) to make sure no extra characters are added or no characters are missing. For Example,

    Vehicle Identification Number (VIN)

    4890CP3482958746357890

- Check for alignment errors when proofreading lists of numbers. For example, numbers with decimals should align on the decimal point; numbers with dollar signs should align the dollar signs.

      345,189.269 $1,510.00

   1,560,208.32493 $ 853.95

- Verify any calculations that involve addition, subtraction, multiplication, or division. Such calculations are used to determine amounts on invoices and totals on financial documents, to name a few examples.

PRODUCT NAME	QUANTITY PURCHASED	UNIT COST	TOTAL
Pencils, Boxed	36 Boxes	$1.99	$ 71.64
Pens, Boxed	12 Boxes	$3.99	$ 47.88
		Total	$119.52

SOFTWARE TIPS

The *table* feature of most document processing software allows you to set a decimal tab to ensure the proper alignment of numbers containing decimals.

Complete the following exercise to practice your skill at proofreading numbers.

CHECKUP 12-1   The cars in the handwritten list are being placed on the year-end clearance sale list in this order: Mercedes, BMW, and Volvo. For each car make, the cars should be listed from the oldest model year to the newest. Cars with the same model year will be sequenced from highest to lowest mileage. Proofread the printed list against the handwritten list. Use revision symbols to mark corrections in the printed list.

1985 300 TD Mercedes; White; Red; 130,320 (mileage); 11,300 (price)

1987 300 SDL; Mercedes; Blue; Gray; 154,332 (mileage); 14,800 (price)

1989 300E Mercedes; Yellow; Cream; 100,940 (mileage); 12,500 (price)

1995 S320 Mercedes; Silver; Gray; 101,002 (mileage); 43,500 (price)

1995 E3210 Mercedes; Green; Tan; 100,200 (mileage); 29,500 (price)

1994 325I BMW; Green; Tan; 36,299 (mileage); 24,950 (price)

1995 Z3CV BMW; Gray; Black; 27,914 (mileage); 25,900 (price)

1990 760T Volvo; White; Tan; 124,895; (mileage); 9,500 (price)

1995 850T Volvo; Black; Cream; 49,624 (mileage); 22,900 (price)

1996 850T Volvo; Black; Cream; 47,254 (mileage); 23,900 (price)

1996 850T Volvo; Pewter; Cream; 42,750 (mileage); 23,900 (price)

1997 960 Volvo; Pewter; Gray; 32,650 (mileage); 25,500 (price)

1997 960 Volvo; Blue; Cream; 29,759 (mileage); 26,000 (price)

1998 S70 Volvo; Blue; Tan; 45,500 (mileage); 24,500 (price)

SPECIAL YEAR-END CLEARANCE						
Sell Ends December 31						
Year	Model	Make	Ext. Color	Int. Color	Mileage	Price
1985	300TD	Mercedes	White	Red	130,320	11,300
1987	300SDL	Mercedes	Blue	Gray	154,332	14,800
1989	300E	Mercedes	Yellow	Cream	100940	12,500
1995	E3210	Mercedes	Green	Tan	100,200	29,500
1995	S320	Mercedes	Silver	Gray	101,002	43,500
1094	3251	BMW	Green	Tan	36,299	24,950
1995	Z3CV	BMW	Gray	Black	27,914	25,900
1995	850T	Volvo	Black	Cream	49,624	22,900
1996	850T	Volvo	Black	Cream	47,254	23,900
1996	850T	Volvo	Peuter	Cream	42,750	23,900
1997	960	Volvo	Blue	Cream	28,759	26,000
1997	960	Volvo	Pewter	Gray	32,650	25,500
1989	S70	Volvo	White	Cream	46,650	23,800
1098	S70	Volvo	Blue	Tan	45,500	25,400

Special Number Formats

Percentages, calculations, and measurements present an additional challenge in proofreading numbers. You must verify each number against the original source as well as double-check all calculations and measurements. You can do this by using a calculator.

Be familiar with the units of measurement used in your line of work, such as feet, yards, milligrams, and cubic tons. Refer to a dictionary or other reference for a list of common measurements.

Complete the following exercise to test your ability to check calculations involving measurements.

The College of Chemistry at the University of California, Berkeley, offers a list of common weights and measures on its Web site. Go to **http://www.cchem .berkeley.edu /ChemResources /Weights-n-Measures /index.html** for a comprehensive list of U.S. measurements and their metric equivalents.

CHECKUP 12-2 The following chart lists the figures for converting inches to feet and feet to yards (12 inches = 1 foot; 3 feet = 1 yard). Proofread the figures in the second and third columns (the figures in the first column are correct). To check the figures in the "Number of Feet" column, divide the number in the "Number of Inches" column by 12. To check the figures in the "Number of Yards" column, divide the number of feet in the second column by 3. Use revision symbols to mark corrections.

CONVERSION CHART

NUMBER OF INCHES	NUMBER OF FEET	NUMBER OF YARDS
89	7.47	2.472
3568	297.333	199.111
5984	489.667	166.222
6660	555	185

In addition to working with measurements, you should know how to perform basic calculations, such as converting a number to a percentage. To convert a number to a percentage, multiply the number by 100. For example, multiplying the number .67 by 100 would give you an answer of 67 percent.

Complete the following exercise to test your ability to check calculations involving percentages.

CHECKUP 12-3 Verify the following conversions of numbers to percentages in the chart on page 260. Place a check mark beside each number in the "Percent" column that is correct. Use appropriate revision symbols to mark corrections.

NUMBER	PERCENT
.25	25%
45.	450%
.057	57%
1.75	.0175%
.0365	36.5%

Tables

Data that is listed in a table presents an extra proofreading challenge. In addition to checking factual information, you must make sure that the material in the columns and rows is formatted consistently. For example, are all numbers aligned at the right? Are all numbers with decimals aligned on the decimal? Is boldface used consistently for column headings? Are all column headings aligned in the same way? That is, are they all centered, aligned at left, or aligned at right?

TIPS

PROOFREADING COLUMNS AND ROWS

To make it easier to proofread material that appears in columns and rows, use a ruler or a piece of paper as a guide. Line up the rule or paper along the edge to guide your eyes down a column or across a row. Using the guide will help you concentrate on small segments of material at a time.

CHECKUP 12-4 Proofread the following table for any formatting errors dealing with alignment and consistency in the use of boldface and italics. (The column headings and the row headings should be in boldface). Also look for any errors in spacing and in formatting numbers. Use appropriate revision symbols from the inside front cover to mark corrections. If a row has no errors, put a check mark in the answer column.

	North	South	East	West		Answer
Division A	115,000	120,000	118000	21,000		1. _____
Division B	23,000	90,000	54,000	77,000		2. _____
Division C	80,000	106,000	83,000	110,500		3. _____
Division D	60,000	85,000	73,000	441,000		4. _____
Division E	54,000	0	35,000	60,000		5. _____
Division F	111,000	130,000	185,000	38,500		6. _____
Division G	93,400	65400	95,000	28,000		7. _____
Division H	103,000	112,400	38,700	248,930		8. _____
						9. _____
Division I	87,350	94,600	53,200	31,430		10. _____

PROOFREADING SPECIALIZED DOCUMENTS

Spreadsheets, databases, and forms such as invoices and purchase orders contain numbers and calculations that must be proofread carefully to ensure the information is correct.

Spreadsheets

A *spreadsheet*, a tool used to make business decisions, can be computerized or paper based. Spreadsheets display data in a series of columns and rows, allowing the user to analyze and evaluate information easily. Spreadsheets (also called worksheets) are used for financial reporting, inventory management, and other accounting functions. For example, spreadsheets may be used to list the sales history for a product.

A computer spreadsheet contains a formula feature that is used to perform automatic calculations. You must pay particular attention to these documents because managers depend on the accuracy of these reports in making decisions. A sample computerized spreadsheet follows:

An official for a festival reported that a recent event attracted $85,000 people and raised 50,000. Should it be the other way around? (Were there 50,000 attendees and was $85,000 raised?)

	A	B	C	D
1	ANN'S ALMOST ANTIQUES Profit per Item Statement			
2	Product	Price	Cost	Profit
3	Armoire	1,500	1,175	325
4	Sideboard	975	500	475
5	English tea set	450	200	250
6			Total Profit	1,050

Verify all figures in the totals column in the following spreadsheet. In the answer column, place a check mark beside accurate totals. Use revision symbols to mark corrections to inaccurate totals.

	A	B	C	D	E		Answer
1	REGIONAL SALES BY QUARTER						
2		JAN	FEB	MAR	TOTAL		
3	A1 Distributing	2,200.15	1,890.71	1,751.23	5,842.09	1.	_____
4	AB Engineering	1,784.66	1,273.88	1,656.82	4,751.36	2.	_____
5	Absolute Enterprises	2,974.84	3,007.51	4,476.02	10,458.27	3.	_____
6	Action Supply	8,105.33	7,064.84	6,968.40	22,138.57	4.	_____
7	Collin Industries	5,689.90	3,475.89	6,597.33	15,763.12	5.	_____
8	Crown, Etc.	12,890.11	7,999.34	8,587.89	29,447.34	6.	_____
9	Engle, Ltd.	8,974.68	3,467.99	7,878.80	20,321.47	7.	_____
10	Tex-OK Planning	2,288.00	2,973.08	2,305.97	7,657.05	8.	_____
11	United, Inc.	3,216.88	3,462.33	3,598.76	10,277.97	9.	_____
12	Westside Company	12,884.88	10,986.44	11,178.99	35,050.31	10.	_____

Databases

A company's files may be computerized or paper based or both. Computerized filing systems, often called *databases*, allow for easy entry and retrieval of information. Companies use databases to maintain customer lists, inventory lists, and employee rosters. Databases present challenges to the proofreader due to the massive quantity of material to be verified. Since databases are updated on a continuing basis, you must proofread carefully to ensure accuracy.

Item Number	Description	Cost	Circa	Condition
A495	English tea set	$250	1910	Good; one cup chipped
A515	Sideboard	$550	1890	Excellent
A537	Armoire	$1175	1845	Good

The following table represents correct inventory information. Using revision symbols, mark any corrections in the inventory database that follows the table.

PRODUCT CODE	QUANTITY	COST	INVENTORY TOTAL
TX438190	14	8.99	125.86
GTX230984	23	2.43	55.89
HTX983658	62	1.89	117.18
STX3869047	45	7.24	325.80
ITX1245779	89	6.45	574.05
LTX0986875	123	3.33	409.59
ZTX56984327	92	7.11	654.12
PTX09856984	44	2.59	113.96

	Product Code	Quantity	Cost	Inventory Total
	TX438190	14	8.98	125.86
	GTX230948	23	2.43	55.89
	HTX983658	62	1.89	117.18
	SX3869047	54	7.24	352.89
	ITX124579	89	6.45	574.05
	LTX0986875	123	3.33	409.59
	ZTX56984327	92	7.17	654.12
	PTX9856984	44	2.59	133.96

Forms

Other technical documents that challenge the proofreader include purchase orders, invoices, payroll registers, expense reports, and any other document that includes calculations and material that is organized according to special headings or formats.

Complete the following exercise to test your ability to check calculations in a specialized form.

Proofread the following invoice.
Be sure to check the calculations in the total column. Assume that the
quantities, the unit prices, and tax and freight charges are correct.
Use revision symbols from the inside front cover to mark corrections

---

North Star Computers
564 Buckeye Avenue
Lansing, Michigan 48915
517-555-8787 (phone or fax)

INVOICE

Invoice #: 1152
Date: 2/15/02
Customer ID: 0935

Bill To:

Orion Graphics
45 Starlight Way
Columbus, Ohio 43240

Ship To:

45 Starlight Way
Columbus, Ohio 43240

Your #	Our #	Sales Rep	FOB	SHIP VIA	Terms
15-A	257	B. Williams	Lansing	Midwest Freight	net 30 days

Qty	Item	Units	Description	Unit Pr	Total
2	1	45A	MegaPro Printer 1500 AX	$329.95	$ 659.99
3	2	76B	OptiView 215 17-inch monitor	$455.95	$1,357.85
3	3	93C	Askar MIL 5200 digital camera	$229.45	$ 688.35

Subtotal	$2,706.10
Tax	$ 216.48
Freight	$ 180.25
Misc	
Bal Due	$3,102.73

Application 12-A

A draft of an income statement for Internet Travel Company for August follows. Using the handwritten draft as the source document, proofread the final typed copy at the bottom of the page. Use appropriate revision symbols to mark corrections on the typed version. Be sure to check the math calculations.

INTERNET TRAVEL COMPANY
Income Statement
Month Ended August 31, <YEAR>

Revenues:

Commission income	$32,935
Airline tickets	7,900
Cruises	14,250
Tours	5,139
Other operating revenues	2,350
Total revenues	$62,574

Expenses:

Salaries expense	$23,075
Commissions paid	2,975
Other operating expenses	3,005
Total expenses	$29,055

Net income before taxes $33,519

INTERNET TRAVEL COMPANY
Income Statement
Month Ended August 30, <YEAR>

Revenues:

Commission income	$32,935
Airline tickets	7,800
Cruises	14,250
Tours	5,193
Other operating revenues	2,350
Total revenues	$62,574

Expenses:

Salaries expense	$23,705
Commissions paid	2,975
Other operating expenses	3,000
Total expenses	$29,055

Net income before taxes $33,519

NAME _____ DATE _____

Application 12-B

Laura Garcia, an oil company executive, received a $2000 cash advance for a business trip to New York. When she returned, she used her daily expense slips to complete her expense report for the trip. Proofread the expense report on the next page, and compare the figures there with the expense slips below. Be sure to check the math calculations for correctness.

Monday, May 9, <YEAR>

Home to airport
    (20 miles at 33 cents/mile)
Air fare to LaGuardia $650

Taxi $35
Dinner $22.50
Hotel $165/night

Convention Registration $250

Tuesday, May 10, <YEAR>

Breakfast $14.75
Lunch $22.50
Dinner $27.95
Taxi $15.00
Hotel $165/night

Fax/Phone $14.45

Wednesday, May 11, <YEAR>

Breakfast $12.85
Lunch $15.75
Dinner $32.90

Taxi $10.00
Hotel $165/night

Thursday, May 12, <YEAR>

Breakfast $9.95
Taxi $35
Parking $32

Mileage to home
    20 miles at 33 cents/mile

Telephone $6.55

Application 12-B (continued)

EXPENSE REPORT FOR Laura Garcia   **WEEK ENDING** May 15, <YEAR>

Date	Transportation		Personal Automobile		Hotel	Meals	Other Expenses		Daily Total
	Type	Amount	Mileage	Amount	Amount	Amount	Itemize	Amount	
5/9	Air fare	$650.00	20 @ $0.33	$6.60	$165.00		Convention Reg.	$250	$1132.10
	Taxi	$35.00				$25.50			
5/10	Taxi	$15.00			$165.00	$14.75			$259.24
						$22.00	Fax	$14.54	
						$27.95			
5/11	Taxi	$10.00			$165.00	$12.85			$236.50
						$15.75			
						$32.90			
5/12	Taxi	$35.00	20 @ $0.33	$6.60		$9.95	Airport Parking	$32.00	$90.10
							Telephone	$6.55	

Weekly Total: $1717.94

Advance: $2000.00

Due Employee:

Due Company: $282.06

Purpose of Travel: Attend Oil Producers' Convention

Submitted by: *Laura Garcia*   Date: 5/16/<YEAR>

Approved by: Date:

Billing Code:

Application 12-C

Proofread the roster at the bottom of this page, comparing it against the handwritten list on this page. Use revision symbols to mark corrections to the roster.

Name	Department	Extension	E-mail Address
Allen, Barbara L.	Human Resources	1829	ballen@mallenkoff.us.cc
Cavanett, Mildred Z.	Production	2239	mcavan@mallenkoff.us.cc
David, Zachary T.	Sales	1993	zdavid@mallenkoff.us.cc
Franks, Elizabeth R.	Human Resources	1831	efrank@mallenkoff.us.cc
Hillyard, Hortense S.	Advertising	1535	hhily@mallenkoff.us.cc
Lemmon, Larry L.	Production	2238	llemmo@mallenkoff.us.cc
Offhaven, Nikki A.	Marketing	3303	noffha@mallenkoff.us.cc
Pastures, Jason P.	Sales	1994	jpastu@mallenkoff.us.cc
Post, Lillianne L.	Sales	1995	llpost@mallenkoff.us.cc
Purvicel, Jennifer M.	Marketing	3330	jpurvi@mallenkoff.us.cc
Richland, Jonathan B.	Production	2293	jrichl@mallenkoff.us.cc
Ruston, Martha M.	Production	2294	mrusto@mallenkoff.us.cc

NAME	DEPARTMENT	EXTENSION	E-MAIL ADDRESS
Allen, Barbara L.	Human Resources	1829	ballen@mallenkoff.us.cc
Cavanett, Mildred Z.	Production	2239	mcavan@malenkoff.us.cc
David, Zachary T.	Sales	1993	zdavid@mallenkoff.us.cc
Franks, Elizabeth R.	Human Resources	1831	efrank@mallenkoff.us.cc
Hilyard, Hortens S.	Advertising	1535	hhily@mallenkoff.us.cc
Lemmon, Larry L.	Production	2238	llemmo@mallenkoff.us.c
Offhaven, Nikki A.	Marketing	3303	noffha@mallenkoff.us.cc
Pastures, Jason P.	Sales	1949	jpastu@mallenkoff.us.cc
Post, Lillianne L.	Sales	1995	llpost@mallenkof.us.cc
Purvcel, Jennifer M.	Sales	3330	jpurvi@mallenkoff.us.cc
Richland, Jonathan B.	Production	2294	jrich@mallenkoff.us.cc
Ruston, Martha M.	Production	2293	mrusto@mallenkoff.us.cc

Application 12-D

Compare the following list of employee information with the database at the bottom of the page. Use appropriate revision symbols to mark corrections in the database.

EMPLOYEE ID	LAST NAME	FIRST NAME	MIDDLE INITIAL	DATE HIRED	SALARY
2667	Harris	Vance	J.	12/2/97	$26,681
2990	Perez	Oleta	S.	12/30/98	$29,346
3209	Pressley	Benjamin	K.	4/21/93	$36,264
3892	Morley	Kaitlyn	E.	8/6/93	$32,600
3898	Danfield	Wayne	J.	8/4/95	$31,600
3971	Reagan	Cathy	D.	10/28/94	$29,364
4687	Creighton	Carol	M.	1/31/97	$19,520
4705	Newton	Nicole	L.	2/19/97	$18,400
4758	Saunders	Lena	F.	11/9/98	$23,642
4782	O'Reilly	Frances	D.	12/10/96	$20,586
4951	Seton	Nichole	A.	3/6/99	$19,560
5020	Sleen	Charity	D.	11/29/97	$27,778

Employee ID	Last Name	Frist Name	Middle Initial	Date Hired	Salary
4687	Creighton	Carol	M.	1/31/97	$19,520
3898	Danfeild	Wayne	J.	8/4/95	$31,600
2676	Harris	Vance	J.	12/2/97	$26,681
3892	Morley	Katilyn	E.	8/6/93	$33,600
4750	Newton	Nicole	L.	2/19/97	$18,450
4782	O'Reillly	Francis	D.	12/1/96	$20,568
3209	Pressley	Benjimin	K.	4/21/93	$36,246
3971	Reagan	Cathy	D.	10/28/94	$29,634
2990	Perez	Oleta	S.	12/30/93	$28,346
4758	Saunders	Lena	f.	11/9/98	$23,642
4951	Seton	Nichole	A.	3/6/98	$19,560
5002	Sleen	Chasity	D.	11/29/97	$27,978

CD-ROM Application 12-E

You are responsible for entering updates to your company's customer database. Use the names from the card file, shown below, to compare against the database entries on the next page. Using your word processor, open the file DPES12E from the CD-ROM. Proofread the database against the card file; then correct any errors. Save the database using your initials in place of the DPES. Print the corrected database.

Card file

Mr. Don Briceton, 132 Battle Rd., Highlands, TX 77523

Mrs. Randi Bridges, 211 Stoney Way, Gonzales, LA 70774

Ms. Christie Casey, 145 Court St., Houston, TX 77229

Dr. Sue Davis, 14 Windchase, Houston, TX 77008

Ms. Anna Duitch, 711 Lucky Rd., Grapeland, TX 77630

Mr. Harry Fisher, 9 Shaky Hollow, Houston, TX 77375

Ms. Ann Gibson, 1765 San Felipe, Katy, TX 77057

Mrs. Patrizia Gonzales, 712 Maple Dr., Humble, TX 77931

Mr. John Gormak, 9307 Oak Ridge, Houston, TX 77048

Dr. Charles Hanson, 222 Foxgate, Spendora, TX 77372

Mr. Lyndon Howell, 6522 Ella Lee, Baton Rouge, LA 70775

Mrs. Victoria Hoye, 4301 Locust, Houston, TX 77471

Dr. M. G. Joseph, 2211 Holly, San Antonio, TX 78226

Mrs. Mary Keatly, 3100 Park Vista, Houston, TX 77007

Mr. Bruce Keeler, 1491 Bates, Monroe, LA 70655

Mrs. Lindsey Keith, 813 Clover, Channelview, TX 77530

Mr. Gilbert Lincoln, 7390 Mayfair, Houston, TX 77068

Mr. Jose Lucasa, 240 Seaside, Seabrook, TX 77490

Mr. Gene Manual, 2023 Augusta, Seguin, TX 78156

Miss Lula Mark, 9802 Bering Rd., Houston, TX 77028

Mr. Ely Nations, 143 Ave. A, San Antonio, TX 78228

Ms. Michele Norman, 5118 Orchard, Columbus, TX 78445

Ms. Eliza Powers, 6550 McKinney, Houston, TX 77022

Miss Mimi Presley, 6926 Hammerly, Monroe, LA 70655

Miss Julia Rede, 1110 K St., Shreveport, LA 70522

Ms. Lavania Salvado, 15 Crestline, Houston, TX 77068

Mr. Brett Salyer, 811 Grand Ave., Houston, TX 77029

Miss Alma Santos, 811 Shangrila, Houston, TX 77022

Ms. Kara Shelton, 16914 Knob St., Pasadena, TX 77409

Dr. Annette Tate, 142 E. Morgan, Houston, TX 77020

Mr. Homer Thompson, 1107 2nd St., Giddings, TX 77566

Mr. Kenneth Turlock, 326 N. Mill Rd., Houston, TX 77228

Mrs. Donna Vasula, 1727 Spurlock, Channelview, TX 77530

Mr. Pablo Wardale, 9306 San Ramon, San Antonio, TX 78229

CD-ROM Application 12-E (continued)

Database

TITLE	FNAME	LNAME	ADDRESS	CITY	ST	ZIP
Mr.	Don	Briceton	132 Battle Rd.	Highlands	TX	77523
Mrs.	Randi	Bridges	211 Stoney Way	Gonsales	LA	70774
Ms.	Christe	Casey	145 Court St.	Houston	TX	77229
Dr.	Sue	Davis	14 Windchase	Houston	TX	77080
Ms.	Anna	Duitch	711 Lucky Rd.	Grapeland	TX	77630
Mr.	Harry	Fisher	9 Shaky Holow	Houston	TX	77375
Ms.	Ann	Gibson	1765 San Felipe	Katy	TX	77057
Mrs.	Patricia	Gonzales	712 Maple Dr.	Humble	TX	77931
Mr.	John	Gromak	9307 Oak Ridge	Houston	TX	77148
Dr.	Charles	Hansen	222 Foxgate	Spendora	TX	77372
Mr.	Lyndon	Howell	6522 Ella Lee	Baton Rouge	LA	70775
Mrs.	Victoria	Hoye	4301 Locust	Houston	TX	77471
Mr.	M. G.	Joseph	2211 Holly	San Antonio	TX	78226
Mrs.	Maria	Keatly	310 Park Vista	Houston	TX	77007
Mr.	Bruce	Keeler	1941 Bates	Monroe	LA	70655
Mrs.	Lindsey	Keith	813 Clover	Channelview	TX	77530
Mr.	Gilbert	Lincoln	7390 Mayfair	Houston	TX	77068
Mr.	Jose	Lucasa	240 Seaside	Seabrook	TX	77490
Mr.	Geane	Manual	2023 Augusta	Seguin	TX	78156
Miss	Lula	Mark	9802 Bering Rd.	Houston	TX	77028
Mr.	Ely	Nation	143 Ave. A	San Antonio	TX	78228
Ms.	Michelle	Norman	5118 Orchard	Columbia	TX	78445
Miss	Mimmi	Presley	6926 Hammerly	Monroe	LA	70655
Miss	Julia	Rede	11110 K St.	Shreveport	LA	70522
Ms.	Lavania	Salvado	15 Crestline	Houston	TX	77068
Mr.	Brett	Salyer	811 Grand Ave.	Houston	TX	77029
Miss	Alma	Sandos	811 Shangrila	Houston	TX	77022
Ms.	Cara	Shelton	16914 Knob St.	Pasadena	TX	77409
Dr.	Annette	Tate	142 E. Morgan	Houston	TX	77020
Mr.	Homer	Thompson	1107 2nd St.	Giddings	TX	77566
Mr.	Kenneth	Turlock	326 S. Mill Rd.	Galveston	TX	77228
Mrs.	Donna	Vasula	1727 Spurlock	Channelview	TX	77530
Mr.	Pablo	Wardale	9306 San Ramon	San Antonio	TX	78229

CD-ROM Application 12-F

Ms. Carston has requested some information from your company about herbs that your company sells. Using your word processor, open the file DPES12F from the CD-ROM. Proofread the letter and correct any errors. Save the letter using your initials in place of the DPES. Print the corrected letter.

April 4, <YEAR>

Ms. N. B. Carston
590 West 5th Street
Birmingham, AL 35607

Dear Ms. Carston:

Thank you for you're interest in our plants. The following provide the information you requested for the herbs you specifically asked about. We believe you will be highly satisfied with the quality of our plants.

Common Name	Description	Price
Hyssop	Excellent for popourri	$5.89
Echinacea	Pink Cone Flower	6.99
Woolly Grass	Good for borders	4.50
Oregano	Woody perennial with pungent leaves	3.79

We can ship these plants immediately if you wish too order. We have also enclose a price list for our other herbs as well. Please let us know, if we can be of farther service to you. Call me if you have any questions.

Sincerly,

J. M. Walters

bd

Enclosure

Correcting Inconsistencies

In Chapter 8 you learned about lack of parallelism, which is a grammatical inconsistency. There are other kinds of inconsistencies that occur frequently in business writing. Some of them are obvious, such as using two different formats for a date. Other types of inconsistencies are harder to detect.

You need to proofread carefully in order to spot inconsistencies. By not catching inconsistencies, you give the impression that you lack attention to detail and that you don't care about the document. Such carelessness reflects negatively on you and your organization.

Inconsistencies that you should be alert to fall into four main categories:

1. Treating similar things differently.

2. Conveying unintentional bias.

3. Making sequencing errors, resulting in illogical order.

4. Overlooking contradictory information, such as in math calculations, facts, dates, and source documents.

This chapter will give you practice in identifying and correcting inconsistencies as you proofread.

PROOFREADING FOR CONSISTENCY

An experienced business communicator or other office professional should be skilled in detecting a variety of inconsistencies. In most cases, inconsistencies are simply the result of treating similar items differently. However, being consistent also involves much more, as you will see in the following examples.

Types of Inconsistencies

The following types of errors are the most commonly found inconsistencies in documents:

1. Treating similar things differently within the same document.

    a. *Formats:* Using different styles for formatting, such as indenting one paragraph when all other paragraphs are not indented.

    b. *Punctuation style in letters:* Using both open and standard punctuation styles in the same letter, such as using a colon after the salutation but omitting the comma after the complimentary closing.

    c. *Headings:* Treating headings of the same level differently alike. For example, if one side heading is underlined, then all of them should be underlined. If a specific heading is typed in bold, then all related headings should be typed in bold.

    <u>INTRODUCTION</u>   **INTRODUCTION**

    d. *Phone numbers:* Using two different styles, such as *(803) 555-2718* and *803-555-6982*.

    e. *Dates in tables:* Using two different styles, such as *12-25-99* and *12/25/99*.

    f. *Book titles:* Using different styles, such as THIRD WAVE, *The Editorial Eye,* and <u>The Power of Concentration</u>. All three styles are correct, but the styles should not be mixed within a document.

    g. *Numbers:* Mixing spelled-out numbers and figures, such as *12* printers and *eight* computers.

    h. *Abbreviations:* Using both an abbreviation and a spelled-out word for the same term, such as 2 *ft* and 3 *feet*.

    i. *Spelling:* Spelling someone's name in different ways, such as *Lynn* and *Lynne*.

j. *Courtesy titles:* Using different courtesy titles for the same person, such as *Ms. Reynolds* and *Dr. Reynolds.*

k. *Punctuation style:* Using different comma styles in the same document, such as *Daniel Smith, Jr.,* and *Daniel Smith Jr.* (The comma here is neither right nor wrong but a matter of Mr. Smith's preference.)

l. *Enumerations and lists:* Mixing number or letter styles. For example,

1.		A.
2.	or	b.
(3.)		C.

2. Conveying unintentional bias.

a. *Names and other items in lists:* Not alphabetizing items in a list. For example, listing the names in a memo distribution as *Eric Bradley, Aileen Wilson,* and *Carlotta Kirby* may cause a reader to assume that someone or something is more important if the name appears first on the list. Putting items in alphabetical order helps avoid any bias when listing names. *Note:* In résumés, the titles of select courses are often listed in order of importance rather than in alphabetical order.

b. *Men and women:* Treating the names of men and women differently, such as *Scott Bradley, Ms. Brenda Kirby,* and *Ed Wilson. (Ms.* should be omitted from the woman's name or *Mr.* added to the men's names.)

3. Making sequencing errors.

a. *Alphabetical order:* Listing names without following any particular order, such as *Wexler, Bellon,* and *Manning.*

b. *Chronological order:* Listing dates out of sequence, such as *April 6, May 12,* and *February 1.*

c. *Numerical order:* Listing numbered items out of sequence, such as Invoice *1823,* Invoice *1825,* and Invoice *1824.*

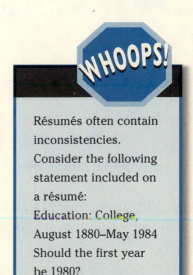

Résumés often contain inconsistencies. Consider the following statement included on a résumé:
Education: College, August 1880–May 1984 Should the first year be 1980?
Source: Accountemps

4. Overlooking contradictions.

   a. *Math calculations:* Using calculations without checking them, as in the following example: You paid *$10* of your *$40 invoice,* which leaves an unpaid balance of *$20.* (The unpaid balance should be *$30.)*

   b. *Facts:* Using facts without checking for accuracy, as in the following example: The speed limit increases from *45* mph to *35* mph in residential areas. (The verb should be *decreases.*)

   c. *Dates:* Using dates without verifying them, as in the following example: Please call me Friday, May 6. (Verify that Friday is the sixth of May.)

   d. *Source documents*: Using information in a document that contradicts a source document, as in this example: An e-mail message says that the flight leaves at *10:05* p.m., but the printed itinerary lists the departure time as *10:50* p.m.

As you can see from the preceding examples, inconsistencies can occur easily in business writing. Bear in mind one word of caution: These are only some of the types of inconsistencies that may appear in documents. You likely will find other inconsistencies in the documents that you work on.

TIPS
SPOTTING INCONSISTENCIES

Some inconsistencies are noticed only during a second reading of a document. Others can be spotted more easily by quickly skimming the copy either before or after it is read word for word. Noticing the use of two different letter formats, for example, may be more obvious during a quick read rather than when they are read word for word.

As with many other skills, expert proofreading is developed only through practice. The next exercises will help you learn to spot inconsistencies.

Look for inconsistencies in the following sentences. If a sentence has inconsistencies, circle them and write *Yes* in the space provided. If a sentence has no inconsistencies, write *No* in the space provided.

Yes/No

1. Our accountant wrote three checks: 2839, 2841, and 2840.

1. _____

2. Film is on sale this week. We can buy four rolls of 35 millimeter film for $9 instead of $10. This is a saving of $10.

2. _____

3. Should Jacob Thomas be transferred to Memphis, Birmingham, or Philadelphia?

3. _____

4. Southern Produce, Inc., shipped 500 pounds of potatoes today and 400 lb yesterday.

4. _____

5. Dr. Jennifer Cox will be our employment consultant. Ms. Cox has much experience recruiting sales representatives.

5. _____

6. Our company has two toll-free numbers for customer orders: (800) 555-2862 and 800-555-2864.

6. _____

7. Send copies of all correspondence to Oscar Owensby, David Pratt, and Mrs. Susan Travis.

7. _____

8. We hired 12 computer specialists, two programmers, and one network administrator.

8. _____

9. Mr. Sam Pittmon will arrive at 3 p.m. today. Will you please meet Mr. Pittman at the airport.

9. _____

10. His first letter was dated April 12, 2001; the second one was dated April 15, 2001.

10. _____

TIPS

VERIFYING INFORMATION

- Use a calculator to verify mathematical computations.

- Refer to a reliable source (such as past correspondence) to check factual information.

- Check a calendar to verify dates.

Using these resources will help you to avoid inconsistencies in figures, facts, and dates.

Within each grouping, put the proper nouns in alphabetical order. In the spaces provided, write the identifying letter of each item in the correct sequence.

1. a. Whitaker, Jane

   b. Yeager, Grace

   c. Tyburski, William

   d. Carinelli, Michelle

   e. Davis, Stanley

1. _____

   _____

   _____

   _____

   _____

2. a. Hawaii

   b. Iowa

   c. Montana

   d. Minnesota

   e. Illinois

2. _____

   _____

   _____

   _____

   _____

3. a. Eastridge Mall

   b. Estridge Advertising Agency

   c. Andover Industries

   d. Hull and Associates, Inc.

   e. Hurleigh Enterprises

3. _____

   _____

   _____

   _____

   _____

4. a. Roger Wallace

   b. Robert Weston

   c. Angela Wellington

   d. Amelia Earnheart

   e. Nancy Williams

4. _____

   _____

   _____

   _____

   _____

5. a. Data Processing Department

   b. Accounting Department

   c. Quality Control Department

   d. Shipping Department

   e. Manufacturing Department

5. _____

   _____

   _____

   _____

   _____

CHECKUP 13-3

Within each grouping, put the items in chronological order, starting with the earliest item. In the spaces provided, write the identifying letter of each item in the correct sequence.

1. a. December 28, 2000
   b. December 20, 2000
   c. December 24, 2001
   d. December 25, 2001
   e. December 23, 2002

   1. _____ _____ _____ _____ _____

2. a. summer
   b. fall
   c. spring

   2. _____ _____ _____

3. a. 1 a.m.
   b. 1 p.m.
   c. 12 noon
   d. 12:30 p.m.

   3. _____ _____ _____ _____

4. a. Friday, June 4
   b. Wednesday, June 2
   c. Monday, May 31
   d. Sunday, May 30
   e. Thursday, May 27

   4. _____ _____ _____ _____ _____

5. a. Fall 2001 semester
   b. Spring 2001 semester
   c. Fall 2000 semester
   d. Summer 2001 semester

   5. _____ _____ _____ _____

6. a. Friday
   b. Wednesday
   c. Monday
   d. Tuesday
   e. Thursday

   6. _____ _____ _____ _____ _____

7. a. April 2001
   b. May 2002
   c. July 2000

   7. _____ _____ _____

8. a. March
   b. January
   c. August
   d. June

   8. _____ _____ _____ _____

9. a. 9:30 a.m.
   b. 5:45 a.m.
   c. 7:30 a.m.
   d. 10:15 a.m.
   e. 9:45 a.m.

   9. _____ _____ _____ _____ _____

10. a. Week of 3-13-02
    b. Week of 3-27-02
    c. Week of 3-6-02
    d. Week of 3-20-02

    10. _____ _____ _____ _____

CHECKUP 13-4

Within each grouping, put the items in numerical order, beginning with the lowest or earliest number. In the spaces provided, write the identifying letter of each item in the correct sequence.

1. a. 55 years old
   b. 50 years old
   c. 52 years old
   d. 60 years old
   e. 59 years old

   1. _____ _____ _____ _____ _____

2. a. Invoices due in 7 days
   b. Invoices due in 14 days
   c. Invoices due in 5 days
   d. Invoices due in 12 days
   e. Invoices due in 16 days

   2. _____ _____ _____ _____ _____

3. a. 65.1   3. _____
   b. 62.625   _____
   c. 61.787   _____

4. a. $10,725   4. _____
   b. $11,080   _____
   c. $12,500   _____
   d. $11,039   _____

5. a. Invoice 3204 5. _____
   b. Invoice 3203   _____
   c. Invoice 3202   _____
   d. Invoice 3210   _____

6. a. Purchase Order 2712   6. _____
   b. Purchase Order 2710   _____
   c. Purchase Order 2714   _____
   d. Purchase Order 2711   _____
   e. Purchase Order 2713   _____

7. a. Check 3192   7. _____
   b. Check 3190   _____
   c. Check 3191   _____

8. a. 20 years   8. _____
   b. 15 years   _____
   c. 17 years   _____
   d. 22 years   _____

9. a. 6 feet 2 inches   9. _____
   b. 2 feet 8 inches   _____
   c. 3 feet 9 inches   _____
   d. 4 feet 10 inches   _____

10. a. Account 1403   10. _____
    b. Account 1613   _____
    c. Account 1219   _____
    d. Account 1519   _____
    e. Account 1103   _____

REVISION SYMBOLS FOR MARKING INCONSISTENCIES

Often when proofreading you may read something that doesn't sound right or that you think is incorrect. If you do not know for sure if something is correct or not, you should query it—do not change the copy to what you "think" is correct. Use revision symbols for querying text as shown in the following list. Verify all material that you query, and make any needed corrections.

In addition to the revision symbols introduced in previous chapters, the following revision symbols will be useful in marking inconsistencies.

Revision	Edited Draft	Final Copy
Remove bold	**IMPORTANT**	IMPORTANT
Remove underscore	E-Business Boom	E-Business Boom
Select block	and the fruit will be shipped by truck.	(no final copy)
Insert selected block	The coffee will be shipped by truck.	The coffee and the fruit will be shipped by truck.
Delete selected block	The coffee and the fruit will be shipped by truck.	The coffee will be shipped by truck.

A form letter that was mailed routinely to customers each year was mailed again this year. The date line was changed to May 12, but the reply date in the letter was the same date as in last year's letter–May 10. The letter writer and the company could have been spared embarrassment if the calendar dates had been checked and the entire letter had been proofread for consistency.

Revision	Edited Draft	Final Copy
Move selected block	The coffee|and the ^A ^move[A] fruit|will be shipped by truck. The vege- tables[A]_will be sent by train.	The coffee will be shipped by truck. The vegetables and the fruit will be sent by train.
Query selected block	He cast his first ballot when he was|81.^A| [A]? (Verify the age. Are the figures transposed?)	He cast his first ballot when he was 18.
Query conflicting blocks	The shipment arrived ^A Friday|morning|at 8|p.m.^B| [A] ? [B] (Verify the time. Morning or evening?)	The shipment arrived Friday morning at 8 a.m.

If two similar items are treated differently, select one way to use as the correct way; then use revision symbols to change the treatment of the other item so that both items are handled the same way. The following exercise will give you practice in using revision symbols to mark inconsistencies.

CHECKUP 13-5 Use appropriate revision symbols to query conflicting blocks (segments) of text, to query blocks of text that you feel may be incorrect, or to indicate other inconsistencies. Write *C* for *Correct* beside any sentence that has no inconsistencies.

1. Denise got her driver's license at age 61.

2. We mailed 250 invitations to select customers for our special sale. Our responses included 215 who said that they would attend and 35 who could not attend. (Assume that the total number of invitations is correct.)

3. The roller blades, which are priced at $130, are discounted 10 percent today. This $10 savings has convinced me to buy the roller blades. (Assume that the $130 is correct.)

4. Today is Monday, August 5; the meeting will be Friday, August 10.

5. The painting contractor charged $245.18 for the gray paint. We have already reimbursed him $45.18 of that amount, and we still owe him $200.18. (Assume that the $245.18 is correct.)

6. I read two books during the holidays: <u>Taking Professional Photographs</u> and PACKING FOR INTERNATIONAL TRAVEL.

7. The company president recommends that we consider Max McMillan, John Sheridan, Sheila Allen, and Jill Townsend for the assistant manager's position.

8. Mr. George Carouthers has excelled in his management training program. Mr. Carothers will definitely advance in this company.

9. Our telephone number is 316-555-2842, and our fax number is (316) 555-2840.

10. The following checks have not cleared our account: 1315, 1323, 1372, 1384, and 1401. (Assume that each check number is correct.)

11. Our profit percentage decreased from 3.5 percent to 4.2 percent since Betty began to work full-time on reducing expenses. (Assume that the percentages are correct.)

12. We have three choices of dates for the dinner: April 15, 7, or 22.

13. Janice Kettner, Tamara Levison, and Wayne Moyer have submitted the top four money-saving ideas for the month. As you know, each person is limited to one entry. Which one should be awarded the cash prize?

14. Dr. Adelyn Symboski, who has her doctorate from the University of North Carolina, is an authority on personality disorders. Even though her calendar is quite crowded, Ms. Symboski has agreed to help profile the perpetrator of these malicious crimes.

15. We will consider opening subsidiaries in Illinois, Florida, and Michigan.

16. Several factors should be considered in our relocation: 1. Availability of truck lines for shipping, 2. Institutions for training our workers, and (3) proximity to the airport.

17. John said that there were 28 applicants for the two positions: 18 people applied for the executive assistant's position and 9 people applied for the engineer's position. (Assume that the total number of applicants is correct.)

18. We ordered 35 gallons of ice cream for the picnic: 10 gal. of chocolate, 10 gal. of strawberry, and 15 gal. of vanilla. (Assume that the total number of gallons is correct.)

19. Ray Montieth, Paul Pasley, and Ms. Teresa Rosmon are on the committee to examine our current insurance coverage.

20. To cast an absentee ballot in the November 7 election, you must submit the ballot 30 days prior to the election, which would be October 7.

SOFTWARE TIPS

Most document processing software programs have a feature that you can use to highlight text. You select the text to be highlighted, then choose the option that highlights the text. If you are proofreading a document on the computer screen rather than looking at a printout, the highlighting feature is a good way to query blocks of information.

Use the following calendar to verify dates in the applications at the end of the chapter. Assume that the calendar is correct for the current year.

		JAN							APR							JULY							OCT				
S	M	T	W	T	F	S	S	M	T	W	T	F	S	S	M	T	W	T	F	S	S	M	T	W	T	F	S
1	2	3	4	5	6	7							1							1	1	2	3	4	5	6	7
8	9	10	11	12	13	14	2	3	4	5	6	7	8	2	3	4	5	6	7	8	8	9	10	11	12	13	14
15	16	17	18	19	20	21	9	10	11	12	13	14	15	9	10	11	12	13	14	15	15	16	17	18	19	20	21
22	23	24	25	26	27	28	16	17	18	19	20	21	22	16	17	18	19	20	21	22	22	23	24	25	26	27	28
29	30	31					23	24	25	26	27	28	29	23	24	25	26	27	28	29	29	30	31				
							30							30	31												

		FEB							MAY							AUG							NOV				
S	M	T	W	T	F	S	S	M	T	W	T	F	S	S	M	T	W	T	F	S	S	M	T	W	T	F	S
			1	2	3	4		1	2	3	4	5	6			1	2	3	4	5				1	2	3	4
5	6	7	8	9	10	11	7	8	9	10	11	12	13	6	7	8	9	10	11	12	5	6	7	8	9	10	11
12	13	14	15	16	17	18	14	15	16	17	18	19	20	13	14	15	16	17	18	19	12	13	14	15	16	17	18
19	20	21	22	23	24	25	21	22	23	24	25	26	27	20	21	22	23	24	25	26	19	20	21	22	23	24	25
26	27	28					28	29	30	31				27	28	29	30	31			26	27	28	29	30		

		MAR							JUNE							SEPT							DEC				
S	M	T	W	T	F	S	S	M	T	W	T	F	S	S	M	T	W	T	F	S	S	M	T	W	T	F	S
			1	2	3	4					1	2	3						1	2						1	2
5	6	7	8	9	10	11	4	5	6	7	8	9	10	3	4	5	6	7	8	9	3	4	5	6	7	8	9
12	13	14	15	16	17	18	11	12	13	14	15	16	17	10	11	12	13	14	15	16	10	11	12	13	14	15	16
19	20	21	22	23	24	25	18	19	20	21	22	23	24	17	18	19	20	21	22	23	17	18	19	20	21	22	23
26	27	28	29	30	31		25	26	27	28	29	30		24	25	26	27	28	29	30	24	25	26	27	28	29	30
																					31					

Application 13-A

Proofread the following memo for inconsistencies. Use appropriate revision symbols to indicate corrections when you have a choice of the correct form or when you are sure of the intended content. Use a different pair of letters (A/A, B/B, and so on) to query inconsistencies in the treatment of related items such as dates. Assume that the calendar on page 283 is correct for the current year. Today is March 6.

MEMO TO: All Staff Members

FROM: Joyce Meade, Human Resource Department

DATE: March 6, <YEAR>

SUBJECT: Staff Development Sessions

Our fall staff development sessions are scheduled for Tuesday, April 12. Dr. Susan Eldridge, Professor of Business Communications at Valley State University, will be our guest speaker.

Ms. Eldridge received her doctorate from the University of Tennessee and is considered an expert in customer relations. Dr. Eldridge will address our associates on how to deal with difficult customers. She has authored two books: <u>The Customer and You</u> and CUSTOMERS WITH AN ATTITUDE.

You may choose one of the three times specified below. There is one morning session and three afternoon sessions. The last session begins at 6:15 a.m.

Session A	8:15–9:45 a.m.
Session B	1:15–2:45 p.m.
Session #C	3:00–4:45 p.m.
Session D	6:15–7:45 p.m.

By Monday, March 28, please call Ms. Heather Lowe at extension 4375 or Ray Queen at extension #4378 to reserve your place. Each session is limited to the first 35 people who register.

c: Sheri Jones, Allen Miklaus, Grace Cole

Application 13-B

Proofread the following block style letter (with standard punctuation)
for inconsistencies. Use revision symbols to indicate corrections when
you have a choice of the correct form or when you are sure of the
intended content. Use a different pair of letters (A/A, B/B, and so on) to
query inconsistencies in the treatment of related itms. Assume that the
calender on page 283 is correct for the current year. Today is July 3.

Post Office Box 4629
Denver, Colorado 80204-4620
(303) 555-3470   ccs@westmtn.net

July 3, <YEAR>

Dr. Jonathan Settlemeyer
4326 Washington Street
Denver, CO 80204

Dear Mr. Settlemeyer:

Thank you for agreeing to speak at next month's City Civic Society staff meeting. As
you know, we meet the first Monday night of each month at 7 a.m. in the hospital
auditorium.

We are very much looking forward to hearing your talk on August 8. We are
especially eager to hear the results of the patient survey that was conducted during the
last two months. Ms. Betty Mitchell, your researcher, said that his findings were
significant. Mr. Mitchell also mentioned that 750 of the 850 people surveyed
responded. This is a high percentage of response; only 200 people did not return the
questionnaire.

   Your presentation should take about 40 minutes. Please let me know if you need
any special equipment such as projectors or screens. As mentioned earlier, you and I
will have lunch at noon one week from today, Monday, July 11, at your office to
discuss your presentation.

Sincerely

Denise Smith

Denise Smith
Education Coordinator

lt

Application 13-C

Proofread the following job application letter. It should be formatted in the personal business style with open punctuation. Check for all types of errors, including inconsistencies. Use appropriate revision symbols to mark corrections. Assume that the calendar on page 283 is correct for the current year. Today is August 8.

325 Kessler Avenue
Shelby, NC 28151
August 8, <YEAR>

Mr. Steven Arendas, Recruiter
United States Secret Service
Department of the Treasury
3294 Graham Boulevard, Suite 268
Charlotte, NC 28322

Dear Mr. Arendas:

Please consider me for the position of Special Agent with the United States Secret Service. After speaking with Special Agent Abigail Rodriques at a recent career fair at Greensboro College, I am confident that I meat or exceed all your requirements.

From the enclosed résumé you can see that my major in criminal justice, combined with specialized training, have given me a solid foundation for criminal investigation work. My years of experience both as an officer with a sheriff's department and as a police detective has honed my investigative skills and has contributed to my over 78 percent success rate in solving cases.

Completing coursework in psychology, political science, psychology, and sociology has assisted me in dealing with the public and with offenders. Currently I am taking courses in computer applications and management science to keep abreast of the latest trends in law enforcement.

I look forward to participating in your group information and interview session that is scheduled two weeks from today, Tuesday, August 23.

Sincerely,

Steve Mellbye

c: Abigail Rodriques

Application 13-D

Proofread the following résumé. Check for all types of errors, including inconsistencies. Use appropriate revision symbols to mark corrections.

---

325 Kessler Avenue
Shelby, NC 28151
Telephone: 704-555-2818 (Home)
Telephone: 704-555-4284 (W)
E-Mail: smellbye@highlands.net

Steve Mellbye

Objective:	Position as Special Agent in the United States Secret Service
Education:	Bachelor of Science in Criminal Justice—Awarded May 15, 2000 Greensboro College, Greensboro, North Carolina Associate of Science Degree—Awarded May 15, 1998 Gaston Community College, Gastonia, North Carolina
Selected Specialized Training	Finger print and Identification Comparison Criminal Investigation Trends Firearms In-Service Training and Qualification Pepper Mace Training Fraud Awareness and Prevention Training Standardized Field Sobriety Testing Arson Investigation Electronic Surveillance Techniques Pepper Mace Training
Employment:	Detective, Shelby Police Department, Shelby, North Carolina, 1996-Present Officer, Cleveland County Sheriff's Department, Shelby, North Carolina, 1994-1996 Campus Security Officer, Greensboro College, 1993-94
Selected Activities:	President, Cleveland County Law Enforcement Association, 1999-Present Vice President, Students Against Drug Drivers (SADD), 1996-1998 Bored Member, Youth Assistance Program of Shelby, 1998-1999
References:	A list references will be furnished one request.

CD-ROM Application 13-E

In the following memo, similar items were treated differently. Correct all of these inconsistencies, using one consistent treatment for similar items. Open the file DPES13E from the CD-ROM. Proofread the memo and correct any inconsistencies. Save the revised memo using your initials in place of DPES. Proofread the memo on the screen and make any additional corrections. Save and print the corrected memo.

MEMO TO: Craig Milligan, Public Information Services

FROM: Jillian Allendale, Manager

Date: September 10, <YEAR>

SUBJECT Autographing Session

Mr. Jorge Santos will be at our bookstore on Wednesday, September 27, from 2:30 to 5:30 p.m., to autograph copies of his new book, <u>Managing Work-Related Stress</u>. His autographing session will certainly boost our sales. To prepare for his visit, please do the following:

First, order 500 copies of Mr. Santos' new book and 100 copies of his other book, STRESSED SPELLED BACKWARD IS DESSERTS.

2. Draft a press release announcing Mr. Santos' visit, emphasizing his recent television appearance on the Early Show.

Caley Lassiter is meeting Mr. Santos' flight (Western Airlines No. 735) at 11:55 a.m. and driving him to and from the airport. His departing flight (Western Airlines Number 835) leaves at 7:45 p.m.

lrs

CD-ROM Application 13-F

Open the file DPES13F from the CD-ROM. Proofread the résumé and correct inconsistencies as well as any other types of errors. (*Note:* The present tense is used to describe current job duties; the past tense is used to describe previous job duties.) Save the revised résumé using your initials in place of the DPES. Print the corrected résumé.

Dana R. Holcomb
2328 Bonaventure Place
Nashville, TN 37208

Telephone: 615-555-2894   Fax: (615)555-8829   E-Mail: holcomb@country.net

Objective: To accept a challenging position as human resource manager.

Education: Bachelor of Science Degree in Business Administration Awarded May 2001
Taylor University, Nashville, Tennessee

Associate of Arts Degree Awarded May 1999
Stevens Community College, Nashville, Tennessee

Related Experience: Director of Human Resources—1997–Present
Memphis Manufacturing Company, Memphis, TN
- Recruit and hire new associates
- Negotiate benefits with providers
- Administer benefits for 500 employees

Office Manager—1995–1997
Memphis Medical Associates, Memphis, Tennessee
- Organized tracking system for medical personnel
- Coordinated payroll and benefits functions
- Arranged on-call schedules for six doctors and 8 nurses

Appointment Assistant—1993–95
Sharpe Dental Associates, Memphis Tennessee
Establish new patient database
Scheduled patient appointments

Skills: Mastery Level
- Microsoft Office and Corel Suite
- Bilingual in English and Spanish

Activities Taylor University
Vice President, Phi Beta Lambda
President, Student Government Assocaition

Editing for Clarity, Conciseness, and Completeness

OBJECTIVES

After completing this chapter, you should be able to:

1. Edit to use simple words and proper English.

2. Edit to eliminate trite language and minimize the use of passive voice.

3. Edit to avoid wordiness, redundancy, overused words, and too many phrases and clauses.

4. Use software tools to improve readability.

5. Edit to make sure all details are included.

Written business communication must be clear, concise, and complete. These three qualities make a message easier and quicker to read, thus making it more likely that the desired action will be accomplished. Making sure a message is clear, concise, and complete helps to avoid the problem of miscommunication.

Business people need to be able to understand a message the first time they read it because:

1. They might not have time to read the message a second time.

2. They might not have time to ask the writer for clarification.

3. They might misunderstand the message and then act on the basis of incorrect assumptions.

In the previous chapters you learned how to proofread to detect and correct keyboarding, grammatical, and formatting errors. In this chapter you will learn how to edit a document for clarity, conciseness, and completeness.

EDITING FOR CLARITY

All writing—especially business communication—must be clear. Editing for clarity involves choosing the right words. Use the following techniques to make messages clear:

- Use simple words.

- Use proper English.

- Eliminate trite language.

- Minimize the use of passive voice.

Use Simple Words

Often simple words can replace more difficult words without changing the meaning of the message. In the following pairs of examples, both sentences are correct, but the second sentence in each pair is easier to understand.

Sherita Hunt is *contemplating* a job transfer.

Sherita Hunt is *thinking about* a job transfer.

Paramedics should be *cognizant* of applicable laws.

Paramedics should be *aware* of applicable laws.

The detective will *ascertain* the facts from the witnesses.

The detective will *get* the facts from the witnesses.

Utilize the safest method for installing the wiring.

Use the safest method for installing the wiring.

Mauricio was *obstinate* about using the new procedures.

Mauricio was *stubborn* about using the new procedures.

CHOOSING SIMPLER WORDS

Use a thesaurus to locate simpler versions of words. Look up the word that you want to replace, then locate synonyms for the word. Make sure the synonym you select has the same meaning as the word you are replacing.

Use Proper English

Using proper English means avoiding slang or incorrect usage. Such substandard English is incorrect in business writing. Notice how the first sentence in each of the following pairs uses substandard English. The second sentence in each pair corrects the error.

Wrong   Our college has classes *irregardless* of the weather.

Right   Our college has classes *regardless* of the weather.

Wrong   Steve will *try and* hire six people.

Right   Steve will *try to* hire six people.

Wrong   Emily should *of* met me at the airport.

Right   Emily should *have* met me at the airport.

Wrong   Oleta was *kind of* irritable after the incident.

Right   Oleta was *rather* irritable after the incident.

Wrong   Jeanne got the information that she needed *off* Joel.

Right   Jeanne got the information that she needed *from* Joel.

CHECKUP 14-1   Replace each underlined word in the following sentences with a simpler word. Use a dictionary or a thesaurus as needed. Write your answers in the space provided.

1. Make sure you submit all the <u>obligatory</u> paperwork.

   _____

2. The hotel guests told the manager that the service they
   received was <u>copacetic</u>.

   _____

3. She was <u>beleaguered</u> by the statement he made.

   _____

4. We <u>concurred</u> that the endangered species should be protected.

   _____

5. Each student who qualifies will be recognized for <u>exemplary</u>
   volunteer service to the community.

   _____

Eliminate Trite Language

Business jargon or terms that have lost their effectiveness through overuse are considered trite. Trite expressions are ones that have lost their freshness and originality. Such expressions can be reworded, as shown in the following examples. The first sentence in each pair contains a trite expression that is shown in italics; the second sentence is reworded to eliminate the expression.

No *Enclosed please find* your new CD-ROM
player. (Was it lost?)

Yes Your new CD-ROM player is enclosed.

No *We would be favored with a written reply.*
(Trite and out of date)

Yes Please write us.

No The replacement parts will be sent
under separate cover. (Trite and out of date)

Yes The replacement parts will be sent *separately*.

Participial closings in letters are considered trite because they sound out of date. These closings are phrases that begin with a participle (a word ending in *–ing*) such as *Remaining*. Compare the following pairs of examples.

No   Thanking you for your order, I remain,

           Sincerely yours,

Yes   Thank you for your order.

           Sincerely yours,

No   Expecting your check soon, I remain,

Yes   Please send us your check promptly.

No   Looking forward to meeting you, I am . . .

Yes   I look forward to meeting you.

CHECKUP 14-2   In the following memo, replace each underlined word or phrase with the correct usage. For example, change difficult words to easier words, correct improper English, and reword trite expressions. Use the appropriate revision symbols from the inside front cover to mark the changes.

MEMO TO: Beth Winslow

FROM: Cecil Steward

DATE: October 5, <YEAR>

SUBJECT: Company Communications

<u>In regards to</u> your suggestion, Harvey Dexter, of Consultants, Inc., will conduct a seminar for all associates on October 15 to discuss customer service issues. Mr. Dexter will <u>try and</u> call you tomorrow about the details. <u>Please find enclosed herewith</u> a copy of his outline for the seminar.

<u>Kindly</u> notify all associates that is <u>of the utmost importance</u> that they attend the seminar. They are welcome to ask any questions or share any suggestions they might have for improving our customer service.

Enclosure

Minimize the Use of Passive Voice

Messages are usually written in the active voice. In the active voice, the subject performs the action. In the passive voice, the subject is the receiver of the action. Note the difference between the italicized verbs in the following examples.

Passive Voice   The announcement *was made* by the publisher.

Active Voice   The publisher *made* the announcement.

Passive Voice   Today the contract *will be signed* by us.

Active Voice   Today we *will sign* the contract.

Sentences written in active voice are easier to read and understand than sentences written in passive voice. You should write in active voice most of the time except when there is a specific reason for using passive voice. In business writing the passive voice is usually used to deliver bad news. Compare the following two sentences, and note how the passive voice in the second sentence softens the delivery of bad news.

Active Voice   We *are unable* to credit your account due to an outstanding check.

Passive Voice   Your account *will be credited* as soon as all outstanding checks are received.

CHECKUP 14-3   Edit each of the following sentences to use the active voice. Write your answers in the spaces provided.

1. After much debate, the policy was changed by the vice president.

   _____

   _____

2. The package was delivered by a parcel delivery service last Friday.

   _____

   _____

3. Darlene was offered a promotion by Mr. Nelson.

_____

_____

4. Changes to the employee investment plan were discussed by Melinda Sorrentino.

_____

_____

5. The results of the lab tests were reviewed by the physician.

_____

_____

EDITING FOR CONCISENESS

Business communications should be concise and to the point. Being concise doesn't mean that your message is so short that it is incomplete or abrupt in tone. Instead, being concise means that you have expressed your thoughts so clearly that only a few words are needed. Use the following techniques to edit a message for conciseness.

- Use fewer words.

- Eliminate redundancy.

- Avoid overusing words.

- Eliminate unnecessary phrases and clauses.

Use Fewer Words

Wordiness is the use of words that add little or no information to the sentence. If you can omit words, phrases, or even sentences without changing the meaning, the message is wordy.

In each of the following pairs of sentences, the first sentence is wordy; the second sentence in the pair is concise.

Wordy   We *were under the impression* that the changes would not be made.

Concise   We *assumed* that the changes would not be made.

Students on Long Island who were taking the Medical College Admissions Test received booklets that had a series of incorrect questions. The questions did not go with the accompanying reading passage. The company that prepared the tests said the mistake was due to a printing mixup and sloppy proofreading. Students with the incorrect version of the test were given the option of retaking the test or having their score recalculated.
Source: Newsday

Wordy	Steve managed the project *until such time* as it was completed.
Concise	Steve managed the project *until* it was completed.

Wordy	They traveled to Oregon *by means of train*.
Concise	They traveled to Oregon *by train*.

Sometimes wordiness is the result of using an unnecessary preposition. Note how the italicized prepositions in the following examples do not add anything to the meaning.

help *from*   opposite *to*

start *up*   where . . . *at*

The following exercises will give you practice in finding and removing unnecessary words.

Net Link

For additional information on how to eliminate wordiness, go to *Grammar and Writing Helps* at **www .valdosta.edu/comarts /grammar.html** on the Valdosta State University Web site.

CHECKUP 14-4   The following numbered phrases are examples of wordy language. For each phrase, write the letter of one of the concise words from the list that has the same meaning.

a. usually	e. before	i. always
b. helped	f. weekly	j. soon
c. if	g. while	
d. now	h. because	

1. in the event that   1. _____
2. every seven days   2. _____
3. at all times   3. _____
4. at the present time   4. _____
5. gave assistance to   5. _____
6. during the time that   6. _____
7. due to the fact that   7. _____
8. in almost every instance   8. _____
9. prior to   9. _____
10. in the near future   10. _____

Use the appropriate revision symbol to eliminate one unnecessary word in each of the following sentences.

1. The groundbreaking ceremony will start promptly at about 10 a.m.

2. Sort out the inventory by category.

3. Samuel and Teresa opened up the restaurant before 5:30 a.m.

4. Communication skills are more important than ever before.

5. Do you know where Marilyn is moving to?

6. Type up the accident report and submit it to the insurance adjuster.

7. The merger proposal must be redone over.

8. What time do you need the decision by?

9. The sales items were sold out in an hour.

10. Where is my laptop computer at?

CHECKUP 14-6 The following sentences contain wordy language. Choose a concise word or words from the list, and use appropriate revision symbols to correct the wordy sentences.

annually	reported	each December
believes	for	

1. Automobile insurance premiums are paid once each year.

2. Our check in the amount of $39.99 is enclosed.

3. Jorge gave a report to the effect that the quality is better.

4. We set our performance goals in the last month of each year.

5. Patricia is of the opinion that the plan will work.

Eliminate Redundancy

Redundancy is the needless repetition of words. Redundant words say essentially the same thing.

   Please give me the *true facts* in the case.

The words *true* and *facts* are saying the same thing. *Facts* are *truths*. Substituting *truths* for *facts* makes the redundancy obvious.

   Please give me the *true truths* in the case.

Here are some other examples of redundancies.

both alike	over with	exact same
cooperate together	past experience	repeat again
refer back	same identical	

Completing the following exercise will give you practice in recognizing and correcting redundancies.

CHECKUP 14-7   All the following sentences contain redundancies. Use appropriate revision symbols to delete the unneeded words.

1. The machine was repaired by 12 a.m. midnight.

2. Planning in advance will be helpful.

3. We tried your new idea today. We plan to repeat it again soon.

4. Prices were reduced down.

5. Jay asked him to return back the equipment.

Use the appropriate revision symbol to eliminate wordiness in the following draft of a memo. There are ten corrections to be made (four wordy phrases that should be replaced by one word, four redundant words, and two unneeded words).

MEMO TO: Belinda Bergman

FROM: Steven Ellerby

DATE: August 18, <YEAR>

SUBJECT: Reducing Stationery Cost

Prior to the time that we bought a word processing system, all letters were typed up on stationery. In almost all instances, we didn't use verification drafts because retyping a correct letter again was more expensive than the stationery used on letters that had to be redone over. Frequently, new errors occurred when letters were retyped again.

To reduce down stationery cost, please print out a verification draft on plain paper should it be that the same letter is going to five or more people. Ask the originator to edit the draft. In the event that changes are needed, they can be made before expensive stationery is used.

Avoid Overuse of Words

Another problem in writing is the overuse of words. For example, the same adjectives and adverbs are often used over and over within a document. Some examples include *really, very,* and *good.* Overused words are often not detected by the writer because the words are part of the writer's usual vocabulary. However, the overused words may be obvious to the reader and take the reader's attention away from the message. As a result, the message loses effectiveness.

Consider the overuse of the word *very* in the following sentence.

Thank you *very* much for the *very* thoughtful gift.

There are four ways to correct the overuse of *very*. Any of these ways can be used to correct a pattern of overuse.

1. Delete all occurrences. (*Much* must also be omitted.)

Thank you for the thoughtful gift.

2. Delete one occurrence.

Thank you very much for the thoughtful gift.

3. Use a synonym.

Thank you very much for the extremely thoughtful gift.

4. Reword the sentence. (You may need to form two sentences.)

Thank you very much for such a thoughtful gift.

Thank you very much. I appreciate the thoughtful gift.

SOFTWARE TIPS

Use the Search feature of word processing software to locate overused words. For example, suppose you are editing the first page of a three-page report and the word *very* appears twice. Is this word overused in the report as a whole? Find out by using the Search feature. This feature can count the occurrences of a specific arrangement of keystrokes. The arrangement can be words, groups of words, or figures.

CHECKUP 14-9 In each of the following sentences, underline the overused word or words. Then rewrite the sentences as specified.

1. I appreciate your most generous donation to this most deserving cause.

   a. Delete all occurrences.

   _____

   _____

   _____

   b. Delete one occurrence.

   _____

   _____

   _____

c. Use a synonym for one occurrence.

_____

_____

_____

2. Craig thinks that the plan will work. He thinks it will save money.

   a. Reword the sentences. (*Hint:* Combine the sentences.)

   _____

   _____

   _____

3. In my opinion, Sarah will do a good job in the new position. Sarah, in my opinion, may not want to leave the good job she has now.

   a. Select an appropriate method to correct the overused words. (*Hint:* Combine the sentences.)

   _____

   _____

   _____

Eliminate Unnecessary Phrases and Clauses

Phrases and clauses are useful in business writing. However, too many phrases and clauses can interrupt the flow of a message and make the meaning unclear.

The following examples illustrate some ways to eliminate or to improve the wording of phrases and clauses.

1. Use a modifier.

   Change *sales manager for the region* to *regional sales manager.*

2. Use a possessive. (Note the apostrophe.)

   Change *home of our manager* to *our manager's home.*

3. Use an appositive. You'll recall from Chapter 7 that an appositive is a word or term that refers to the noun or pronoun that immediately precedes it. (Note the commas around the appositive.)

   Change *Charles, who is our stockbroker, said* to *Charles, our stockbroker, said.*

4. Use better wording.

Change *He came on the first day of last week.* to *He came last Monday.*

CHECKUP 14-10 Without changing the meaning, edit the following sentences to remove as many clauses and phrases as possible in order to clarify the meaning. Use appropriate revision symbols to make changes. *Note*: Follow the example.

0. She applied for the position that was new.

   She applied for the new position.

1. Julio sold three trucks that were new and five cars that were used.

2. The meeting will be held in the conference room on the fourth floor at 8:30 a.m.

3. Most of the associates in the computer department have personal computers at home.

4. Please fax Amelia a list of the merchandise that was damaged.

5. The new policy is effective on the first day of the first month of the calendar year.

IMPROVE READABILITY

Readability refers to how difficult or how easy a document is to read. The readability of a document is based on the difficulty of words, the number of words, the length of sentences, and the number of sentences in a paragraph.

Most word processing software includes readability indexes that count the number of characters per word, the average number of words per sentence, and the average number of sentences per paragraph. The software also displays the computed readability index, which can be a grade level or a reading ease index that ranges from 0 to 100. Grade levels are designed to correspond to grade levels in school. The reading ease index score, however, reflects the ease with which a document can be read. The higher the ease index score, the greater the number of people who can easily understand the document.

Business documents should be written at a level that is comfortable for the intended receiver to read and understand. Although professionals in all fields are well-educated, they should not have to consult a dictionary to understand routine e-mail, memos, letters, or reports.

When editing a document for readability, consider both your audience and your purpose. If the readability index indicates that a document is too difficult, edit the document to use simpler words as well as fewer words.

EDITING FOR COMPLETENESS

Editing a message to make sure it is complete is important. Leaving out a detail such as a name, date, place, or amount can make the message useless. You need to look at the content as well as the format to make sure a message is complete.

Edit for Content

Details are necessary. Have you ever received a message that left out a very important detail? For example, maybe you were invited to a meeting. All details were given except the time.

Messages are often incomplete because the writer is so familiar with the content that omitted details are not obvious. Omitted details are, however, obvious to the reader.

A good way to check for details is to ask yourself the questions a reporter would ask when gathering information: Who? What? Where? When? Why? How?

Edit for Format

In addition to editing for completeness of details, you should also edit for completeness of format. Do the following to make sure that the format of a communication is complete.

- In an e-mail, a memo, or a letter, check that all the parts and the special notations have been included and are in the correct position and sequence. For example, it is easy to omit an enclosure notation or forget to include the date. It also is easy to place the enclosure notation before the reference initials when it should be just the opposite.

Not paying attention to details can be extremely costly. The Georgia Court of Appeals rejected an appeal submitted by the state Attorney General's office because the appeal was filed in the Times New Roman font instead of the Courier font. (The court specified that legal briefs must use the Courier font. Doing so prevents attorneys from using a smaller font to fit more words within the set page limit.) The appeal was rejected twice. As a result, the state settled with the accident victim for one million dollars.
Source: The Florida Times-Union

- In a report, check to see that all appropriate pages, such as the title page, table of contents, works cited page, and so on, have been included and are in the correct sequence.

Complete the following exercise to help you be alert to editing for details.

CHECKUP 14-11 Indicate the detail from the list that would appropriately complete each numbered item by placing the letter of the detail in the blank provided. Use each letter only once.

a. p.m.
b. stationery
c. at the Italian Garden Restaurant
d. 803-555-8824
e. size extra large

_____ 1. Please ship two sweatshirts, Catalog No. 2830-S. Ship them by UPS to Jacob Anderson, 324 Murphy Drive, Pawtucket, Rhode Island 02864.

_____ 2. Order these three items: ink cartridges and disks.

_____ 3. To avoid conflict with most class times, Dr. Dennis Walrutta's lecture will be at 6:30.

_____ 4. Let's discuss the proposal tonight at dinner. I'll meet you at 7:30 p.m.

_____ 5. Call me at my pager number 704-555-2483 or my home number.

Application 14-A

Use appropriate revision symbols to remove wordy, trite, and sub-standard English expressions from the following draft letter. Replace any difficult words with words that are easier to understand. Harry Friedman hopes he helped Jack Carter by returning the questionnaire Mr. Carter enclosed with his October 5 letter. The completed questionnaire is enclosed with Mr. Friedman's letter.

Travel Consultants, Inc.

132 Elizabeth Avenue, Boiling Springs, NC 28017
Telephone: 704-555-2841   •   Fax: 704-555-2844   •   travelco.bs.net

October 15, <YEAR>

Mr. Jack Carter
Director of Marketing
Smart Communications
3281 Felter Street
Charlotte, NC 28219

Dear Mr. Carter:

We are in receipt of yours of the fifth asking us to complete a questionnaire regarding our company communications. Please find same completed and enclosed herewith.

In regard to your suggestion, we will initiate a study to try and find ways of facilitating our company's communications. We will explain the study to our staff and elicit their assistance. They should be involved in the study and the subsequent decisions.

Looking forward to working with you to improve our communications, we remain,

Sincerely yours,

Harry Friedman
Manager

lc
Enclosure

Application 14-B

Edit the following draft of a two-page letter to Mrs. Elizabeth Thomas that appears on pages 307–308. Be especially alert to wordiness, redundancies, overused words, improper English, trite phrases, unnecessary phrases and clauses, and the unnecessary use of difficult words. Use revision symbols to mark corrections.

October 28, <YEAR>

Mrs. Elizabeth Thomas
Director of Corporate Travel Services
Step-by-Step Seminars Inc.
2772 Carolina Causeway
Wilmington, NC 28403

Dear Mrs. Thomas:

Thanks for sharing the taxi with me from LaGuardia Airport into midtown Manhattan last week. During rush hour traffic that very long ride is very much more interesting with pleasant conversation.

I'm eager to talk with you further about our services that you and your company can utilize. As I understood from our conversation, a primary problem you face is coordinating arrangements with hotels and convention facilities for the seminars and workshops your organization offers in major cities around the United States. Although participants rank your organization very high in program and presentation content, problems with meeting rooms, refreshment and meal services, and accessibility for physically challenged registrants have drawn very strong criticism during the past two consecutive years. We can help your organization improve in these areas.

As I told you in New York, our agency specializes in planning and coordinating meeting and convention gatherings for groups of 25 to 2500. Our services range from making hotel reservations to coordinating conventions that are one week long. The following list describes some of the services we can provide.

1. <u>Meeting rooms and audiovisual services</u>. We handle arrangements with hotels and convention centers to tailor meeting room size, outfitting, and climate control to the needs of the presentation. Our service includes arranging for rental, delivery, setup, testing, and return of audiovisual equipment.

2. <u>Housing</u>. If your staff and clients need housing at or near the site of the meeting, we can coordinate those accommodations and will provide rooming lists for convenience in distributing messages, agendas, materials, and so on.

3. <u>Travel arrangements</u>. My understanding is that you need travel arrangements primarily for your staff and presenters rather than for meeting participants. We will develop a travel profile for each traveler that describes preferences in airline, seat assignments, and special dietary needs.

4. <u>Participants list</u>. Our specialist of computer services provides a detailed participants list including name, billing address, specialized medical needs and/or physical limitations, dietary requirements and/or preferences, and VIP status. We also can provide client histories that are cumulative.

5. <u>Special activities</u>. If you wish to offer any activities that are special during your meeting, we can research and coordinate arrangements for those events. Such events might include group tickets for the theater, concerts, or sports events; visits to theme parks or museums; or sightseeing tours.

6. <u>Event scheduling</u>. Our researchers maintain a master calendar of events throughout the United States. We can help you schedule your meetings to stay away from or to coincide with other major events.

Your organization would benefit from our specialists' expertise in the following areas: travel, housing facilities, presentation services, social events, and computer services.

In the event that you have questions or need additional information, please call me up or e-mail me at karen@blassingame.com.

Looking forward to hearing from you soon, I remain

Sincerely yours,

Karen Blassingame
Manager of Corporate Services

Application 14-C

Edit the following letter to eliminate passive voice, wordiness, redundancies, overused words, and trite expressions. Use appropriate revision symbols to mark corrections.

Post Office Box 33299, Georgetown, SC 29442
•Telephone: 803-555-2284 •Cell Telephone: 803-555-8824 •Pager: 803-555-2285

May 18, <YEAR>

Mr. Joshua Ephraim
Post Office Box 5284
Winston-Salem, NC 27113

Dear Mr. Ephraim:

Enclosed herewith please find the exact same expensive luggage that was damaged on your recent trip to Georgetown, South Carolina. The expensive luggage has been repaired by Ace Luggage Company, which is the manufacturer.

Kevin, who is the luggage handler, has been reprimanded by his supervisor. He is at the present time assigned to retraining. Kevin was concerned about your expensive damaged luggage and asked that I express his apologies for any inconvenience.

Thank you, Mr. Ephraim, for flying Marlin Airlines. We look forward to serving you again on your flights in the future.

Sincerely,

Stephen R. Stover

sdk
Enclosure

Application 14-D

Below is information that should appear on the Web site for T-Shirt Express. Proofread the information from the Web site that appears on the following page, comparing it to the information shown below. (Information on the Web site may appear in a different order than shown below.) Use appropriate revision symbols to mark needed changes.

Information for Web Page

Company Name: T-Shirt Express
Address: Post Office Box 5224, Cincinnati, Ohio 45201
E-Mail Address: tshirtexp@ohio.net
Telephone Number: 513-555-6874
Fax Number: 513-555-6876

Order Personalized T-Shirts
Design your own T-Shirts for your company, family, or friends.
Choose the printed text, background design, and color.
Use your own photos (submitted electronically or by snail mail).

Ordering is Easy!

First Quality T-Shirts
Available Colors

| White | Cream | Blue | Yellow |
| Pink | Green | Lilac | Orange |

T-Shirt Prices and Sizes

Pictures–$5 Extra
Text–10 Words–Free
Extra Words–$1 Per Word

Children's Sizes–$15
1T to 4T
Youth Sizes–$20
Small, Medium, and Large
Adult Sizes–$25
Small, Medium, Large, Extra Large

Shipping and Handling
$2 per Shirt
Next Day Air Available at Additional Cost

Application 14-D (continued)

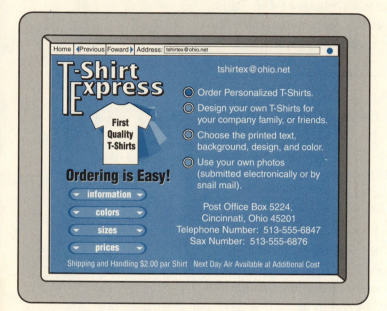

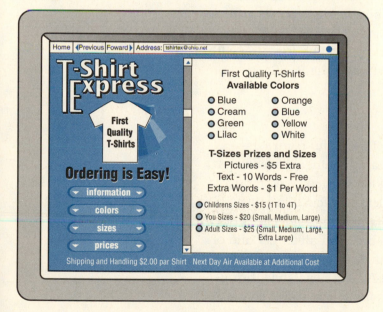

CD-ROM Application 14-E

Using your word processor, open the file DPES14E from the CD-ROM. Edit the brochure copy to eliminate passive voice, wordiness, redundancies, overused words, and trite expressions. Use revision symbols to mark corrections. Save the revised brochure copy using your initials in place of the DPES. Proofread and edit the brochure copy on the screen; make any additional corrections. Save and print the corrected document.

LOOKING FOR A CHANGE OF SCENERY?

Let us help you plan something different this year with exciting vacation packages to the Pacific Northwest and Canada.

Westwinds Tours

Why not do something fun by combining a spectacular land tour of Alaska's Pacific Mountain region with a cruise along the famous Inside Passage? This itinerary offers a fabulous vacation value and the best of both worlds—land and sea! You'll spend an entire day in spectacular Glacier Bay National Park. Think of your neighbors back home sweating through the heat of summer as you scrutinize glorious Mt. McKinley and spectacular Denali National Park on a scenic ride aboard a glass-domed railcar. You will be traveling with a company that has been introducing visitors to the Pacific Mountain region for over 25 years.

Alaska Seas

Also awaiting you is a summer vacation of beautiful contrasts— from whales and icebergs in Alaska to quaint fishing villages set amid the breathtaking beauty of the Rockies' rugged peaks and sparkling lakes. Our Alaska Seas cruise lets you focus in on the cosmopolitan seaports of British Columbia and the wilderness of the Northwest Territories. No two cruises are both alike. Let one of our travel consultants tell you how Alaska Seas can facilitate your enjoyment of Canada's best in the famed Alaska Seas style, bringing you unforgettable memories. Contact one of our travel consultants in the near future for details.

CD-ROM Application 14-F

Open the file DPES14F from the CD-ROM. Use the grammar checker and the readability indexes in your software to detect passive voice in the following memo. Edit to remove most of the passive voice and to lower the reading level. Reword the memo as necessary but do not change the intended meaning. Save the revised memo using your initials in place of the DPES. Five lines below the memo, type and complete the following statement: I reduced the reading grade level from _____ to _____ and the percentage of passive voice from _____ to _____. Proofread and edit the memo; then save and print the corrected memo.

Memo To: Nancy S. Williams, County Manager

From: David A. Bennett, Administrative Assistant

Date: December 20, <YEAR>

Subject: Preparation for the Council Meeting

During our regularly scheduled encounter yesterday, you solicited my assistance in summarizing the issues that may be controversial at our next council meeting. Below are three issues that we should be prepared to discuss.

1.   The Traffic Advisory Committee verbally evaluated the potentiality of converting the street in front of the Court House to bi-directional traffic. The committee will present its conclusions at our meeting.

2.   A survey on the property adjoining the Court House has been completed by Jones and Company. This property, if purchased, would be used for a three-tier parking facility. An appraisal was completed by Crowe Surveying and Appraisals, Inc. We do not know the figures yet but anticipate that they will be exorbitant.

3.   An upward adjustment in compensation has been proposed for the Court House security guard by the maintenance engineer. The effect on the budget is inconsequential, but there will be opposition because the security guard has been employed less than two months.

The remainder of the upcoming matters are routine. Please communicate with me if you want additional information on these issues.

Editing for Language Use

After completing this chapter, you should be able to:

1. Edit documents so that they reflect the you-attitude.

2. Edit documents to achieve a consistent point of view.

3. Edit documents to eliminate biased language and stereotypes.

The final steps in editing involve polishing a document to make it the best, most effective communication that you can transmit. Obviously, you should proofread and edit documents to find and correct all content, mechanical, and typographical errors, but you need to go beyond these basics.

Chapter 15 gives you a look at some of the finer points of editing, specifically applying the you-attitude, maintaining a consistent point of view, and eliminating stereotypes and biased language. Doing so will increase the likelihood that your document will convey the intended message and that your reader will respond in the way you want him or her to respond. Let's look first at using the you-attitude.

USING THE YOU-ATTITUDE

Effective use of the you-attitude can increase the likelihood of getting a positive response to your communication. Using the you-attitude involves focusing on the reader's point of view and considering how he or she might interpret your message. In other words, you make the communication reader-centered (you-attitude) as opposed to writer-centered (I-attitude).

The following examples illustrate the difference between using the I-attitude and the you-attitude. Note how the you-attitude places the emphasis on the reader.

I-attitude:	I would like to congratulate you on your promotion to vice president.
You-attitude:	Congratulations on your promotion to vice president.

I-attitude:	I need to receive your report by Monday, April 10.
You-attitude:	Please send me your report by Monday, April 10.

Positive words help convey the you-attitude by creating a pleasant impression in the reader's mind. Using positive words where appropriate—such as *succeed* instead of *fail*—can increase the positive feeling the reader has about your communication. On the other hand, negative words such as *blame* and *refuse* can make the reader feel angry or upset.

The following are some examples of negative words. Look for these and other negative words in the documents you edit. Where appropriate, edit sentences to use positive words.

cannot	failure	incompetent	never
deny	fault	mistake	unreliable
disagree	inability	neglect	wrong

Using a negative word with *you* or *your* seems to verbally accuse, attack, or downgrade the reader, so you should avoid this usage. Compare the use of negative and positive words in the following examples.

Negative:	You neglected to tell us that you had moved.
Positive:	We did not know that you had moved.

Negative:	Due to your error, the project is delayed.
Positive:	Due to an oversight, the project is delayed.

Negative:	You failed to notice that you have reached your credit limit on your charge card; thus, your purchase is being denied.
Positive:	You may be unaware that you have reached your credit limit. We recommend that you postpone this purchase until you check with your credit card company.

TIPS

SELECTING POSITIVE WORDS

To replace a negative word with a positive one, use a dictionary or thesaurus. Look up the negative word, then find an antonym (a word with an opposite meaning) for the negative word.

CHECKUP 15-1 In the space provided, rewrite each sentence to use the you-attitude and positive words.

1. Your quarterly report for the holiday sales season should not show a loss.

   _____

   _____

2. I want to wish you and your family much happiness in the New Year.

   _____

   _____

3. Kristin is not incapable of completing the audit.

   _____

   _____

4. I want to thank you for not interpreting my comments in the wrong way.

   _____

   _____

5. There should be no problem with the computer software.

   _____

   _____

6. We hope you will not refuse the offer.

   _____

   _____

7. I believe that your proposal has the most merit.

   _____

   _____

8. He was misinformed about the accident.

   _____

   _____

9. Cheryl neglected to tell us about the appointment.

   _____

   _____

10. She almost never disagrees with us.

   _____

   _____

ACHIEVING A CONSISTENT POINT OF VIEW

Using a consistent point of view in a message is important. Point of view involves using the first, second, or third person consistently throughout a document. Doing so makes the message easier to understand.

First person refers to the person who is speaking. *Second person* refers to a person who is spoken to. *Third person* refers to a person who is spoken about. Verbs as well as personal pronouns change forms in order to show which person is being used. Note how the following personal pronouns are used for first, second, and third person.

First Person: I, we

Second Person: you, your

Third Person: he, she, it, one, they
                    (*the student*, *the volunteers*, and so on)

First and second person usually are used in informal writing and in conversation. Third person usually is used in formal writing to demonstrate an objective viewpoint. For example, the third person would be used in documents such as reports, reviews, policy statements, and term papers.

A common error in stating the point of view is shifting person from singular to plural, as in the following example.

> *We* are planning a trip to Asheville, and *I* should arrive there by 4 p.m.

Using the third person *We* and the first person *I* is confusing since one is plural and one is singular. It indicates that more than one person is planning a trip but only one person is arriving in Asheville. The sentence is unclear.

Complete the following exercise for practice in identifying and correcting inconsistencies in point of view.

CHECKUP 15-2 In the space provided, rewrite each sentence to achieve a consistent point of view.

1. One becomes easily frustrated when you can't get the photocopier to work properly.

   _____

   _____

2. Citizens should realize that you cannot lower the crime rate without hiring more police officers.

   _____

   _____

3. We offered to purchase the house, and the owner agreed to sell it to me.

   _____

   _____

4. If you dial 911, one can get emergency help immediately.

   _____

   _____

5. People frequently offer their opinion even when they are not asked.

   _____

   _____

ELIMINATING BIASED LANGUAGE AND STEREOTYPES

An important part of editing is to eliminate any biased language. Biased language refers to wording that is gender-specific, discriminatory, or stereotyped.

Use Gender-Neutral Words

Gender-neutral words do not show bias on behalf of either men or women; *gender-specific* words demonstrate a preference for one gender over the other. For example, the term *stewardess* is gender-specific because it refers only to women; the preferred term is *flight attendant*. The term *flight attendant* is considered gender-neutral—it refers to both men and women without mentioning gender. Other examples of gender-specific and gender-neutral terms appear in the following list.

The contents of a man's wallet and a woman's purse were taken while they slept in their home between 1:30 p.m. Thursday and 7:30 a.m. Friday. *Source:* Police report

Gender-Specific	Gender-Neutral
businessman	businessperson, business worker
chairman	chairperson, chair
foreman	supervisor
mailman	mail carrier
newsman	newscaster
policeman	police officer
salesman	sales associate, salesperson
spokesman	spokesperson

Gender bias involves making an assumption that any group of people or people with specific job titles are of a specific gender. For example, all doctors are not male and all nurses and secretaries are not female. A blunder in this category could be costly as it was when David, a job applicant, entered the human resources office for an interview. David asked the woman seated at the desk, "May I see the human resource manager, please?" She replied, "I am she." His awkward response was, "Oh, I thought you were the receptionist." Needless to say, David didn't make a positive impression.

In writing, avoid expressions that imply that people in a certain group are of the same gender. Look at the following pair of sentences:

Gender-specific: Wives of the executives who are receiving awards should be invited to the awards luncheon. (Implies that all executives are male.)

Gender-neutral: Spouses of executives who are receiving awards should be invited to the awards luncheon.

Many grammar checkers are designed to check for gender-specific language. When the software recognizes a gender-specific term, as shown in Figure 15-1, it displays choices of gender-neutral language. For example, the word *chairman* in Figure 15-1 may be replaced by the gender-neutral terms *chair* or *chairperson*.

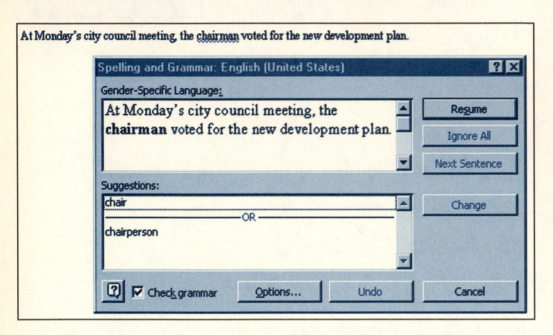

Figure 15-1. Grammar checker in Microsoft Word® showing alternatives for gender-specific language.

Use Nondiscriminatory Words

Communicating successfully in today's business environment demands that we be courteous and considerate in communicating for ethical as well as legal reasons. For example, classified ads for positions should not be gender-specific because they would be discriminatory.

Compare the following two examples. The ad on the left is gender-specific and the ad on the right is gender-neutral. Note how removing the gender-specific words makes the ad on the right gender-neutral.

Gender-Specific	Gender-Neutral
Large medical office needs experienced office manager. Her duties would include developing employee work schedules, administering payroll, and making investment recommendations. Excellent benefits. Salary commensurate with her education and experience.	Large medical office needs experienced office manager. Duties would include developing employee work schedules, administering payroll, and making investment recommendations. Excellent benefits. Salary commensurate with education and experience.

Net Link

For additional information on using gender-neutral language, go to **http://www.rpi.edu /dept/llc/writecenter /web/text/gender.html** and read the article "Writing with Gender-Fair Language" on the Rensselaer Polytechnic Institute Web site.

You and everyone you work with should strive to treat all persons equally. To accomplish this, you need to respect each person's characteristics and beliefs, even though they may be different from your own. Remember, there are laws stating that discrimination on the basis of race, religion, age, sex, physical abilities, and national origin is illegal. Thus, care must be taken to avoid discriminatory words and stereotypes when communicating. You should think before you communicate so that you do not offend someone, even unintentionally.

Some words are discriminatory because they focus on a person's physical condition. Note the following examples.

Discriminatory	Nondiscriminatory
blind	visually impaired
crippled, disabled	physically challenged
deaf	hearing impaired
fat	overweight

Other words are discriminatory because they make unnecessary references to a person's age, appearance, ethnicity, or gender, as in the following examples.

Discriminatory: Despite being elderly, Mr. Turner exercises quite a bit.

Nondiscriminatory: Despite his age, Mr. Turner exercises quite a bit.

Discriminatory: The Asian doctor performed the surgery.

Nondiscriminatory: The doctor performed the surgery.

Complete the following exercise for practice in eliminating discriminatory language.

CHECKUP 15-3   In the following sentences, delete any discriminatory language or replace any discriminatory language with unbiased language. Use revision symbols to mark corrections.

1. If you hire Jeremy, he will do a great job, even though he is confined to a wheelchair.

2. The doctor told the patient that being fat made his condition worse.

3. A speeding car struck the elderly woman as she crossed the highway about 9 p.m.

4. Our Hispanic taxi driver got a speeding ticket on the way to the airport, making us miss our plane.

5. We plan to hire 20 drivers in November. Each of the drivers should give us a copy of his driver's license.

6. Please invite all local businessmen to the luncheon.

7. Yvette is unable to play softball because she is deaf.

8. Our attractive assistant will prepare the report.

9. Will Christina serve as chairman of the committee?

10. All hospitals offer special parking passes for the crippled.

Avoid Stereotyping and Prejudice

Making an assumption, either positive or negative, about an individual based on the group to which the individual belongs is called *stereotyping*. For example, assuming that John, a teenager, is rebellious simply because all teenagers are rebellious is an example of stereotyping. Stereotyping leads to *prejudices,* which are usually negative (rather than positive) attitudes about a group, a race, or someone who has a certain characteristic. Some examples would be to say that African-Americans are good athletes or that Asians have excellent math skills.

The next exercise will give you practice in detecting and correcting language that leads to stereotypes or prejudice.

Each of the following sentences
uses language that contributes to stereotypes and prejudice. In the
space provided, rewrite each sentence to eliminate the stereotype
or prejudice.

1. Jimmy, from South Carolina, takes a long time doing anything. He puts three syllables in the word *yes*.

   _____

   _____

2. The house has a swimming pool and a three-car garage. A
   doctor must own it.

   _____

   _____

3. That guy is almost seven feet tall. He must be a basketball
   player.

   _____

   _____

4. Those women can't figure out the right course of action. Do
   they all have blonde hair?

   _____

   _____

5. Don't expect a kind word from Claire; she is a northerner.

   _____

   _____

Application 15-A

Use revision symbols to correct point-of-view errors and eliminate stereotypes and the I-attitude in the following memo.

MEMO TO: Administrative Staff, Tampa Volunteer Association

FROM: Randall Hobbs

DATE: March 18, <YEAR>

SUBJECT: Annual Clean-Up Day

I would like to announce that on Friday, April 1, we will be having our Annual Clean-Up Day. This year, we will concentrate our efforts in the covered picnic area that is used frequently for lunch and for organized functions.

In addition to cleaning up the area, we also will be planting trees, shrubs, and flowers. Both plants and trees have been donated by area businessmen. I want to ask the men to please bring their chain saws, shovels, and hedge trimmers.

Please call my secretary, T. J. Parsons, to sign up for a specific work assignment. Lunch will be provided. Women, we especially need some help in serving lunch and providing iced beverages throughout the day.

Several of you, because of your specific job responsibilities, have been asked to remain on the job on Clean-Up Day. Everyone else may participate in our cleaning and planting venture. I want to encourage everyone, unless you are crippled, to participate in some way.

In previous years we have enjoyed working together in an outdoor environment. Let's hope that the weather is good and that we can get much done on April 1.

Application 15-B

Edit the following letter to use the you-attitude. Also correct any point-of-view errors and eliminate stereotypes. Use revision symbols to mark corrections.

April 22, <YEAR>

Ms. Maxine Aldridge
3244 Park Lane
Denver, CO 80209

Dear Ms. Aldridge:

I want to take this opportunity to congratulate you on your graduation from college next month. I am sure that you worked hard, because you made the dean's list almost every semester.

I am sure that you, as a member of a sorority, will be taking some time off before accepting your first full time position. Thus, we have allowed several weeks between graduation and your first day on the job. However, I want to confirm our offer to you for employment beginning June 1. I have attached a contract outlining the specific details. I ask that you sign the contract and return it to me within 10 days of the date of this letter.

I thoroughly enjoyed working with you when I supervised your internship at our company. I look forward to having you back as my assistant.

Sincerely yours,

Anita Gordon, Manager

Enclosure

Application 15-C

Proofread and edit the following draft of a cover letter that will accompany a questionnaire being mailed to customers. Use appropriate revision symbols to correct language use errors as well as other types of errors.

January 27, <YEAR>

Ms. Alisa Esteban
1863 East Humboldt Drive
Columbus, OH 43230

Dear Ms. Esteban:

We are currently updating our product line and I would appreciate some feedback from you. To that end, we wood like to know more about the outdoor activities you enjoy.

Please take a few moments to complete the enclosed questionnaire. By doing so, you will help us to develop quality products that are tailored to your needs. Your responses will be kept confidential.

Please mail you completed questionnaire to Willis Research Associates, an independant research firm that will tabulate the responses from our male and female customers. You may use the enclosed postage-paid envelope that I have provided.

I wish to thank you for participating in this important survey.

Sincerly,

Davis L. Rush,
  Sales Manager

Enclosures

Application 15-D

Proofread the following balance sheet very carefully, especially the calculations. Use revision symbols to mark all errors.

Bill's Auto parts, Inc.
Balance Sheet
June 30; <YEAR>

Assets

Current Assets

Cash	$10,260	
Short Term Investments	2,000	
Accounts Receivable	8,100	
Notes Receivable	35,200	
Merchandise Inventory	61,400	
Prepaid Insurance	5,600	
Office Supplies	1,000	
Ware House Supplies	6.560	
Total Current Assets		$130,220

Property Plant, and Equipment

Land		$ 6,500	
Building	$21,650		
Less Accumulated Depreciation	8,640	13,010	
Office Equipment	$ 9,600		
Less Accumulated Depreciation	5,000	4,600	
Delivery Equipment	$20,400		
Less Accumulated Depreciation	9,450	10,950	
Total Property, Plant, and Equipment			35,060

Total Assets	$165,180

Liabilities

Current Liabilities

Notes Payable	$16,000	
Accounts Payable	24,602	
Salaries Payable	2,083	
Total Current Liabilities		$42685

Long Term Liabilities

Mortgage Liabilities	17,800	
Total Liabilities		$60,485

Owner's Equity

Bill Morgan, Capitol	$104,695
Total Liabilities and Owners Equity	$165,180

CD-ROM Application 15-E

Using your word processor, open the file DPES15E from the CD-ROM. Edit the policy statement to change the wording to third person and to correct any sexist language. Save the revised policy using your initials in place of the DPES. Proofread and edit the policy on the screen and make any additional corrections. Save and print the corrected policy.

VACATION POLICY

DAVIS CORPORATION

Effective January 1, <YEAR>

Associates who have been continuously employed for at least one year as of January 1 are eligible for one week of vacation. Male and female associates continuously employed from two to nine years are eligible for two weeks of vacation. If you have been employed for over ten years, you are eligible for three weeks of vacation.

Vacation time must be requested and confirmed in writing (Form #5894) by the appropriate foreman one month in advance. To maintain adequate health and safety resources, each company nurse should request her vacation days at least three months in advance.

You must use vacation time in the year that it is earned. I have determined that all request decisions are based primarily on the date the request is received and secondarily on seniority. Men and their wives requesting the same vacation dates should note this in the appropriate place on the form. Such requests will be honored if possible.

CD-ROM Application 15-F

Using your word processor, open the file DPES15F from the CD-ROM. Edit the memo to eliminate language use errors as well as other types of errors. Use revision symbols to mark corrections. Save the revised memo using your initials in place of the DPES. Proofread and edit the memo on the screen and make any additional corrections. Save and print a copy.

MEMO TO: Rebecca O'Neal, Commuter Specialist

FROM: Leslie Compton, Manager

DATE: October 5, <YEAR>

SUBJECT: Customer Invoicing

Rebecca please examine our procedures for invoicing customers. I have tired three different methods; tow of them was complete disasters. The third method is the one we are using now, and it is unsatisfactory. There should be a better way.

Enclosed is a software package that is designed specifically for invoicing. The software company has offered it to us free on a trail basis. We don't have to buy the software unless it works for use.

I would like to get your recomendations as soon you have had time to evaluate our existing procedures and the new software. As our computer specialist, you should be able to tell if this software will improve our invoicing procedures.

Enclosure

Proofreading and Editing and Voice - Recognition Technology

After dialing an 800 number to request a home decorating magazine, the caller was surprised to hear the following computerized voice message. "May I send you a *Leisure Home Catalog*? If so, say <u>yes</u> now." The caller responded in the affirmative, and the computerized voice instructed the caller to say her last name. The caller responded and continued answering additional prompts until she had given the necessary address information that would enable the company to mail the catalog to her. The computer had changed the spoken address to a typed address and stored the information in its files. This is an example of voice-recognition technology. The address information was not typed; instead, it was spoken and changed into text.

The next section gives an overview of what voice-recognition technology is and how it is used.

VOICE-RECOGNITION TECHNOLOGY

Very simply explained, voice-recognition software uses the human voice instead of the keyboard and a mouse to enter information into a computer. Voice-recognition technology is available for the personal computer with the addition of voice-recognition software, a microphone, a sound card, and more computer memory, if needed. Speaking into a microphone, the user dictates the document. As the words are spoken, they appear as typed text on the screen.

To format a document, the user tells the program the type of document that is being dictated. Based on macros or templates that the user has set up, the program formats the document accordingly. The user also must tell the program where to start and end paragraphs. To punctuate a sentence, the user speaks the punctuation as part of the dictation, as shown by the following example.

Sentence to dictate:	The highest accuracy rate, according to the latest report, is 98 percent.
Actual dictation:	The highest accuracy rate [comma] according to the latest report [comma] is 98 percent [period]

The early versions of voice-recognition software programs had problems that prohibited wide acceptance. For example, it took hours to train the software to recognize your voice. Also, the software had a limited vocabulary and had difficulty distinguishing words when a speaker had an accent. Most of these problems have been conquered with the latest versions of voice-recognition software. For instance, training the software to recognize your voice now takes as little as fifteen minutes. With improvements in the ability to recognize a person's speech patterns plus expanded software vocabularies, most voice-recognition programs can achieve an accuracy rate of 95 to 98 percent.

Net Link

For a short demonstration of how voice-recognition software works, go to **http://www-4.ibm.com /software/speech** and select the link for the demo of the latest IBM voice-recognition software.

Advantages of Voice-Recognition Technology

You can readily see several advantages for this technological advancement.

- **Assists physically challenged persons in using computers.** Voice-recognition technology allows people who are visually impaired and those who lack hand or finger mobility to use computers more easily.

- **Saves time and makes computer use easier for those who lack typing skills.** Computer users who lack typing skills will find voice-recognition technology a much easier and faster way to enter text.

- **Reduces the number of spelling errors.** Most voice-recognition software programs have extensive vocabularies. If the word is pronounced correctly and is recognized by the software, it should be spelled correctly. When a word is used that may be spelled in more than one way, such as the homonyms *to* and *too*, voice-recognition software uses the context (the surrounding text) to determine which usage is correct. Note the following examples.

It was <u>too</u> early <u>to</u> go <u>to</u> the <u>two</u> o'clock show.

We <u>knew</u> who would be the <u>new</u> vice president.

- **Frees hands for other tasks, and reduces the opportunity for repetitive stress injuries.** The computer operator is free to perform other tasks such as looking through materials to get needed information for the document being dictated. By reducing the amount of time spent in repetitive activities such as typing, voice-recognition programs could reduce the number of repetitive stress injuries, which are very common in today's work environment.

SOFTWARE TIPS

Most voice-recognition software programs have a vocabulary feature that allows you to add specialized terms and often-used phrases as part of the vocabulary the program recognizes. Whenever the user includes one of the terms or phrases as part of the dictation, the software will recognize the words and enter them in the dictation.

Disadvantages of Voice-Recognition Technology

As with any new technology, there are some drawbacks to voice-recognition programs.

- **The cost of voice-recognition programs.** Although the cost of the latest voice-recognition programs is lower than that of earlier versions, there is still cost involved in making sure the computer has the memory and sound capabilities to run voice-recognition software programs.

- **Training the software to recognize your voice.** The software must become accustomed to the inflections of the computer user's voice plus any accent that the user may have. The software also must deal with occasional changes in the user's voice due to conditions such as a cold or allergy. In addition, the user will have to continue training the software to recognize new words and phrases.

- **Distraction of dictating aloud.** Dictating aloud, rather than typing, increases office noise and causes distractions. Using voice-recognition programs in an open office setting or an office with cubicles is especially distracting.

- **Need for improved dictation skills.** Document originators must improve their dictation skills. The most important thing is to speak clearly and use a natural pace. As part of the dictation, the user must tell the software what formatting to use as well as the punctuation marks to use.

Applications of Voice-Recognition Technology

Professionals in a variety of occupations, such as doctors and lawyers, already use voice-recognition technology on the job. Doctors usually dictate information about their patients soon after each examination is completed. The dictation must be transcribed and subsequently placed in the patient's file. Voice-recognition programs reduce the need for transcription, which saves time and money. Lawyers also spend much time dictating information related to each client and each case. Here again, voice-recognition software saves time and money. To meet the growing demand for voice-recognition technology, software vendors offer specialized packages for various professions. For example, some voice-recognition programs offer specialized dictionaries and features for users in the financial, legal, computer, and medical fields.

With continuous improvements in accuracy and ease-of-use, voice-recognition programs may soon become the primary means of inputting text on a computer.

A physician who was using a voice-dictation program dictated the following sentence: "Recommend CAT scan if symptoms persist." The program typed the sentence as: "Recommend casket if symptoms persist." *Source: Reader's Digest*

Correction Features of Voice-Recognition Programs

The accuracy of dictation when using voice recognition depends on how clearly you speak, how well you train the software, and how you position the microphone. For example, if the microphone is not positioned correctly, the software may pick up background noise or misinterpret your words. As a result, the software may insert extra words in your dictation, such as *to* and *an*. To avoid this problem, position the microphone as recommended, and speak at a natural pace that does not include long pauses.

If the voice-recognition program makes a mistake, you have the option of correcting the mistake either as you dictate or after you are finished. Some voice-recognition programs allow you to correct a mistake by using voice commands. For example, say the word "Correct," then say the incorrect word followed by the correct word. Each time the program hears the incorrect word, it will use the correct one in its place. Other voice-recognition programs require you to use a combination of voice commands, the mouse, and the keyboard to edit words.

Most voice-recognition programs allow you to play back your dictation. The playback option is especially helpful if someone other than the person who dictated the document will be proofreading and editing the document.

The most frequently made errors occur when the program mistakenly recognizes the word the user spoke as another word. For example, the person may say "cut <u>and</u> paste" and the software may enter "cut <u>in</u> paste." Contractions also may be entered incorrectly. For example, instead of "<u>shouldn't</u>" the software may enter "<u>should dent</u>."

Although voice-recognition programs offer automatic correction features, proofreading and editing are still needed. Polished documents do not result the first time around.

Complete the following exercise to gain experience in detecting the types of errors that often result when using voice-recognition software.

CHECKUP 16-1 Use revision symbols to mark needed corrections in the following sentences.

1. Each camper should have his or her own fork in spoon.

2. At dessert time, the hostess served the guests a pizza pie.

3. Having the board meeting on the coast offers a siren atmosphere.

4. Your bank account will accumulate enter rest at a low rate.

5. How many bites of memory does your computer have?

6. We will be held a cannibal for completing the project.

7. Most of our reports assent as e-mail attachments.

8. There is much for us to disgust at the next meeting.

9. Our new building has offices forever 500 employees.

10. The board of directors in tents to make a decision this week.

The contents of a man's wallet and a woman's purse were taken while they slept in their home between 1:30 p.m. Thursday and 7:30 a.m. Friday.

Application 16-A

Proofread the following memo that was dictated using voice-recognition software. Be especially alert for words that may have been mispronounced and were not recognized correctly by the software. Use appropriate revision symbols from the inside front cover to mark corrections.

MEMO TO: All Employees

FROM: Edward Custer, Vice President

DATE: March 21, <YEAR>

SUBJECT: Promotion of Lisa Moharas

I ham pleased to announce the promotion of Lisa Moharas to the Manager of Electronic Publishing.

Since joining the company last tear, Lisa has been a key member of the electronic publishing department. Most recently, Lisa held the position of Special Projects Administrator for the Art, Design, and Production departments. In that role Lisa add rest a variety of issues surrounding the electronic publishing process. In Lisa's new role, her primary focus will be to head the internal electronic pub fishing activities. Lisa will also have an active role in implementing new electronic publishing technologies.

Please join me in congratulating Lisa and witching her much success in her new position.

Application 16-B

Proofread the following letter that was dictated using voice-recognition software. Be especially alert for words that may have been mispronounced and were not recognized correctly by the software. Use appropriate revision symbols from the inside front cover to mark corrections.

August 16, <YEAR>

Mr. Jacob Miller
Shelby Learning Systems
111 South Lane Avenue
Westerville, OH 43081

Dear Mr. Miller:

Thank you for you'll recent order for sick teen boxes of Pensco drawer ring pens. Your complete order is enclosed.

You will find these pens to be durable and comfortable farm most students to use. I feel sure that the drawer ring class that your company is sponsoring will be happy with these find pens.

As the class progresses, led us know these students' reactions to the special pens and to the work that you are doing with them. Meeting your needs in this way is important to us. Please call as again way we may be on service to you.

Sincerely,

Sharon Quick
Sales Manager

CD-ROM Application 16-C

Using your word processor, open the file DPES16C from the CD-ROM. Proofread and edit the memo to correct any mistakes that may have resulted from using voice-recognition technology to dictate the memo. Make corrections and save the revised memo using your initials in place of the DPES. Print the corrected memo.

MEMO TO: Entire Staff

FROM: Dean Coleman, LAN Administrator

DATE: March 21, <YEAR>

SUBJECT: Network Upgrades

We well need to make upgrades to our computer network this weekend, March 20 and 21. On toes days you will be unable to abscess any data files you half saved to the network. In addition, the e-mail system will not be available.

If you need to word with any files you have saved to the net worth, please copy ten to your computer hard drive by Friday March 19.

Pleas contract Andrea Pattee in the Computer Systems Group, Extension 6007, if you have any questions.

CD-ROM Application 16-D

Using your word processor, open the file DPES16D from the CD-ROM. Proofread and edit the letter to correct any mistakes that may have resulted from using voice-recognition technology to dictate the memo. Make corrections and save the revised letter using your initials in place of the DPES. Print the corrected letter.

April 3, <YEAR>

Ms. Althea Thomas
President
Fair Reporting, Inc.
11624 East 42nd Street
New York, NY 10021

Dear Ms. Thomas:

Thank you for agreeing to provide the expertise and personnel to staff the Hanson Enterprises, Inc., Employee Hotline. I'm looking for to working with you.

As we discussed on March 20, the hotline is indented as a convenient resource for employees to report there concerns about cup rate policies and workplace issues. The hotline as to be available seven days a week, 24 hours a day, for employee in booth our U.S. and international operations.

To maintain each caller's anonymity, no caller-identification or recording devices will be used. Instead, each call will be issued a control numb her to be used for tracking purposes. Booth the caller and the hotline will use the control numb her to track the status of the caller's concern.

Let's arrange a meeting next week to determine the means for handling international calls.

Sincerely,

Barbara Seagate
Director of Human Resources

NAME _____ DATE _____

Posttest

Part 1. Is the copy in the first column identical to the copy in the second column? If it is, write *Yes* in the space provided. If it is not identical, write *No*. Circle the errors in the second column.

1. Dr. Gordon Tarazi   Dr. Gordon Tarazi   1. _____
   879 Pembleton Lane   879 Pembleton Lane
   Savannah, GA 31460   Savanah, GA 31460

2. Account 2589503146   Account 2589503416   2. _____
   Account 1016523177   Account 1016522177

3. Jay B. Guiardina   Jay B. Guiardina   3. _____
   jaybga@00216.net   Jaybga@00216.net

Part 2. Proofread each of the following sentences for errors in keyboarding, spelling, word use, capitalization, word division, punctuation, grammar, sentence structure, number style, and consistency. Use revision symbols from the inside front cover to mark corrections.

4. Our new telecommunications center is located in Denver Colorado.

5. Both of the accountants has passed the CPA exam.

6. See that the article is is posted on our Internet site.

7. Many employees like the independance of working at home.

8. Either the associates or the manager are able to handle that request.

9. You need to order eighteen cubic yards of topsoil for the garden.

10. Norman's and Maria's house is being remodeled.

11. On April 1 2003, we will have been in business 20 years.

12. All salespersons are required to provide their won transportation.

13. The leading candidate for the position would be her.

14. Rosemarie manages the project development;Chris handles the marketing.

15. Of the 8 artists in the department, Sherry has the most experience.

16. See me at end of the day to discuss plans for tomorrow's meeting.

17. Ethan, Gary and Michael will open their new business in September.

18. We hired a well known consultant to review our business plan.

19. New employees will receive the following benefits overtime pay, stock options, and flexible hours.

20. Do you know whom is the new marketing manager?

21. Three are three main competitors in our target market.

22. Sue contacted the client about the contract she also called the attorney.

23. Beth our production manager has a knack for solving difficult problems.

24. Refer to the glossary for an explanation of terms see page 462.

25. After we review the proposal we will make a decision.

26. Sharon's new job involves a transfer to los Angeles.

27. Accounts 27695, 27730, and 27726 have been activated.

28. Two-thirds of our employees participate in volunteer activitys.

29. Everyone of our customers deserves outstanding service.

30. The two research assistants will complete the project by next week and send the results to Mr. Stowe.

31. Neither of the books are ready for publication.

32. We should recieve a refund on the defective software.

33. What would you say were the initial affects of the merger?

34. Each franchise owner is responsible for updating their inventory.

35. Brendas proposal has the best ideas for attracting new investors.

36. About sixty percent of our employees work overtime each month.

37. We recomended that our client take the settlement.

38. Miguel completed his degree in record time and he was soon hired.

39. Doug would you be willing to relocate?

40. Tony and Melissa work on the twenty second floor of the building.

41. Have you read the book Investing Carefully In Today's Market?

42. Do you know if its possible to fly nonstop to Japan?

43. If there is a change in travel plans. Let me know the details.

44. The Franklin Conservatory will open at 9:00 a.m. on weekends.

45. A fitness trainer will chose the equipment for our exercise room.

46. The new policy was rewritten to add new rules, for clarifying unclear rules, and to confirm existing rules.

47. Dallas, Miami, and Boston are the three citys where we have lived.

48. Is there a new deadline for completing the project.

49. The 9 am press conference has been rescheduled for tomorrow.

50. In the Fall we will launch our new product line for next year.

WORDS FREQUENTLY MISSPELLED IN BUSINESS COMMUNICATION

ability	altogether	bankruptcy
absence	always	basically
abundant	amortize	basis
accede	analysis	beginner
acceptable	analyze	believe
accessible	angle	beneficiary
accidentally	annual	benefited
accommodate	answer	biannual
accompanying	apologize	biased
accomplish	apparent	biennial
accountable	appetite	biggest
accustom	applicable	bought
achievement	appreciable	boundary
acknowledgment	approaches	breakfast
acquaintance	appropriate	breath
acquisition	approximate	breathe
activities	arbitrary	brochure
address	architect	brought
adjacent	area	budget
administrative	argument	bulletin
advantageous	arrangement	buried
advertise	article	business
advice	assessment	
advisable	assistance	cafeteria
advise	association	calendar
affiliate	athletics	campaign
agencies	attendance	canceled
aggressive	attorney	cannot
aisle	authorize	capabilities
all right	autumn	capacity
allege	auxiliary	capital
allowed	available	careful
already	average	cashier
alter		catalog
alternative	balance	categories

ceiling
certificate
choose
chose
chronological
claimant
client
coarse
coincidence
collateral
column
commission
commitment
committee
companies
comparison
compensation
competitive
complaint
complement
compliance
conceivable
conceive
conference
confidential
conscientious
conscious
consensus
consultant
continuous
contractor
controversy
convenience
cooperate
coordinator
corporate
correlate
correspondence
council
counsel
course
courteous
criticism
current
customer

debt
deceive
decision
defendant
defense
deficit
definite
delivery
dependent

describe
description
design
desirable
destroy
destruction
determined
detrimental
development
difference
different
dilemma
disability
disappear
disappoint
discussion
dissimilar
distribution
document
doesn't
double
duplicate
dying

efficient
either
electrical
eligible
embarrass
emphasize
employee
empty
enough
enrollment
enterprise
enumerate
environment
equipment
equipped
especially
essential
estimate
evaluate
exaggerate
exceed
excellent
exception
executive
exhibition
existence
expenditure
experience
extension
extraordinary
extremely

facility
facsimile
familiar
feasible
field
financial
fiscal
foreign
foresee
forfeit
forty
forward
fourteen
fourth
franchise
freight
friend
fulfill
further

gauge
generally
government
grammar
grateful
grievous
growth
guarantee
guardian

handicapped
happiness
harass
health
hear
height
here
hopeful
humor
hygiene

illegal
imitate
immediately
implement
importance
incidentally
inconvenience
increase
indicated
influence
initial
innovation
insurance
inventories

irrelevant
it's
itinerary
its

judgment
justifiable

knew
knowledge

labeled
laboratory
lease
leisure
lessen
lesson
liability
liaison
library
license
lieutenant
likelihood
listen
loose
lose
loss
lying

maintenance
manageable
maneuver
manufactured
material
meant
mileage
miniature
minimum
miscellaneous
modification
morale
mortgage

necessary
negotiate
neighbor
neither
nineteen
ninety
ninth
noticeable
notify

objective
occasion
occasionally

occur
occurrence
offense
offered
omission
operating
opinion
opportunity
ordinance
organization
organize
orientation
original

paid
pamphlet
paragraph
parallel
partially
participant
particularly
patience
patients
payable
percentage
performance
permanent
permissible
persistence
persistent
personal
personnel
persuade
pertinent
phase
phenomena
physical
physician
piece
planning
pleasant
policy
portion
position
possess
possession
possibility
potential
practically
precede
precedent
preferable
preference
preferring
preliminary
premise

prerogative
presence
principal
principle
privilege
procedure
proceed
production
professor
programmed
prove
provision
publicly
pursue

quality
quantity
question
questionnaire

receipt
receiving
recipient
recognize
recommend
recruit
reference
referral
registration
regular
relevant
relieved
repellent
representative
request
requirement
rescind
resistance
responsibility
responsible
restaurant
résumé
review

schedule
science
secretary
security
seize
seminar
separate
sergeant
serial
shipment
signed
significant

similar	supervisor	truly
simultaneous	suppose	two
sincerely	surgeon	
site	surveillance	usable
situation	survey	useful
sizable	symbol	utilization
source	symmetrical	
special		value
specification	tariff	variety
sponsor	technique	vendor
standard	technology	versus
stationary	temperature	volume
stationery	temporary	
statue	tenant	waiver
stature	termination	warehouse
status	theater	weather
statute	their	welfare
strength	there	where
subpoena	they're	whether
substantial	thorough	who's
succeed	thought	whole
successive	through	wholly
sufficient	to	whose
suggestion	too	written
summary	totaled	
superintendent	toward	yield
supersede	transferred	you're
	traveler	your

ABBREVIATIONS OF STATES AND TERRITORIES OF THE UNITED STATES

AL	Alabama	Ala.	IA	Iowa	…	MP	Northern Mariana Islands	…
AK	Alaska	…	KS	Kansas	Kans.	OH	Ohio	…
AS	American Samoa	…	KY	Kentucky	Ky.	OK	Oklahoma	Okla.
			LA	Louisiana	La.	OR	Oregon	Oreg.
AZ	Arizona	Ariz.	ME	Maine	…	PW	Palau	…
AR	Arkansas	Ark.	MH	Marshall Islands	…	PA	Pennsylvania	Pa.
CA	California	Calif.	MD	Maryland	Md.	PR	Puerto Rico	P.R.
CO	Colorado	Colo.	MA	Massachusetts	Mass.	RI	Rhode Island	R.I.
CT	Connecticut	Conn.	MI	Michigan	Mich.	SC	South Carolina	S.C.
DE	Delaware	Del.	MN	Minnesota	Minn.	SD	South Dakota	S. Dak.
DC	District of Columbia	D.C.	MS	Mississippi	Miss.	TN	Tennessee	Tenn.
			MO	Missouri	Mo.	TX	Texas	Tex.
FM	Federated States of Micronesia	…	MT	Montana	Mont.	UT	Utah	…
			NE	Nebraska	Nebr.	VT	Vermont	Vt.
FL	Florida	Fla.	NV	Nevada	Nev.	VI	Virgin Islands	V.I.
GA	Georgia	Ga.	NH	New Hampshire	N.H.	VA	Virginia	Va.
GU	Guam	…	NJ	New Jersey	N.J.	WA	Washington	Wash.
HI	Hawaii	…	NM	New Mexico	N. Mex.	WV	West Virginia	W. Va.
ID	Idaho	…	NY	New York	N.Y.	WI	Wisconsin	Wis.
IL	Illinois	Ill.	NC	North Carolina	N.C.	WY	Wyoming	Wyo.
IN	Indiana	Ind.	ND	North Dakota	N. Dak.			

Use the two-letter abbreviation on the left when abbreviating state names in addresses. In any other situation that calls for abbreviations of state names, use the abbreviations on the right; if no abbreviation is given, spell the name out.

Checkup Answer Keys

Checkup 1-1

1. No, Mr. Larry M. Berstorf
2. No, Mrs. Alicia Ann Efird
3. No, Mr. H. Baxter Smith, Sr.
4. Yes
5. Yes
6. No, William Ray Bergman
7. No, Ky Chin Nguyen
8. No, Ms. Catherine R. Roessner
9. Yes
10. Yes
11. No, Melinda Fritz Schaeffer
12. Yes
13. No, J. Franklin Widenhouse
14. Yes
15. Yes
16. No, Teresa Rudisill McDowell
17. Yes
18. No, Gretchen Joy Nichols
19. No, Wyatt J. Roggenkemp, III
20. Yes

10. Yes
11. No, 6084 Tittabawassee Road
12. Yes
13. Yes
14. No, 7261 Knottingham Drive
15. Yes
16. No, 325 Playa Del Reyes
17. Yes
18. No, 728 Gehgring Road
19. No, 1231 Altamonte Spring Road
20. No, Post Office Box 24587

Checkup 1-2

1. No, 1344 Heather Way
2. No, 6728 Third Avenue South
3. Yes
4. Yes
5. No, 1534 Cypress Boulevard
6. Yes
7. No, 3265 43rd Avenue, SE
8. No, Pizza Emilia, 8
9. Yes

Checkup 1-3

1. No, IL
2. Yes
3. No, TX
4. No, PA
5. No, OH
6. No, UT
7. No, VT
8. Yes
9. No, WY
10. No, CT
11. Yes
12. Yes
13. Yes
14. No, CO
15. Yes
16. No, ME
17. Yes
18. No, ID
19. No, MT
20. Yes

Checkup 1-4

1. Yes
2. No, 93542-2251
3. No, 85037
4. Yes
5. Yes
6. No, 02186
7. No, 31419-5634
8. Yes
9. Yes
10. No, 53224-3697
11. Yes
12. Yes
13. No, 63147
14. Yes
15. No, 06851-7834

Checkup 1-5

1. Yes
2. No, New Dehli

Checkup Answer Keys

3. No, Columbus, OH 44430

4. Yes

5. Yes

Checkup 1-6

1. No, 317-384-2835

2. Yes

3. Yes

4. No, (260)532-4841

5. No, 1-900-303-3827

6. No, 405.533.8824

7. Yes

8. Yes

9. No, 011-52-16-541-3286

10. Yes

11. No, (505)839-6687

12. No, 913-351-4857

13. Yes

14. Yes

15. No, 1-800-562-33881

Checkup 1-7

1. A	6. C	11. B	16. A
2. C	7. B	12. A	17. C
3. B	8. B	13. C	18. A
4. B	9. A	14. C	19. C
5. C	10. A	15. B	20. A

Checkup 1-8

1. Yes	6. Yes
2. No	7. No
3. Yes	8. Yes
4. No	9. No
5. No	10. Yes

Checkup 1-9

1. No, 002-865-8299

2. No, Mr. Leon Leonardi

3. No, Rockford, ILL 61109

4. Yes

5. Yes

6. No, October 18, 2001

7. Yes

8. Yes

9. Yes

10. No, 089-55-1973

11. Yes

12. No, 011-61-14-34-1793

13. No, Lincoln, NE 68512-2348

14. No, 1-800-492-4782

15. Yes

16. Yes

17. No, Francis G. Smythe

18. No, Billing, MT 59106

19. Yes

20. Yes

Checkup 1-10

1. scheduled

2. C

3 999

4. as the best as the best

5. 222

6. for or five

7. time managment

8. for for creating

9. C

10. candidates, ^only^ two have

Checkup 1-11

1. jmfrieght@harrisville.net

2. October 13

3. Athens, Greece

4. 008-56-1293

5. service calls every day

6. 420-04-2189

7. Dayton, OH 45459-4373

8. Most of us recieved the

9. C

10. The plane should at be the

Checkup 1-12

1. our of

2. is 61 age 51

3. turn 81

4. 81 years old . . . used to be 12

5. ages of 62 and 07

Checkup 1-13

1.	0	11.	1
2.	1 or 2	12.	1 or 2
3.	1	13.	1
4.	1	14.	0
5.	0	15.	1 or 2
6.	0	16.	0
7.	1 or 2	17.	1
8.	0	18.	1
9.	1	19.	1 or 2
10.	0	20.	1 or 2

Checkup 1-14

work settings— from hospitals

customer 's request

the situation be positive

what is wanted, (2) listening carefully,

remember : put the customer first.

Checkup 2-1

1. resistant
2. preferred, carpeting
3. exercising, manageable
4. deceiving
5. attorneys, summarized, arguments
6. achievements
7. referred, weight
8. dependable, inexpensive
9. flies
10. assistance, planning

Checkup 2-2

1. recognised
2. cuped
3. programed, formating
4. temporaryly
5. hopful, acheivements
6. cielings
7. perishible, useable
8. immediatly
9. assistent
10. flexability, arrangeing

Checkup 2-3

1. ~~weather~~ whether   3. ~~sight~~ site
2. ~~threw~~ through   4. ~~two~~ too

Checkup Answer Keys

5. pole

6. C

7. aide

8. pared

9. you're *your*

10. fare *fair*

Checkup 2-4

adapted *adopted*

affect *effect*

moral *morale*

~~aloud~~ allowed

then *than*

suites *suits*

chose *choose*

Checkup 2-5

1. may be
2. Everybody
3. instill
4. something
5. anyway
6. a while
7. on to
8. indirectly
9. any more
10. sometime

Checkup 2-6

1. realestate
2. pass port
3. sales person
4. C
5. feed back
6. check list
7. halfhour
8. Spread sheets
9. timeframe
10. good will

Checkup 2-7

(Answers will vary.)

1. tour
2. significant
3. accurate
4. attractive
5. exceptional

Checkup 2-8

(Answers will vary.)

1. new, recent
2. definite, specific
3. early, prompt, punctual
4. insignificant, irrelevant, nonessential
5. detrimental, disadvantageous

Checkup 3-1

1. SUCCESSFUL EXPORTING
2. dishes
3. for
4. a.m.
5. professor
6. Day
7. • Employee
   • Health
   • Guide
8. credit cards
9. Ms.
10. OSHA

Checkup 3-2

1. computer science
2. Flight 1628
3. south
4. Hispanic
5. Medical Office Procedures
6. Policy 301429
7. Japanese
8. JavaScript
9. West Coast
10. PowerPoint

Checkup 3-3

1. 5
2. 7
3. 10
4. 16
5. 2 or 18
6. 7
7. 6
8. 5
9. 8
10. 19

Checkup Answer Keys

Checkup 3-4
1. September
2. OH
3. credit application
4. references
5. charge account
6. percent
7. October
8. fall
9. yours
10. Manager

Checkup 3-5
1. CPA
2. Mayor
3. Professor
4. college professor
5. flight reservations
6. 8:30 a.m.
7. Dear
8. HEALTH FOR COLLEGE STUDENTS
9. Labor Day
10. prices

Checkup 3-6
1. sunday
2. 8:45 P.M.
3. Fortran
4. jill Kline
5. South
6. Ibm
7. maxwell house
8. BOARD
9. States
10. after-christmas
11. internet
12. Attorney
13. lake
14. flight 2375
15. Modems

Checkup 3-7

Paragraph 1
Assistant Coordinator

los angeles

Volunteers

Program

Paragraph 2
The Green Thumb Florist, inc.

february 21

University of south dakota

Worldwide

Spring and Summer

Paragraph 3
ansley electronics

West side of

Nashville, tennessee

Expansion

september

Checkup 4-1
1. delays
2. runners-up
3. videos
4. opportunities
5. get-togethers
6. R.N.s
7. viruses
8. embargoes
9. choices
10. brushes
11. policies
12. accounts receivable
13. children
14. editors-in-chief
15. supplies
16. women
17. bills of lading
18. beliefs
19. potatoes
20. CD-ROMs

Checkup 4-2
1. analyses
2. crises
3. hors d'oeuvres (preferred)
   hors d'oeuvre (foreign plural)
4. parentheses
5. diagnoses
6. addenda
7. errata
8. censuses
9. agendas
10. stimuli

Checkup Answer Keys

Checkup 4-3
1. Mike's and Elaine's
2. sisters-in-law's
3. Charles and Amber's
4. daughters'
5. Ms. Moss's
6. Nurse's Day
7. witnesses'
8. editor-in-chief's
9. children's
10. Bob's

Checkup 4-4
1. ~~him~~ *his*
2. Sally's
3. box*es*
4. stud*ies*
5. Stephen's
6. staffs
7. manufacturers
8. ~~bushs~~ *bushes*
9. Davis's
10. ~~companys~~ *companies*

Checkup 4-5
1. supporting
2. dependable
3. platter
4. o'clock
5. navigate
6. CEO
7. mediocre
8. thirty-first
9. dripped
10. establishment
11. $23,986
12. http://www.uschamber.org
13. lengthwise
14. April 15, 2004
15. wouldn't
16. privilege
17. beginning
18. around
19. preregister
20. dressing

Checkup 4-6
1. from J. B. Drexler, Inc., a~~bout~~ *bout* our October seminar for CPAs. Please call the hotel and make reservations for seven additional people.
2. their staff to call immediately an*y*time there is a problem with the
3. goals, the programmer will ideal*ly* ~~ly~~ know how to program using
4. corporation when she was almost twen*ty-* ~~ty-~~ nine. Most of the employees were

Checkup 5-1
1. 3223 South Ashwood Drive
   Covington, KY 41011
   January 14, 2002
2. C
3. Very truly yours,
4. Rebecca S. Timmons,
   Vice President
5. Amanda Milligan, Manager

Checkup 5-2
1. St. Louis, Missouri, after
2. Susan Washburn, my . . . roommate, is
3. have, in
4. Bristol, Tennessee, and

Checkup Answer Keys

5. New York City, Doris?

6. November 21, 2020, we

7. portfolio, Tabitha, is

8. October 22, 1998, after

9. Portland, Oregon, until

10. December 9, we

11. should, in . . . opinion, close

12. associate, came

13. know, Graduates

14. temperatures, which . . . the 90s, have

15. Carolyn Esteban, the . . . manager, is

Checkup 5-3

1. Pankaj, have

2. Yes, your

3. C

4. Drive, Akron

5. Quebec, Denise

6. ago, and

7. VA, 22401.

8. contest, mail

9. valuable, beachfront

10. Edwin, Jane

11. highest, and

12. beautiful, scenic

13. members, phoned . . . reservations, and

14. department, or

15. relaxed, less

Checkup 5-4

1.	1	3.	12	5.	11
2.	2	4.	8	6.	14

7.	9	10.	5	13.	9
8.	9	11.	13	14.	3
9.	6	12.	10	15.	4

Checkup 5-5

1. requested, that

2. Dr. Anne Jackson, and

3. year, is

4. received, and

5. applicant, was

6. Harold, called

7. orderlies, and

8. Web site, and

9. Kaufman, or Doris

10. revealed, any

Checkup 6-1

1. Ms.

2. (No punctuation needed.)

3. Reilly:

4. Congratulations!

5. area.

6. May 7—sooner

7. services:

8. profitability—these

9. them.

10. further.

Checkup 6-2

1. signed.

2. Jason, all

3. best. Limit

4. 2 p.m.

5. Melton, she's . . . company, and

6. manual, pages

Checkup Answer Keys

7. Congratulations! You

8. Ph.D.

9. January, all

10. me.

Checkup 6-3

course, but . . . time, consider

convenience, they

instructor; e-mail,

course:

1.

2.

3.

people from

helpful, there's

Checkup 6-4

1. following: (1) opening . . . morning, (2) making . . . and (3) closing

2. twenty-fifth

3. late; however,

4. up-to-date sales

5. today; therefore,

6. Patrick (he . . . .associate) spends

7. two-thirds

8. Tampa, Florida; Raleigh, North Carolina; Denver, Colorado; and Austin, Texas.

9. Chapter 5 (see page 112).

10. three-story building.

11. member (she's a technology specialist) was

12. April 15–19

13. room; Carole

14. generous; for

15. worksites (particularly . . . plants) can

Checkup 6-5

1. Friday?

2. problem

3. job!

4. "Exercise for Executives" . . . Business Today,

5. We . . . . claims, stated

6. We . . . decision, Adam said, but . . . Monday.

7. Arrival?

8. asked, Do . . . settlement?

9. desert . . . dessert.

10. September 10?

Checkup 6-6

country? If

book Do's and Taboos of Using English Around the World,

chapter How to be Understood, he

distinctly.

cool

bad

Checkup 7-1

1. was
2. have
3. were
4. Is
5. was
6. are
7. has
8. is
9. are
10. have
11. Does
12. sell

13. apply
14. participate
15. are
16. has

17. have
18. is
19. have
20. are

Checkup 7-2

1. his
2. its
3. their
4. her
5. his or her
6. she
7. they
8. he

9. his or her
10. his or her
11. his
12. their
13. his
14. her
15. their

Checkup 7-3

1. I
2. me
3. she
4. her
5. I

6. Whom
7. he
8. me
9. she
10. me

Checkup 7-4

1. who
2. whoever
3. who
4. who
5. Who

6. Whom
7. who
8. Whom
9. whom
10. who

Checkup 7-5

1. ~~her~~ *his*
2. ~~he or she wants~~ *they want*
3. ~~I~~ *me*
4. C
5. ~~their~~ *his or her*

6. C
7. ~~are~~ *is*
8. ~~her~~ *she*
9. ~~were~~ *was*
10. Whom

Checkup 8-1

1. <u>You</u> <u>sold</u>
2. <u>should we</u> <u>change</u>
3. <u>They</u> <u>must follow</u>
4. <u>Ms. Chambers</u> <u>has</u>
5. <u>son</u> <u>was born</u>
6. <u>team</u> <u>completed</u>
7. <u>You</u> (understood) <u>Lock</u>
8. <u>Shelly</u> <u>is</u>
9. <u>We</u> <u>sold</u>
10. <u>Harry</u> <u>is satisfied</u>

Checkup 8-2

1. S
2. F
3. F
4. S
5. F

Checkup 8-3

(Answers will vary.)

1. arrive. Be
2. C
3. service. Madeline
4. crew. We
5. deliberation. The
6. early. we took some time off.
7. him. he left.
8. C
9. C
10. market. is the top seller.

Checkup Answer Keys

Checkup 8-4

(Answers will vary.)

1. CS   merger, ~~or~~ it
2. RO   courses; they
3. CS   consuming; ~~so~~ however
4. C
5. CS   printers, ~~or~~ we

Checkup 8-5

(Answers will vary.)

1. getting a job.
2. C
3. or ~~sending him an~~ by e-mail.
4. also to addressing
5. and to the insurance company.
6. and ~~to~~ enjoy
7. and ~~will be~~ expensive.
8. C
9. rewarding and ~~a~~ challenging.
10. talking but also ~~in the ability to~~ listening
11. to repair equipment or replacing it.
12. C
13. graduated
14. repairing cameras.
15. also ~~to~~ punctuates sentences

Checkup 8-6

(Answers will vary.)

1. We saw 24 young children playing ball in the park.
2. During the class roll, each student answered, "Present," when his or her name was called.

3. Turning on the siren, the ambulance driver navigated through the busy, rush-hour traffic.
4. C
5. We purchased the swimming pool, made primarily from concrete, from a local sales representative.
6. The owner had $350 worth of equipment stolen that was in the parked car.
7. Marilyn called the help desk with a question about copying files from the Internet.
8. According to the hospital official, the heart transplant was performed successfully by the surgeon.
9. She saw the ambulance in her rearview mirror while she was driving to work.
10. Kathi found a book in the library that explains how to catch really big fish.

Checkup 9-1

1. eight
2. One thousand
3. April 10
4. 3 1/4
5. 62
6. $8
7. fifteen
8. 32
9. 5
10. fifth

Checkup 9-2

1. five hundred
2. $35,000
3. 8.5
4. 15 percent
5. 9 a.m.
6. $8,500
7. 8
8. 3.5
9. 615-555-4827
10. 2-gallon

Checkup 9-3

1. ~~8th~~ eighth of July
2. ~~5~~ Five members
3. $1,600.
4. 1 of our
5. was ~~thirty thousand dollars.~~ $30,000.
6. a ~~2/3s~~ two-thirds majority

Checkup Answer Keys

7. ~~five~~ of the 15 *(5 written above)*

8. C

9. Three of our (15) *(thousands written below)*

10. ~~1000s~~ of dollars. *(thousands above)*

Checkup 9-4

1. (2nd) trip

2. C

3. (3) ~~five story~~ *(5=story written above)*

4. C

5. ~~seventy-five dollars~~. *($75 written above)*

6. C

7. $1,200. *(crossed out comma, 0 written)*

8. ~~six~~ percent *(6 written above)*

9. 8:00 a.m. and 10:00 a.m.

10. ~~1000~~ people *(one thousand written above)*

11. your ~~50s~~. *(fifties written above)*

12. ~~two-to-one~~ ratio. *(2:1 written above)*

13. ~~1/3~~ one=third

14. C

15. C

16. $68.00 *(comma crossed to period)*

17. (1st) of July.

18. C

19. (12) pine trees

20. ~~five~~ apples, ~~six~~ bananas, and 12 oranges. *(5 and 6 written above)*

Checkup 10-1

1. T	11. one
2. T	12. two
3. F	13. left margin
4. F	14. *Distribution*
5. F	15. two
6. T	16. two
7. T	17. one
8. F	18. alphabetic
9. F	19. lowercase
10. MEMO TO or TO	20. interoffice
FROM	
DATE	
SUBJECT	

Checkup 10-2

DS

MEMO TO: Glenda Turrbyfield, Human Resources Manager

DATE: May 2, <YEAR>
FROM: John Madison, Marketing Director

SUBJECT: Needed Personnel

DS My administrative assistant, Eleanor Wray, has resigned to return to college and finish her accounting degree. She plans to work a three-week notice, making her last day of employment May 23.

SS Please initiate your usual hiring procedures to fill this vacancy. I would like Eleanor's replacement to learn our operation thoroughly before our summer rush begins the end of June.

DS A copy of Myra's job description is enclosed. I would appreciate seeing any résumés for qualified applicants that you now have on file. Incidentally, Myra is interested in returning to work for us when she completes her degree. She should graduate in about two years. You might want to consider her for an internship next summer. Her employment record here has been impeccable.

GT

jks

SS Enclosure

c: Clyde Galinski

Checkup Answer Keys

Checkup 10-3

1. enclosure
2. reference
3. postscript
4. subject
5. attention
6. copy
7. blind copy
8. delivery
9. company name
10. writer's title

Checkup 10-4

1. b
2. c
3. b
4. d
5. b
6. a
7. d
8. b
9. c
10. d

Checkup 10-5

1. 4
2. 2
3. 2
4. 2
5. 2
6. 2
7. 2
8. 4
9. 1
10. 2

Checkup 10-6

1. Begin a new page after the second line.

    The courier personally delivered the package to my office to ensure that it arrived today in *pg* good condition. We now have the information needed to make a decision.

2. Do not begin a new page.

    The courier personally brought the package *no pg*
    Page 2
    to my office to ensure that it arrived today in good condition.

3. Begin a new paragraph after the second sentence.

    . . . . My plane was almost three hours late. The long delay was caused by bad weather.*¶* I was extremely tired and went directly to the hotel.

4. Don't begin a paragraph after the first sentence.

    . . . My plane was almost three hours late. *no ¶*
    The long delay was caused by bad weather.

5. Indicate the only appropriate page break in this paragraph.

    The sale will begin at 10:30 a.m. *pg* on Saturday, May 8. All merchandise will be drastically reduced so that we may close out our inventory.

Checkup 11-1

1. Centered heading.

Heading

Xxxx xxxxxxx xxxxxxx xxxxxxxxxx x xxxxxxxxxx xxxxxxx xxxxxx

xxxxxxx xxxxxxx xxxxxxxxx xxx xxxxxxxx xxxxxxxxxx.

2. Paragraph heading.

Heading. Xxxx xxxxxx xxxxxxx xxxxxxxxx xxxxxxxxx

xxxxxxxxx xxxxxxxxx xxx x xxxxxx xxxxxxxxx xxxxxx xxxxxxx

xxxxxx xxxxxxxxx xxxxxxxx xx xx xxxxxx xxx.

3. Side heading.

HEADING

Xxxxx xxxxxxxx xxxxxxxxxxxxx xxxxxxxxxxx xxxxxxxxxxx.

xxxxxxxxx xxxxxxxxx xxx x xxxxxx xxxxxxxxx xxxxxx xxxxxxx

4. Block-style header.

Mr. Joseph Serrano

   January 5, <YEAR>

Page 2

5. Horizontal-style header.

Mr. Joseph Serrano   2   January 5, <YEAR>

Checkup Answer Keys

Checkup 11-2

TABLE OF CONTENTS

iii

INTRODUCTION

    Xxxxx xxxxxxxx xxxxxx xxxxxxxxxx xxxxxx xxxxxxx

xx xxxxxxx xxxx xxx xxxxxxx xxxx xxxxxxx xxxxxx xxxxxx

xx xxx xxxxxxxxxxxx.

    Xxxxxxxxxxxx xxxxxxx xxxxxxxxxxxx xx x xxxxxx
xx xxxxxxxxxxxx xxxxxxxx xxxxxxxxxx xx xxxxxx xxxx xxxxxx
xxxxxxxxxxxx xx.

FIRST MAIN HEADING

    Xxxxx xxxxxxxx xxxxxx xxxxxxxxxx xxxxxx xxxxxxx

xx xxxxxxx xxxx xxx   xxxxxx xxxx xxxxxxx xxxxxx xxxxxx

xx xxx xxxxxxxxxxxx xxxxxxx xxxxxxxxx x xxxxxx .

Side HEADING *(or Side Heading)*

Xxx xxxxxxx xxxx xxx xxxxxxx xxxx xxxxxxx xxxxxx xxxxxx

xx xxx xxxxxxxxxxxx xxxxx xxxxxxx xxxxx x xxxx.

    Paragraph Heading. Xxxxxxx xxxxxx xxxxxxxxxxxxx

xxxxxxxx xxxxxxx xxxxxxxx.

Checkup Answer Keys

Paragraph Heading. Xxxxxxxxxx xxxxxxxxx xxxxxxxxxxx xxxx xxxxxxxxxx xxxxxxx. X xxxxxxxxxxxx xxxxx xxxxxxxxxxxx x xxxxxxx xxxxx xxxxx xxx xxxxx xx x xxxxxxxx. xxxxxx xxxxx xxxxxx xxxx xxxxxxxxxx.

¶ 1

Checkup 11-3

1. List author's name with the last name first.
2. Delete quotations around article title.
3. Add parentheses for publication information.
4. Use a period instead of a hyphen after the author's name.
5. Use underscore instead of italics for book title.

Checkup 12-1

SPECIAL YEAR-END CLEARANCE
Sale ~~Sell~~ Ends December 31

Year	Model	Make	Ext. Color	Int. Color	Mileage	Price
1985	300TD	Mercedes	White	Red	130,320	11,300
1987	300SDL	Mercedes	Blue	Gray	154,332	14,800
1989	300E	Mercedes	Yellow	Cream	100,940	12,500
1995	E3210	Mercedes	Green	Tan	100,200	29,500
1995	S320	Mercedes	Silver	Gray	101,002	43,500
1994	3251	BMW	Green	Tan	36,299	24,950
1995	Z3CV	BMW	Gray	Black	27,914	25,900
1995	850T	Volvo	Black	Cream	49,624	22,900
1996	850T	Volvo	Black	Cream	47,254	23,900
1996	850T	Volvo	Pewter	Cream	42,750	23,900
1997	960	Volvo	Blue	Cream	28,759	26,000
1997	960	Volvo	Pewter	Gray	32,650	25,500
~~1989~~	~~S70~~	~~Volvo~~	~~White~~	~~Cream~~	~~46,650~~	~~23,800~~
1998	S70	Volvo	Blue	Tan	45,500	25,400
1990	760T	Volvo	White	Tan	124,895	9,500

Checkup Answer Keys

Checkup 12-2

CONVERSION CHART		
NUMBER OF INCHES	NUMBER OF FEET	NUMBER OF YARDS
89	7.47e *(4167)*	2.472
3568	297.333	199.111
5984	489.667	166.222
6660	555	185

Checkup 12-3

NUMBER	PERCENT
.25	25% ✓
45.	450%
.057	57%
1.75	0175%
.0365	36.5%

Checkup 12-4   Checkup 12-5

	North	South	East *(no ital)*	West
Division A	115,000	120,000	118,000	21,000
Division B	23,000	90,000	54,000	77,000
Division C	80,000	106,000	83,000	110,500
Division D	60,000	85,000	73,000	441,000
Division E	54,000	0	35,000	60,000
Division F	111,000	130,000	185,000	38,500
Division G	93,400	65,400	95,000	28,000
Division H	103,000	112,400	38,700	248,930
Division I	87,350	94,600	53,200 *(no ital)*	31,430

Answer

1. _____
2. _____
3. _____
4. _____
5. _____
6. _____
7. ____✓____
8. _____
9. _____
10. _____

Checkup Answer Keys

Checkup 12-5

	A	B	C	D	E
1	REGIONAL SALES BY QUARTER				
2		JAN	FEB	MAR	TOTAL
3	A1 Distributing	2,200.15	1,890.71	1,751.23	5,842.09
4	AB Engineering	1,784.66	1,273.88	1,656.82	4,731.36
5	Absolute Enterprises	2,974.84	3,007.51	4,476.02	10,458.27
6	Action Supply	8,105.33	7,064.84	6,968.40	22,138.57
7	Collin Industries	5,689.90	3,475.89	6,597.33	15,763.12
8	Crown, Etc.	12,890.11	7,999.34	8,587.89	29,447.34
9	Engle, Ltd.	8,974.68	3,467.99	7,878.80	20,321.47
10	Tex-OK Planning	2,288.00	2,973.08	2,305.97	7,637.05
11	United, Inc.	3,216.88	3,462.33	3,598.76	10,277.97
12	Westside Company	12,884.88	10,986.44	11,178.99	35,050.31

Answer

1. ✓
2. 4,715.36
3. 10,458.37
4. ✓
5. ✓
6. 29,477.34
7. ✓
8. 7,567.05
9. ✓
10. ✓

Checkup 12-6

Product Code	Quantity	Cost	Inventory Total
TX438190	14	8.99	125.86
GTX230948	23	2.43	55.89
HTX983658	62	1.89	117.18
SX3869047	54	7.24	362.80
ITX124579	89	6.45	574.05
LTX0986875	123	3.33	409.59
ZTX56984327	92	7.11	654.12
PTX9856984	44	2.59	123.96

Checkup 12-7

North Star Computers
564 Buckeye Avenue
Lansing, Michigan 48915
517-555-8787 (phone or fax)

INVOICE

Invoice #: 1152
Date: 2/15/02
Customer ID: 0935

Bill To:

Orion Graphics
45 Starlight Way
Columbus, Ohio 43240

Ship To:

45 Starlight Way
Columbus, Ohio 43240

Your #	Our #	Sales Rep	FOB	SHIP VIA	Terms
15-A	257	B. Williams	Lansing	Midwest Freight	net 30 days

Qty	Item	Units	Description	Unit Pr	Total
2	1	45A	MegaPro Printer 1500 AX	$329.95	$ 659.99
3	2	76B	OptiView 215 17-inch monitor	$455.95	$1,357.85
3	3	93C	Askar MIL 5200 digital camera	$229.45	$ 688.35

Subtotal	$2,706.10
Tax	$ 216.48
Freight	$ 180.25
Misc	
Bal Due	$3,102.73

Checkup 13-1

1. Yes   2841, and 2840
2. Yes   of $10.
3. Yes   Memphis, Birmingham
4. Yes   500 pounds . . . and 400 lb
5. Yes   Dr. Jennifer Cox . . . Ms. Cox
6. Yes   (800) 555-2862 and 800-555-2864
7. Yes   Mrs. Susan Travis
8. Yes   12 . . ., two . . . and one
9. Yes   Pittmon and Pittman
10. No

Checkup 13-2

1. d, e, c, a, b
2. a, e, b, d, c
3. c, a, b, d, e
4. d, a, c, b, e
5. b, a, e, c, d

Checkup Answer Keys

Checkup 13-3
1. b, a, c, d, e
2. c, a, b
3. a, c, d, b
4. e, d, c, b, a
5. c, b, d, a

6. c, d, b, e, a
7. c, a, b
8. b, a, d, c
9. b, c, a, e, d
10. c, a, d, b

Checkup 13-4
1. b, c, a, e, d
2. c, a, d, b, e
3. c, b, a
4. a, d, b, c
5. c, b, a, d

6. b, d, a, e, c
7. b, c, a
8. b, c, a, d
9. b, c, d, a
10. e, c, a, d, b

Checkup 13-5
1. age, 61. ?A
2. 215 . . . 35 A ? B
3. This $10 savings
4. is Monday, August 5; be Friday, August 10.
5. $45.18 . . . $200.18 A ? B
6. holidays: Taking Professional Photographs and PACKING FOR INTERNATIONAL TRAVEL.
7. Max McMillan, . . . Sheila Allen,
8. George Carouthers . . . Mr. Carothers A ? B
9. is 316-555-2842 . . . is (316) 555-2840.
10. C
11. percentage ~~decreased~~ increased from 3.5 percent to 4.2 percent since
12. April 15, 7,
13. four money-saving . . . to one entry A ? B
14. Dr. Adelyn   crowded, Ms. Dr. Symboski
15. Illinois, Florida, and
16. Relocation: 1. Availability . . . shipping, 2. Institutions . . . and 3. proximity

17. positions: 18 people . . . and 9 people A ? B
18. 35 gallons of ice cream . . . picnic: 10 gal of chocolate, 10 gal of strawberry, and 15 gal of vanilla.
19. and Ms. Teresa
20. C

Checkup 14-1
1. necessary, mandatory
2. satisfactory
3. troubled
4. agreed
5. outstanding

Checkup 14-2
Regarding
call
Enclosed is

Please
important

Checkup 14-3
1. After much debate, the vice president changed the policy.
2. A parcel delivery service delivered the package last Friday.
3. Mr. Nelson offered Darlene a promotion.
4. Melinda Sorrentino discussed changes to the employee investment plan.
5. The physician reviewed the results of the lab tests.

Checkup 14-4
1. c
2. f
3. i
4. d
5. b

6. g
7. h
8. a
9. e
10. j

Checkup Answer Keys

Checkup 14-5

1. at ~~about~~ 10 a.m.
2. Sort ~~out~~ the
3. opened ~~up~~ the
4. ever ~~before~~.
5. moving ~~to~~?

6. Type ~~up~~ the
7. redone ~~over~~.
8. decision ~~by~~?
9. sold ~~out~~ in
10. computer ~~at~~?

Checkup 14-6

1. annually
2. for
3. reported
4. each December
5. believes

Checkup 14-7

1. 12 a.m. ~~midnight~~
2. Planning ~~in advance~~ will
3. again ~~soon~~.
4. reduced ~~down~~.
5. return ~~back~~ the

Checkup 14-8

Before
~~Prior to the time that~~ we . . . typed ~~up~~
        most
In ~~almost all~~ instances,

letter ~~again~~ was

redone ~~over~~.

retyped ~~again~~.

reduce ~~down~~ stationery

print ~~out~~ a verification
              if
paper ~~should it be that~~
      If
~~in the event that~~ changes

Checkup 14-9

1. Most   **a.** I appreciate your generous donation to this deserving cause.   **b.** I appreciate your generous donation to this
   most deserving cause.   **c.** I appreciate
   your most generous donation to this very
   deserving cause.

2. Thinking   Craig thinks the plan will work
   and will save money.

3. In my opinion   In my opinion, Sarah will do
   a good job in the new position; however,
   she may not want to leave the good job
   she has now.

Checkup 14-10

1. three trucks ^{new} ~~that were new~~ and five cars
   ~~that were used~~. ^{used}

2. the conference room ^{fourth floor} ~~on the fourth floor~~ at
   8:30 a.m.

3. Most ~~of the~~ associates ~~in the~~ computer
   department have

4. the merchandise ^{damaged} ~~that was damaged~~.

5. on ^{January 1} ~~the first day of the first month of~~

Checkup 14-11

1. e   2. b   3. a   4. c   5. d

Checkup 15-1

(Answers will vary.)

1. Your quarterly report for the holiday sales
   season should show a gain.
2. Happy New Year to you and your family.
3. Kristin is capable of completing the audit.
4. Thank you for interpreting my comments in
   the right way.

Checkup Answer Keys

5. The computer software will work fine.
6. We hope you will accept the offer.
7. Your proposal has the most merit.
8. He was not told the truth about the accident.
9. We were not told about the appointment.
10. She almost always agrees with us.

Checkup 15-2

(Answers will vary.)

1. You can become easily frustrated when the photocopier will not work properly.
2. Citizens should realize that we cannot lower the crime rate without hiring more police officers.
3. We offered to purchase the house, and the owner agreed to sell it.
4. If you dial 911, you can get emergency help immediately.
5. People frequently offer their opinions even when they are not asked.

Checkup 15-3

1. job ~~even though he is confined to a wheel chair.~~ e
2. being ~~fat~~ made _overweight_
3. the ~~elderly~~ woman
4. Our ~~Hispanic~~ taxi driver
5. a copy of his _or her_ driver's license.
6. business~~men~~ _people_
7. is ~~deaf~~. _hearing impaired_
8. Our ~~attractive~~ assistant
9. chair~~man~~ of the committee _person (or chair)_
10. the ~~crippled~~ _physically challenged_

Checkup 15-4

(Answers may vary.)

1. Jimmy takes his time doing anything.
2. The house has a swimming pool and a three-car garage. The owners must have good jobs.
3. That man is almost seven feet tall. He could be a basketball player.
4. Those women can't figure out the right course of action. Do they know what's going on?
5. Claire has a hard time saying a kind word to anyone.

Checkup 16-1

1. fork ~~in~~ spoon _and_
2. a ~~pizza~~ pie _piece of_
3. a ~~siren~~ atmosphere _serene_
4. ~~enter rest~~ at _interest_
5. ~~bites~~ of memory _bytes_
6. held ~~a cannible~~ _accountable_
7. reports ~~assent~~ as _are sent_
8. to ~~disgust~~ at _discuss_
9. offices ~~forever~~ _for over_
10. ~~in tents~~ to _intends_

Application I-A (continued)

Note that the names in this typed version of the list have been placed in alphabetical order.

Patricia Abbott	patab@battleground.net
Brady S. Bellemy	bbellemy@piedmont.net
Sarah Ann Booth	sboofth@citytower.net
Amber B. Camp	abc@blueridgmti.net
Barbara Goldberg	bgoldberg@citytcwer.net
J. W. Harrison	jwh@battleground1.net
Nancy Hilderbran	nancy@lakeview.net
Branden Koch	koch@piedmont.net
Michael S. Miller	mike@skytel.net
Catherine Mobley	katherine@hiddenvalley.net
Larry Nelson	harryn@blueridgemtn.net
Lynn S. Norman	lnorman@hiddenvalley.net
Evelyn R. Owensby	erowensby@blueridgemtn.net
J. B. Roland	jbroland@hiddenvalley.net
Betty H. Searcey	bettys@skytel.net
William Starnes	bill@skytel.net
Zach W. Taylor	zachwt@hiddenvalley.net
H. Gordon Wexler	wexler@lakeview.net
Mary Elizabeth Wirt	mewirt@piedmont.net
Darlene S. Wray	dsray@citytower.net

Application I-B (continued)

Ms. Benita Branson
Branson Ultrasonics Corp.
19236 Muirfield Court
Grand Rapids, MI 49506
616-897-2182
bransonb@rapids.net

Ms. Amanda S. Browillette
Professional Management Systems
1449 Eucalyptus Drive
Orlando, FL 32181
407-397-4487
asbrowillette@sunshine.net

Ms. J. C. Delachevrotiere
Imperial Graphics and Communications
9218 West Florissant Avenue
St. Louis, MO 63115-9218
301-527-9984
jcd@graphics.net

Mr. J. Michael McCabe
City Office Services
19264 Ginochio Court
Bakersville, CA 93363
805-249-6734
mccabe@bakers.net

Ms. Jacqueline McCrorie
Triangle Technology Group
Post Office Box 17892
Paducah, KY 42002
502-287-6153
jacmcrorie@stables.com

Mrs. Anita Sanchez
Rosenzweig Center, Inc.
1386 Edgemoor Avenue
Boston, MA 02181
617-389-4428
asanchez@mass.com

Dr. Linda S. Spradley
Spradley Communications
1831 Wimbledon Court
South Bend, IN 46613
219-492-8876
spradley@indiana.net

Mr. David Stoesifer
Dexter Data Consultants
2286 Marguerite Avenue
Syracuse, NY 13207
315-864-2613
dstoesifer@syra.net

Dr. Donald J. Tyndall
Datatronics, Inc.
P.O. Box 21198
Broken Arrow, OK 74011-2198
405-568-2247
djtyndall@okla.net

Mr. Malcolm Brantley Wilkinson
Multigraphics, Inc.
12423 Nueces Town Road
Corpus Christi, TX 78410
512-675-3489
brantley@cctx.net

NAME _____ DATE _____

Application 2-A

Proofread the following memo. Use revision symbols to indicate misspelled and misused words as well as errors in words that should be written as one word or as two words. Use a thesaurus to select an appropriate synonym for *noncompulsory* in the third paragraph and for *brochures* in the fourth paragraph.

MEMO TO: Steve Berkowitz, Sales Coordinator

FROM: Alice Daves, Human Resource Coordinator

DATE: April 8, <YEAR>

SUBJECT: Fringe Benefits

As a new associate, you are now ~~elegible~~ *eligible* for most of the fringe benefits offered by our company. You will be pleased to know that you will not have a *break* in your health plan coverage during your employment transition.

Your life ~~assurance~~ *insurance* plan is now in *effect*, and your retirement plan will begin after you have been employed for *one* year. To take advantage of our retirement plan, you must make a contribution of up to *five* percent of your salary. Your contributions will be matched by the company. Most associates take advantage of the *five* percent maximum.

You may be interested in enrolling in noncompulsory coverage at your own expense. We have arranged for dental and vision insurance premiums to be deducted from your check.

Within the next two weeks, you will be receiving brochures that explain each of these benefits in detail. After you have had an opportunity to read the information provided, please let me know if I can help you with your fringe benefit selection in *any way*.

1. Synonym for *noncompulsory:* <u>optional</u>

2. Synonym for *brochures:* <u>pamphlets</u>

NAME _____ DATE _____

Application 2-B

E-mail messages, though often quite informal, should be correct. Proofread the following two e-mail messages. Use appropriate revision symbols to mark misspelled and misused words as well as errors in words that should be written as one word or as two words.

To.. Wendy Horowitz
Cc..
Subject: Absence from Work

Wendy,
Up on the *advise/advice* of my doctor, I will not be into work today because she believes that I may have acute appendicitis. Dr. Moreno has scheduled several tests for me today.

After getting the results of these tests, I will call and let you know my status. My doctor says that it may be some thing else, but she cannot make a definite diagnosis until after the tests.

Please review my appointment calendar and cancel my appointments for today. Also, will you be responsible for making the regular bank deposit at 4:30 p.m.

Thanks for your assistance.

Dave

To.. Dave Mellinger
Cc..
Subject: Your Absence from Work

Dave,
hear
I'm sorry to here about your health problem. I'm happy to take care of your work concerns. As you requested, I'll be handling the bank deposit at 4:30 p.m.

All of your appointments for today have been canceled.

know there
Please let me know if there is anything else that I can do for you.

Wendy

Application 3-A

Proofread the following memo. Use appropriate revision symbols to mark corrections in capitalization.

MEMO TO: Abigail Miller—Corrptroller

FROM: Robert Billingsly—Office Manager

Date: July 2, <YEAR>

SUBJECT: Annual Audit

As mentioned to you in a conversation earlier today, we will begin our annual auditing procedures at 8 A.M. on Monday, July 8. this audit will be for the FISCAL year just ended, running from July 1 to june 30.

Mr. Jeff Snyder, cpa, of Snyder, Hilton, and Berstrom, inc., will have ten accountants with him, and he anticipates completing the audit within two weeks. Ms. ellen Lawrence will be working primarily with the computer part of the process.

Please introduce Mr. Snyder and Ms. Lawrence to all appropriate staff members.

Application 3-B

Proofread the following letter. Use appropriate revision symbols to mark corrections in capitalization. (10 points for each properly marked correction)

Columbia Coastal Savings

14 South Pinehurst Avenue, Columbia, SC 29608-1469 / Tel: 803.555.2272 / colcoastsav.com

August 3, <YEAR>

Ms. Millie Hempstead
Special Accounts Manager
Epic Regency Hotel
3687 East Brentwood Terrace
Columbia, Sc 29602

Dear Ms. hempstead:

On Wednesday, August 15, a group of international students will be arriving in Columbia on their way to various locations throughout the united states. Our company has agreed again this year to pay for their lodging the night they will be in Columbia.

In the past, your hotel has graciously offered a discount to help defray the expenses for lodging international students. Last fall, in fact, you gave us a discount and provided a special continental breakfast for one such group.

Will you help again this year? There will be eight male students and twelve female students, which means that ten double rooms will be sufficient. We have already reserved the rooms.

Thank you for considering this request, please call me as soon as you have reached a decision.

Very truly Yours,

Anita Burns
Manager

skj

NAME _____ DATE _____

Application 4-A

Proofread the following memo. Use appropriate revision symbols to correct errors in plurals, possessives, and word division.

MEMO TO: All Employees

FROM: Jorge Rodriquez, Human Resource Manager

DATE: April 15, <YEAR>

SUBJECT: Parking Lot Regulations

On Monday, April 10, a committee met to finalize regulations that will improve our parking situation. The committee has met diligent-ly for the last six weeks.

The senior management's opinion was that the associates who use the parking facilities should recommend any changes in regulations. As you will recall, you had several opportunities to complete surveys indicating preferences and concerns. The most frequently mentioned concern on both the men's and the women's surveys was safety. This issue has been addressed by employing a security guard for each parking facility around the clock.

Enclosed is a pamphlet that lists the revised regulations. The com-mittee's goal was to implement regulations that would avoid any crises with regard to parking. Please let me know if you have any suggestions.

eap
Enclosure

NAME _____ DATE _____

Application 4-B

The following flyer will be distributed throughout the city to adver-tise a benefit to raise money for hurricane victims. Proofread the flyer and correct any errors in plurals, possessives, and word divi-sion with the appropriate revision symbols.

Benefit
Yard & Bake Sale
for victims of
Hurricane
William

Saturday
September 1, 2001
7:30 a.m. to 7:30 p.m.

Graham Industries, Inc.
128 West Jordan Drive, Marietta, Georgia

The associates of Graham Industries, Inc., are working to raise money for the recent victims of Hurricane William. Our associates have emptied their attics, closets, and garages to provide a variety of furniture, used clothing, and antiques.

Local merchants have donated new products to add to the buying activities. Homemade cakes, pies, and cookies will also be available.

The associates' goal is to raise at least $10,000. Join us on Saturday in this worthwhile humanitarian effort.

Application 5-A

Proofread the following draft of a letter. Use appropriate revision symbols to insert and delete commas as needed.

February 18, <YEAR>

Mr. Alfredo Gonzales
4423 Elmhurst Drive
Norman, OK 73071

Dear Mr. Gonzales:

Thank you for attending the meeting last week that explained our limited partnership. Thank you also for letting me know that you are interested in investing in this venture.

As you requested, I have enclosed a prospectus for the partnership. Also enclosed is a questionnaire that must be completed before we can accept you as an investor.

Please complete, sign, and return the questionnaire to us as soon as possible. The questionnaire should be returned to Ms. Glenda Carpenter, our attorney, at Post Office Box 2843, Norman, OK 73073, by March 1. Once you have been accepted as an investor, you will be asked to submit your check for $15,000.

Incidentally, we need only three more investors before the project can begin. We hope to have these investors identified by the end of March.

Please call Ms. Carpenter or me if you have questions about the prospectus. I look forward to hearing from you soon.

Sincerely,

DAVENPORT PARTNERSHIP

Scott Davenport, General Partner

slc
Enclosures

Application 5-B

Proofread the following letter for correct comma usage. Use appropriate revision symbols to insert or delete commas as needed.

Big Sky Computers
3245 Nelson Avenue, Missoula, MT 59807
Phone: 406.555.1247 • Fax: 406.555.1298 • bsmt@bigsky.com

July 1, <YEAR>

Ms. Gloria Terazzo
Terazzo Accounting Consultants
Post Office Box 7236
Missoula, MT 59807

Dear Ms. Terazzo:

As I mentioned to you on the telephone today, I would like to arrange a time for your annual audit of our books. Our fiscal year, as you know, ended June 30, and we would like to complete the year-end process as soon as possible.

Mr. Joe Hartwell, our new accountant, will be glad to assist you while you complete the audit. He has access to our records, our computer system, and our safe.

I have several questions that are too involved for this letter, and I would appreciate your meeting with me in my office next week. Would Friday, July 8, at 3:30 p.m. suit your schedule? My assistant will telephone you Tuesday to confirm this appointment.

Ms. Terazzo, I appreciate the competent, meticulous job that your staff always does for us. I look forward to meeting with you next week.

Sincerely,

Olida Loaces

Olida Loaces
Accounting Manager

ls

Application 6-A

Use appropriate revision symbols to supply the needed parentheses, hyphens, colons, and semicolons in the following memorandum. In some cases, you will have to change existing punctuation.

MEMO TO: Lana G. Reynolds

FROM: Jeff Wilson

DATE: April 8, <YEAR>

SUBJECT: Promotions and Transfers

After much review, three employees have been approved for promotion. The following criteria (see page 172 of the company policy manual) were used in selecting the branch managers: (1) qualifications, (2) seniority, and (3) job performance.

The branch managers and their new locations are as follows: Victoria Spencer in Danville, Virginia; Dale Ledbetter in Charlotte, North Carolina; and Jackson Fritz in Salem, Oregon. Together these new managers represent forty-one years of manufacturing experience.

The managers may assume their new positions as early as July 1; however, they must report by August 1. Nelson Weinberg (recently appointed as relocation specialist) will help make their moves as smooth as possible.

Each of the new managers will be attending the executive-level conference to be held April 26-28 in New York, New York. Conference details will be mailed today.

mc

Application 6-B

Use appropriate revision symbols to insert needed punctuation—dashes, periods, parentheses, question marks, colons, exclamation points, quotation marks, and underscores—in the following memo. You may need to delete or change existing punctuation.

MEMO TO: Terry Blevins, Human Resource Manager

FROM: Anna Roland, Office Manager

DATE: March 10, <YEAR>

SUBJECT: Office Communications

Did you subscribe to the magazine Office Dynamics for our staff? Melissa Fredrich, who conducted our last staff development session, said, "This magazine should be required reading for all office associates."

Attached is an excellent article that I clipped from the magazine. This article, "Writing on the Job," emphasizes the importance of correct, effective writing at all levels of the organization. The article gives a humorous slant to the term miscommunication as it relates to the office environment. I would suggest that you use the contents of this article in your preparation for next week's staff meeting (Tuesday at 8:30 a.m.) on office communications.

I am looking forward to hearing your comments on how important it is for all associates, both managers and staff, to improve their writing skills. Please emphatically make this point. I think before you write!

Attachment

Application 7-A

Proofread the following draft of a two-page letter. Use appropriate revision symbols to mark errors in subject-verb agreement, pronoun-antecedent agreement, and pronoun case.

March 20, <YEAR>

Mr. Glenn Foxworthy, President
Foxworthy Supply Company
Post Office Box 28448
Wilmington, DE 19808

Dear Mr. Foxworthy:

Thank you for your prompt response to my request for a bid to provide inventory control for our widgets. After reviewing all the bids, I am happy to report that your company has successfully met our requirements for price and delivery.

Widgets play an essential role in our manufacturing operation. Maintaining and controlling inventory items is costly for us. By signing the enclosed agreement, you are accepting the responsibility for performing weekly audits of our widgets and ordering the sizes that have fallen below the minimum stocking requirements. Under this arrangement, one shipment of widgets is expected each week.

It is important for us to form alliances with vendors whom supply the products and services we need. At the end of the six months, we will evaluate the effectiveness of this method of inventory control. If the inventory control is performed satisfactorily, we will consider contracting with your firm to assume the responsibility for controlling other manufacturing materials.

If you have any questions, please contact Jim Decker. You should consider your contact to be him. Jim has over ten years of experience with us, and she will be eager to help your sales representatives. You may also direct questions to Martha Moore, whom is Jim's assistant. Either Jim or Martha are available to help you.

(continued)

Application 7-A (continued)

Mr. Glenn Foxworthy
Page 2
March 20, <YEAR>

Please sign and return the enclosed agreement by March 25 so that our new widget inventory control process may start on April 1. We look forward to your becoming a supplier with who we can enjoy a pleasant, reliable business relationship.

Sincerely,

Ann B. Taylor, President

scc
Enclosure

Application 8-A

Proofread the following job postings that appear on the Web page for a company. Use appropriate revision symbols to indicate corrections in parallel structure and dangling and misplaced modifiers.

Human Resources Staff Assistant

This individual provides secretarial and clerical support to the human resources staff. The position requires interaction with all levels of employees throughout the organization. Duties include typing correspondence, tracking résumés, making travel arrangements, and to organize and maintain files. The assistant also handles inquiries and requests for information. The work is of an extremely confidential nature. Three years of secretarial/clerical experience is required, along with excellent oral and written skills.

Customer Service Representative

This position is responsible for providing accurate and quickly responses to customers. Responsibilities include researching, resolving, and to reply to inquiries from customers and sales representatives. Other responsibilities include maintaining an open line of communication among accounting, sales, marketing, and customers. The ideal candidate will have good interpersonal and communications skills and knowledge of word processing and database software programs. Energy, enthusiasm, and a customer-oriented attitude are a must!

Administrative Assistant

This individual will provide six-person administrative support to a real estate service department. Duties include typing and tracking real estate documents such as leases, subleases, various legal documents, and invoices. Requirements include excellent written and oral communication skills, good administrative and organizational skills, basic math skills, and knowledge of Windows software programs accurate typing.

Application 7-B

Proofread the following e-mail message and mark corrections in subject-verb agreement, pronoun-antecedent agreement, and nominative- and objective-case pronouns.

To...	Office Staff
Cc...	Richard Fielding, Human Resource Manager
Subject:	Job Sharing

As most of you know, Karen, Steve, and me have been appointed to a task force to examine the possibility of job sharing. Several people in the office have mentioned this option as an attractive alternative to full-time employment in his or her particular situations. With their permission, I have included some specific comments below.

• John and Sally Elliott, whom will become new parents within three months, is considering job sharing as an option to provide child care. They are expecting twin girls, and the twins will require much time from her parents.

• Roslyn Roberts, whom plans to retire within the next year, wants to try job sharing as a way to ease into retirement.

• Dan Taylor would like to share a job with someone during the hours that his children are in school.

• Amelia Wexler is interested in sharing a job upon returning to work after her recent illness and hospitalization. Her and me, as her supervisor, are hoping that job sharing can be implemented to make her recovery easier.

We would like to know whom would be interested in job sharing. Please e-mail Lisa Rowe or by June 5, with your suggestions, questions, or concerns.

/I

/their

/are

/their

/She / I

/me

NAME _____ DATE _____

Application 8-B

Proofread the following memo. Use revision symbols to correct sentence structure errors such as sentence fragments, faulty parallelism, misplaced or dangling modifiers, comma splices, and run-on sentences.

MEMO TO: The Executive Staff

FROM: Jeanette Lorenzo, President

DATE: December 1, <YEAR>

SUBJECT: Retirement Banquet

On Friday, December 15, we will honor 20 employees who are retiring from our company. The banquet, to be held in our recreational facilities, is scheduled for 7 p.m.

Each of these employees has 15 or more years of service with our company. We appreciate not only their hard work but also that they were dedicated. A watch will be given to each employee that has been engraved.

Andy and Mary Jean Leonardi will be recognized for their combined total of 60 years with us. Either Dennis Worthy or June Hobbs plans to attend as a representative from our New York office I will let you know later which one is coming.

Please plan to attend the banquet. We have reserved seating for you and a guest; however, please call Gayle Price at extension 3425 if you or your guest is unable to attend.

NAME _____ DATE _____

Application 9-A

Proofread the following two e-mail messages. Use appropriate revision symbols to correct errors in number style. If there is not enough room to write a correction above the line, write the correction in the margin next to the line of copy. Use a caret or draw an arrow to show where the corrected copy goes.

To: George Taylor, Brenna Williams, Camp Reservations
From: Shane Waldrop
Subject: Camp Filled to Capacity

On camp fifteen, our summer program began for teenage campers up to age fifteen. This bunk has filled to our capacity of twenty campers. We had to decline reservations for about sixty campers.

For the first time in three years, we have more girls than boys. In fact, almost three-fourths of our campers are girls. Your recruiting efforts have been enormously successful. Keep up the great work!

Sylvia Vanegsard

10 / 15
300 / 50

first / three−fourths

To: Patricia Adams, Events Coordinator
From: Fredra Nordona
Subject: Concessions at Industrial League Games

Thank you for supervising our company's efforts in the concession stand at the Industrial League softball games this summer. I was glad to volunteer for your three nights this week.

The concession stand sales for Monday night were $413.50. We sold three cases of soft drinks, 5 boxes of candy bars, and 7 helium-filled balloons. Last night, the total sales were $260. We sold 9 cases of soft drinks, 1/2 boxes of candy, and no balloons.

Concession operations have had a profit of $18,000.00 this summer. We have this money in a certificate of deposit earning three percent interest. After the last game on the 30th of September, we will donate this money to the charities we have identified.

Fredra Melson

three

15

3 / tenth

NAME _____ DATE _____

Application 9-B

Proofread the following letter for correct number style. Use appropriate revision symbols to correct the errors.

JASPER PRINTING AND PACKAGING, INC.
3298 Carson Boulevard, Post Office Box 2843, Wayne, MI 48187
jp@mich.net   517-555-2948

March 15, <YEAR>

Mr. Steve Wallenda
Century Sales and Service
1486 Camelot Drive
Wayne, MI 48187

Dear Mr. Wallenda:

Confirming our telephone conversation earlier today, we are quoting you a price of $4295 for printing 500 50-page sales manuals. The pages will be punched for a standard 3-ring binder, which will be furnished by you. The $4295 total includes scanning the photographs and artwork that you will supply. Itemized costs are as follows:

Scanning Photographs and Artwork	$1,500
Proofreading (8 hours at $15 hour)	120
Design & page layout (10 hours at $80 an hour)	800
Printing (500 copies at $3.75 per copy)	1,875
Total	$4,295

You will receive a draft to approve approximately two weeks after you send us the needed information and photographs. Your sales manuals will be delivered one week after you approve the draft.

Our price quote is effective for only fifteen days because of an expected price increase in paper. To assure this $4295 price, please order by March 30. As a new customer, you will receive a 10 percent discount if your payment is received within 9 days of the invoice date. Invoice payments are due by the 15th of the month following delivery.

We look forward to working with you on this project.

Sincerely,

Tom Messer

Tom Messer, Sales Representative

NAME _____ DATE _____

Application 10-A

Proofread the following memo, and use appropriate revision symbols to correct formatting errors. Assume that the top and side margins on the memo are correct.

MEMO TO: Dennis S. Clark, Human Resources Manager

FROM: Edith B. Haroldson, Administrative Assistant

DATE: June 23, <YEAR>

SUBJECT: Reimbursement for Educational Expenses

As you know, I am taking evening courses for credit at the local college. During the first session of summer school, I completed a three-hour course in business communications, bringing my total hours to 90.

Enclosed is a copy of my tuition invoice for $185 and a copy of my most recent transcript showing that I satisfactorily completed the course. My expenses are listed below:

Tuition	$185
Parking	25
Book	45
Supplies	15
Total	$270

I would appreciate your approving this amount for reimbursement. If you need any other documentation, please let me know. Thank you for making this educational benefit available.

_____ expenses23jun
Enclosures

Application 10-B

Proofread the following letter. Use revision symbols to correct any formatting errors. The letter should use the block style format with open punctuation.

Travel Consultants, Inc.

132 Elizabeth Avenue, Boiling Springs, NC 28017 • travelco.bs.net
Telephone: 704-555-2844 • Fax: 704-555-2844

July 5, <YEAR>

Mr. Nathan Harbinger, President
Brentwood Industries
424 Industrial Park
Charlotte, NC 28214

Dear Mr. Harbinger

The arrangements for your excursion to see the Charlotte Knights play the Memphis Volunteers are complete. Every effort has been made to ensure that your company's international visitors relax and enjoy the baseball game.

As a theme for your excursion, we will use "An American Afternoon." We will include everything needed for an old-fashioned picnic lunch, including hot dogs, potato salad, and watermelon.

Your visitors will travel to the game in vintage 1957 Chevrolets. They will be escorted to a luxurious air-conditioned sky booth. Prior to the game, several members of both teams will visit the sky booth to sign autographs.

Your visitors will experience the kind of day that creates unforgettable memories. To personally record these memories, each visitor will receive a disposable camera. Additionally, each visitor will receive a baseball autographed by the Charlotte Knights players.

A detailed itinerary is enclosed. Please call me if you have questions about the excursion.

ds Sincerely
TRAVEL CONSULTANTS, INC.

Gloria G. Paterno, President
Enclosure

harbinger.sjul
ttc

Application 11-A

Use appropriate revision symbols to correct formatting errors in the following two-page memo report. The report uses side and paragraph headings.

MEMO TO: Mr. Calvin Rains, President

FORM: L. Linda Cooper, Maintenance Supervisor

DATE: August 24, <YEAR>

SUBJECT: Annual Facilities Study

The Maintenance Department has concluded its facilities study of our entire complex. The following discussion documents our findings and presents our recommendations for updating and/or repairing the existing facilities.

ADMINISTRATION BUILDING

Carpeting. The carpeting, installed in 1995, shows signs of wear. A high-traffic area such as this requires that carpeting be replaced every 3–4 years. Recommendation: Replace with a high-grade commercial carpet. Cost estimate: 5,000 sq. ft. at $23 = $115,000.

Windows. The original windows, circa 1985, continue to waste valuable electricity. A 1995 study determined that escaping air conditioning and heating cost more than $10,000 per year. Recommendation: Replace the 75 windows with DuraWindows. Cost estimate: $15,000. (Cost recovery period would be less than two years.)

Furnishings. The seating areas in the lobby appear worn and dated. The last refurbishing of the sofas, chairs, desks, and tables occurred in 1994. Recommendation: Purchase new furnishings for the seating areas. Cost estimate with trade-in on old furnishings: $21,000.

Application 11-A (continued)

Mr. Calvin Rains   August 24, <YEAR>

]2[

DS

MANUFACTURING Building

Flooring. The tile has become unsightly and dangerous due to excessive chipping and peeling. Recommendation: After several attempts to repair the danger spots, it appears to be more economical to replace the flooring. Cost estimate: 12,000 sq. ft. at $20 = $240,000.

Doors. The two overhead doors on the west side of the building have warped; therefore, workers have difficulty opening and closing them each day. Repair estimates rival the cost of replacement. Recommendation: Replace the doors. Cost estimate: $2,400.

Restroom Facilities. Although the ADA (American Disabilities Act) required updating these facilities in 1995, employees have indicated a need for additional lavatories. Recommendation: Install three additional lavatories. Estimated architectural and plumbing installation costs: $15,000.

SS

Supply Room. A recent OSHA inspection revealed a safety hazard in the supply room that must be repaired. Estimated Cost: $500.

RECREATION BUILDING

DS

Exercise Equipment. The treadmills and stationary bicycles, purchased in 1993, have become unusable. Recommendation: Replace three treadmills and five stationary bicycles. Cost Estimate:

bk

Application 11-B

Proofread the following manuscript for a newsletter article. Use appropriate revision symbols to correct formatting errors. The manuscript should be double-spaced.

HOW TO BECOME A SOUGHT-AFTER
(AND HIGHLY PAID)
ADMINISTRATIVE ASSISTANT

So now you have finished your college training and accepted that dream position. How do you keep the momentum going and get those raises and promotions? Here's how:

Act Like a Professional

Be that person who never takes supplies home. **Be ethical!** Be that person who never says anything bad about anybody. **Refuse to gossip!** Be that person who always wears a smile and never complains. **Be pleasant!** Be that person who minds his or her own business. **Respect others' privacy!** (no ital)

Look Like a Professional

Wear that good quality suit, those polished shoes, that tasteful hairstyle. Women, be sure your jewelry and other accessories are appropriate. Men, leave out the earrings until you find out if they are acceptable to wear in the office.

ds

Work Like a Professional

Be pleasant, be prepared, and one more BIG thing: do your work efficiently and correctly.

Your Workspace. Keep only the essentials (telephone, legal pad, pen and pencil, and the current work) on your desk. Leave files and projects in your desk drawer or filing cabinet until you need them. When you leave your workstation, push your chair under the desk.

The MAIL. Open and distribute the mail as soon as it arrives. If you open mail for others, place the mail in order of importance with the most important pieces on top.

Your Documents. Develop your own trademark style (but nothing too flashy!). Attractively formatted documents say that you care about your work—that you are a professional who takes pride in what you do.

Application 11-B (continued)

2

Learn to compose e-mail messages that are both brief and well-written. A sloppy or error-filled e-mail message says that you didn't take the time or pride in your work to think the message out before writing it.

Your Phone Manners. Have you ever been "turned off" to a company because of a rude representative of that company? Do just the opposite. Be polite, be patient, and smile when you answer the phone in order to convey a pleasant tone.

It is just as important to be professional with your voice mail. When you leave a message on someone's voice mail, **speak clearly and say your phone number slowly.** If someone cannot identify your name or phone number, your message is useless.

Your Proofreading. Proofreading can make or break a million-dollar deal. If you want to make an impression with your company, always produce **accurate documents.** Sure, we all make an error now and then, but that's just it—it should be only now and then.

Personal Matters. Refrain from sending cute little sayings or chain messages as e-mail—such messages aren't part of the company's business. If you avoid such gimmicks, you will be taken more seriously.

Arrive at work on time, and put in a full day's work! Don't make a habit of leaving early each work day. **Reliability counts!**

Do what you say you will do by the time or date you promised. **Dependability counts!**

Pitch in—never say, "It's not my job." It takes everyone to get the job done. **Teamwork counts!**

Application 12-A

A draft of an income statement for Internet Travel Company for August follows. Using the handwritten draft as the source document, proofread the final typed copy at the bottom of the page. Use appropriate revision symbols to mark corrections on the typed version. Be sure to check the math calculations.

INTERNET TRAVEL COMPANY
Income Statement
Month Ended August 31, <YEAR>

Revenues:		
Commission income	*$32,935*	
Airline tickets	*7,900*	
Cruises	*14,250*	
Tours	*5,139*	
Other operating revenues	*2,350*	
Total revenues		*$62,574*
Expenses:		
Salaries expense	*$23,075*	
Commissions paid	*2,975*	
Other operating expenses	*3,005*	
Total expenses		*$29,055*
Net income before taxes		*$33,519*

INTERNET TRAVEL COMPANY
Income Statement
Month Ended August 30 <YEAR>

Revenues:		
Commission income	$32,935	
Airline tickets	7,900	
Cruises	14,250	
Tours	5,139	
Other operating revenues	2,350	
Total revenues		$62,574
Expenses:		
Salaries expense	$23,075	
Commissions paid	2,975	
Other operating expenses	3,005	
Total expenses		$29,055
Net income before taxes		$33,519

Application 13-A

Proofread the following memo for inconsistencies. Use appropriate revision symbols to indicate corrections when you have a choice of the correct form or when you are sure of the intended content. Use a different pair of letters (A/A, B/B, and so on) to query inconsistencies in the treatment of related items such as dates. Assume that the calendar on page 283 is correct for the current year. Today is March 6.

MEMO TO: All Staff Members

FROM: Joyce Meade, Human Resource Department

DATE: March 6, <YEAR>

SUBJECT: Staff Development Sessions

Our ~~fall~~ *spring* staff development sessions are scheduled for Tuesday,/ [A]? [A] April 12 / Dr. Susan Eldridge, Professor of Business Communications at Valley State University, will be our guest speaker.

~~Ms.~~ *Dr.* Eldridge received her doctorate from the University of Tennessee and is considered an expert in customer relations. Dr. Eldridge will address our associates on how to deal with difficult customers. She has authored two books: The Customer and You and CUSTOMERS WITH AN ATTITUDE.

You may choose one of the ~~three~~ *four* times specified below. There is one morning session and three afternoon sessions. The last session begins at 6:15 *p.m.*

Session A   8:15–9:45 a.m.
Session B   1:15–2:45 p.m.
Session C   3:00–4:45 p.m.
Session D   6:15–7:45 p.m.

By Monday,/ March 28 / please call ~~Ms.~~ Heather Lowe at extension 4375 or Ray Queen at extension /4378 to reserve your place. Each session is limited to the first 35 people who register. [B]? [B]

c: Sheri Jones, Allen Miklaus, Grace Cole

Application 12-B (continued)

EXPENSE REPORT FOR Laura Garcia   WEEK ENDING May 15, <YEAR>

Date	Transportation Type	Amount	Personal Automobile Mileage	Amount	Hotel Amount	Meals Amount	Other Expenses Itemize	Amount	Daily Total
5/9	Air fare	$650.00	20 @ $0.33	$6.60	$165.00		Convention Reg.	$250	$1132.10 / 1129.10
	Taxi	$35.00						$23.50 / 2	
5/10	Taxi	$15.00			$165.00	$14.25	Fax	$22.40 / 14.45	$299.24 / 254.45
						$27.95			
5/11	Taxi	$10.00			$165.00	$12.85		$15.75	$236.50
						$32.90			
5/12	Taxi	$35.00	20 @ $0.33	$6.09		$9.95	Airport Parking	$32.00	$90.10
							Telephone	$6.55	

Purpose of Travel: Attend Oil Producers' Convention   Weekly Total: $1717.94 / 1715.35

Submitted by: *Laura Garcia* Date: 5/16/<YEAR> Advance: $2000.00

Approved by: _____ Date: _____ Due Employee: _____

Billing Code: _____ Due Company: $282.06 / 284.65

Application 14-A

Use appropriate revision symbols to remove wordy, trite, and sub-standard English expressions from the following draft letter. Replace any difficult words with words that are easier to understand. Harry Friedman hopes he helped Jack Carter by returning the questionnaire Mr. Carter enclosed with his October 5 letter. The completed questionnaire is enclosed with Mr. Friedman's letter.

Travel Consultants, Inc.
132 Elizabeth Avenue, Boiling Springs, NC 28017
Telephone: 704-555-2841 • Fax: 704-555-2844 • travelco.bs.net

October 15, <YEAR>

Mr. Jack Carter
Director of Marketing
Smart Communications
3281 Felter Street
Charlotte, NC 28219

Dear Mr. Carter:

received your October 5 letter
We are in receipt of yours of the fifth asking us to complete a questionnaire questionnaire
regarding our company communications. Please find same completed and enclosed
herewith.

begin to
Regarding your suggestion, we will initiate a study to try and find ways of
facilitating our company's communications. We will explain the study to our staff and
ask their assistance. They should be involved in the study and the subsequent
decisions.

We look
Looking forward to working with you to improve our communications, we
remain,

Sincerely yours,

Harry Friedman
Manager

lc
Enclosure

Application 13-B

Proofread the following block style letter (with standard punctuation) for inconsistencies. Use revision symbols to indicate corrections when you have a choice of the correct form or when you are sure of the intended content. Use a different pair of letters (A/A, B/B, and so on) to query inconsistencies in the treatment of related items. Assume that the calender on page 283 is correct for the current year. Today is July 3.

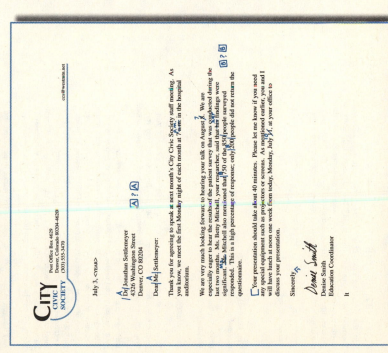

CITY CIVIC SOCIETY
Post Office Box 4629
Denver, Colorado 80204-4620
(303) 555-3470

ccs@westumin.net

July 3, <YEAR>

Dr. Jonathan Settlemeyer
4326 Washington Street
Denver, CO 80204

Dear Mr. Settlemeyer:

Thank you for agreeing to speak at next month's City Civic Society staff meeting. As you know, we meet the first Monday night of each month at 7 p.m. in the hospital auditorium.

We are very much looking forward to hearing your talk on August 7. We are especially eager to hear the results of the patient survey that was conducted during the last two months. Ms. Betty Mitchell, your researcher, said that his findings were significant. Ms. Mitchell also mentioned that 150 of the 350 people surveyed responded. This is a high percentage of response; only 200 people did not return the questionnaire.

Your presentation should take about 40 minutes. Please let me know if you need any special equipment such as projectors or screens. As mentioned earlier, you and I will have lunch at noon one week from today, Monday, July 3, at your office to discuss your presentation.

Sincerely,

Denise Smith

Denise Smith
Education Coordinator

lt

Application 14-B

Edit the following draft of a two-page letter to Mrs. Elizabeth Thomas that appears on pages 307–308. Be especially alert to wordiness, redundancies, overused words, improper English, trite phrases, unnecessary phrases and clauses, and the unnecessary use of difficult words. Use revision symbols to mark corrections.

October 28, <YEAR>

Mrs. Elizabeth Thomas
Director of Corporate Travel Services
Step-by-Step Seminars Inc.
2772 Carolina Causeway
Wilmington, NC 28403

Dear Mrs. Thomas:

Thanks for sharing the taxi with me from LaGuardia Airport into midtown Manhattan last week. During rush hour traffic that very long ride is very much more interesting with pleasant conversation.

I'm eager to talk with you further about our services that you and your company can utilize. As I understood from our conversation, a primary problem you face is coordinating arrangements with hotels and convention facilities for the seminars and workshops your organization offers in major cities around the United States. Although participants rank your organization very high in program and presentation content, problems with meeting rooms, refreshment and meal services, and accessibility for physically challenged registrants have drawn very strong criticism during the past two consecutive years. We can help your organization improve in these areas.

As I told you in New York, our agency specializes in planning and coordinating meeting and convention gatherings for groups of 25 to 2500. Our services range from making hotel reservations to coordinating conventions that are one week long. The following list describes some of the services we can provide.

1. Meeting rooms and audiovisual services. We handle arrangements with hotels and convention centers to tailor meeting room size, outfitting, and climate control to the needs of the presentation. Our service includes arranging for rental, delivery, setup, testing, and return of audiovisual equipment.

Mrs. Elizabeth Thomas   2   October 28, <YEAR>

2. Housing. If your staff and clients need housing at or near the site of the meeting, we can coordinate those accommodations and will provide rooming lists for convenience in distributing messages, agendas, materials, and so on.

3. Travel arrangements. My understanding is that you need travel arrangements primarily for your staff and presenters rather than for meeting participants. We will develop a travel profile for each traveler that describes preferences in airline, seat assignments, and special dietary needs.

4. Participants list. Our specialist of computer services provides a detailed participants list including name, billing address, specialized medical needs and/or physical limitations, dietary requirements and/or preferences, and VIP status. We also can provide client histories that are cumulative.

5. Special activities. If you wish to offer any activities that are special during your meeting, we can research and coordinate arrangements for those events. Such events might include group tickets for the theater, concerts, or sports events; visits to theme parks or museums; or sightseeing tours.

6. Event scheduling. Our researchers maintain a master calendar of events throughout the United States. We can help you schedule your meetings to stay away from/or to coincide with other major events.

Your organization would benefit from our specialists' expertise in the following areas: travel, housing facilities, presentation services, social events, and computer services.

In the event that you have questions or need additional information, please call me up or e-mail me at karen@blassingame.com.

Looking forward to hearing from you soon, I remain

Sincerely yours,

Karen Blassingame
Manager of Corporate Services

308   Chapter 14

Editing for Clarity, Conciseness, and Completeness   307

Application 15-A

Use revision symbols to correct point-of-view errors and eliminate stereotypes and the I-attitude in the following memo.

MEMO TO: Administrative Staff, Ta~~m~~pa Volunteer Association

FROM: Randall Hobbs

DATE: March 18, <YEAR>

SUBJECT: Annual Clean-Up Day

~~I would like to announce that~~ ᵒⁿ Friday, April 1, we will be having our Annual Clean-Up Day. This year, we will concentrate our efforts in the covered picnic area that is used frequently for lunch and for organized functions.

In addition to cleaning up the area, we ~~also~~ will be planting trees, shrubs, and flowers. Both plants and trees have been donated by
                        people
area businessmen. I want to ask the ~~men~~ to please bring their chain
       everyone
saws, shovels, and hedge trimmers.

Please call my secretary, T. J. Parsons, to sign up for a specific
work assignment. Lunch will be provided. ~~Women,~~ ᵂᵉ especially
                                              we
need some help in serving lunch and providing iced beverages
throughout the day.

Several of you, because of your specific job responsibilities, have
been asked to remain on the job on Clean-Up Day. Everyone else
may participate in our cleaning and planting venture. I want to
                                         physically challenged
encourage everyone, unless you are ~~crippled,~~ to participate in some
way.

In previous years we have enjoyed working together in an outdoor
environment. Let's hope that the weather is good and that we can
get much done on April 1.

Application 15-B

Edit the following letter to use the you-attitude. Also correct any point-of-view errors and eliminate stereotypes. Use revision symbols to mark corrections.

April 22, <YEAR>

Ms. Maxine Aldridge
3244 Park Lane
Denver, CO 80209

Dear Ms. Aldridge:
 Congratulations
~~I want to take this opportunity to congratulate you~~ on your
graduation from college next month. I am sure that you
worked hard, because you made the dean's list almost every
semester.

I am sure that you ~~, as a member of a sorority,~~ will be taking
some time off before accepting your first full-time position.
Thus, we have allowed several weeks between graduation
and your first day on the job. However, I want to confirm
our offer to you for employment beginning June 1. I have
attached a contract outlining the specific details. ~~I ask that~~ Please
~~you~~ sign the contract and return it to me within 10 days of
the date of this letter.

I thoroughly enjoyed working with you when I supervised
your internship at our company. I look forward to having
you back as my assistant.

Sincerely yours,

Anita Gordon, Manager

Enclosure

Application 16-A

Proofread the following memo that was dictated using voice-recognition software. Be especially alert for words that may have been mispronounced and were not recognized correctly by the software. Use appropriate revision symbols from the inside front cover to mark corrections.

MEMO TO: All Employees

FROM: Edward Custer, Vice President

DATE: March 21, <YEAR>

SUBJECT: Promotion of Lisa Moharas

I am pleased to announce the promotion of Lisa Moharas to the Manager of Electronic Publishing.

Since joining the company last ~~tear~~ [year] Lisa has been a key member of the electronic publishing department. Most recently, Lisa held the position of Special Projects Administrator for the Art, Design, and Production departments. In that role Lisa ~~a dressed~~ [addressed] a variety of issues surrounding the electronic publishing process. In Lisa's new role, her primary focus will be to head the internal electronic ~~pub lishing~~ [publishing] activities. Lisa will also have an active role in implementing new electronic publishing technologies.

Please join me in congratulating Lisa and ~~witching~~ [wishing] her much success in her new position.

Application 16-B

Proofread the following letter that was dictated using voice-recognition software. Be especially alert for words that may have been mispronounced and were not recognized correctly by the software. Use appropriate revision symbols from the inside front cover to mark corrections.

August 16, <YEAR>

Mr. Jacob Miller
Shelby Learning Systems
111 South Lane Avenue
Westerville, OH 43081

Dear Mr. Miller:

Thank you for ~~you'll~~ [your] recent order for ~~sick teen~~ [sixteen] boxes of Pensco ~~drawer ~~flag~~pens~~ [drawing pens]. Your complete order is enclosed.

You will find these pens to be durable and comfortable ~~farm~~ [for] most students to use. I feel sure that the ~~drawer ~~flag~~ class~~ [drawing class] that your company is sponsoring will be happy with these ~~fine~~ pens.

As the class progresses, ~~let us~~ [let] know these students' reactions to the special pens and to the work that you are doing with them. Meeting your needs in this way is important to us. Please call ~~again way ~~have~~~~ [us when] we may be of service to you.

Sincerely,

Sharon Quick
Sales Manager

INDEX